Building Your Business with Google™

FOR

DUMMIES®

Building Your Business with Google™

FOR

DUMMIES®

by Brad Hill

WILEY

Wiley Publishing, Inc.

Building Your Business with Google™ For Dummies®

Published by
Wiley Publishing, Inc.
111 River Street
Hoboken, NJ 07030-5774

WILEY

About the Author

Brad Hill has worked in the online field since 1992 and is a preeminent advocate of the online experience. As a bestselling author of books and columns, Hill reaches a global audience of consumers who rely on his writings to help determine their online service choices.

Brad's books include a *Publishers Weekly* bestseller and a Book-of-the-Month Club catalog selection. Brad's titles in the *For Dummies* series include *Internet Searching For Dummies*, *Google For Dummies*, and *Yahoo! For Dummies*. In other venues, Brad writes about cybercultural trends, digital music, virtual investing, and all sorts of online destinations. He is often consulted about the media's coverage of the Internet. He appears on television, radio, Webcasts, and is quoted in publications such as *Business Week*, *The New York Times*, *USA Today*, and *PC World*.

Brad is a staff blogger at Weblogs Inc. (www.weblogsinc.com), where he runs the Search Engine Marketing weblog (SEM.weblogsinc.com) and contributes to several others. He also operates The Digital Songstream (www.Digital Songstream.com), a news and review site for digital music. Brad's personal site (www.bradhill.com) describes all his current projects and provides an e-mail link.

Brad doesn't get outdoors much. Sunshine baffles him. As compensation, he is listed in *Who's Who* and is a member of The Authors Guild.

Author's Acknowledgments

Every book is a partnership of author and editor. Susan Pink is the editor of this book and a collaborator in other projects as well. Besides laughing at my worst jokes, Susan's keen eye for clarity and incisive comments make me look good. She also remains calm in the face of deadlines. Too calm. I scheme to make her panic but nothing works.

Karen Wickre at Google pored over this manuscript with a relentless attention to detail that would cause brain-cell loss in a less robust individual. Her refinements improved this book's accuracy tremendously.

Ana Yang at Google was an enthusiastic and helpful partner in this book from the beginning. My sincere thanks to Ana for her time and diligence. Also at Google, Michelle Vidano and Joel Slovacek clarified my questions and gave generously of their busy schedules.

Melody Layne at Wiley Publishing nursed this project from the start and saw it through to the end. I'm very thankful.

I send a warm and admiring thank-you to the marketing experts who provided extensive quotes to the manuscript. Amazingly generous, these pros contributed an extra dimension that will benefit every reader.

Continued thanks to Mary Corder at Wiley.

Many thanks to all the copy editors and production experts who lent their expertise to every page of the manuscript.

Publisher's Acknowledgments

We're proud of this book; please send us your comments through our online registration form located at `www.dummies.com/register/`.

Some of the people who helped bring this book to market include the following:

Acquisitions, Editorial, and Media Development

Project Editor: Susan Pink

Acquisitions Editor: Melody Layne

Technical Editor: Karen Wickre

Editorial Manager: Carol Sheehan

Permissions Editor: Laura Moss

Media Development Supervisor: Richard Graves

Editorial Assistant: Amanda Foxworth

Cartoons: Rich Tennant, `www.the5thwave.com`

Composition

Project Coordinator: Courtney A. MacIntyre

Layout and Graphics: Karl Brandt, Andrea Dahl, Lauren Goddard, Denny Hager, Stephanie D. Jumper, Lynsey Osborn, Heather Ryan, Jacque Schneider, Mary Gillot Virgin

Proofreaders: Carl William Pierce, Brian H. Walls; TECHBOOKS Production Services

Indexer: TECHBOOKS Production Services

Publishing and Editorial for Technology Dummies

    Richard Swadley, Vice President and Executive Group Publisher

    Andy Cummings, Vice President and Publisher

    Mary C. Corder, Editorial Director

Publishing for Consumer Dummies

    Diane Graves Steele, Vice President and Publisher

    Joyce Pepple, Acquisitions Director

Composition Services

    Gerry Fahey, Vice President of Production Services

    Debbie Stailey, Director of Composition Services

Contents at a Glance

Table of Contents

Introduction

*I*n the Introduction of *Google For Dummies* I wrote, "There has never been an Internet phenomenon like Google." The book you're holding now doubles the truth of that statement, revealing and illuminating the hidden half of Google. Taken together, Google's front end (the consumer search engine) and back end (the business services) make up an online juggernaut arguably more significant to online society than eBay, Amazon.com, or Yahoo! right now. And Google's momentum as a revenue-generating media company is just starting to pick up speed.

Until recently, Google's radical impact on Internet citizenry, and society generally, was focused on the consumer experience of searching. The quality of that experience was established in a revolutionary triple whammy (*whammy* being the technical term):

- **The clutter-free home page.** In crisp contrast to the ad-clotted and frantically informational Web portals that previous search engines had morphed into, Google's spare appearance is exhilarating in its announcement that search — pure Search, with a capital *S* — was back, and back hard.

- **The quality of results.** This factor, of course, built Google's fame and planted "Googling" in the global lexicon. Does Google read your mind? Or do the uncanny results derive from groundbreaking technology? Well, it's the latter. But those who prefer imagining that they have a telepathic relationship with Google should go for the fantasy with gusto.

- **The speed of results.** Lightning-quick results have pushed Google into the little cracks in everyone's work day. People Google because the engine matches speed with the online lifestyle. Google never thinks of itself as the destination; hence, it is the most important destination. (Ahh . . . Zen insight.)

Google's unprecedented performance is underlined by its much-publicized traffic statistics: more than 200 million searches each day and more than 55 billion searches per year, servicing at least 50 percent of all search queries. Approximate and changeable as these metrics are, they emphasize the impressive command Google has established in the consumer searching arena.

But Google has another side — and another personality. Behind the scene of any simple search lies a frenzy of competition and a wealth of opportunity. Web sites wrestle with each other and with Google for position on the search results page. Advertisers bid for attention-getting placement on that same page. Other sites all over the Web vie for the privilege of showing Google ads.

The quests for visibility and traffic — the twin imperatives of online marketing — are played out against the world's most important search engine. To the people who start this chain reaction by typing keywords into the search box, Google is about searching the Web. To Webmasters, entrepreneurs, and marketing executives, Google is about being found. The latter group populates the world of Google business services.

About This Book

This book is about Google as a business partner. Google's business services (especially the AdWords advertising program and the AdSense publishing program) are now getting as much attention as the search engine did during Google's early years. The business services are bound closely to the search engine; they can't be approached as an isolated set of tools. Building your business with Google involves knowing how Google constructs its index, improving your site's visibility on search results pages, and hooking into Google's advertising programs as an advertiser, a publishing partner, or both. (Google also offers other business tools based on peripheral search technologies and products.)

Accordingly, this book is like a mirror of *Google For Dummies,* which won a Pulitzer Prize for literature. (No, it didn't.) Whereas that book blazed a trail to power-using Google's front end (the search engine), this book instructs in power-using Google's back end (the business services). The two books together provide a complete initiation to the hidden arts of more effectively using Google, approaching from both the front and the rear.

Actually, because Google marketing types are obsessively focused on the quest for visibility and traffic, to these poor souls Google's business side appears as the only part of Google that counts, the *real* consumer interface. All that stuff people do on Google's home page and in the Google Toolbar — entering keywords and finding destinations — happens in the background, like the constant rolling of the ocean to fishermen on a boat. Online marketers cast their lines into the ever-heaving Google index, trolling for their share of the Internet populace swimming through endless search results. And that is the last time I'll bring up the ocean-fishing metaphor.

Anyway, you don't need *Google For Dummies* to make full use of this book. So if you haven't picked up your copy (yet), don't get nervous. (Just know that the author requires tremendous amounts of dark chocolate to stay at the top of his game, and that stuff isn't cheap. The imported stuff, that is.) This book keeps its sight set on Google's consumer side in recognition of the fact that Google's customers are also *your* customers. And what is good for Google's customers on the front end tends to benefit Google's customers on the back end (that would be you). It's all part of the relentless interdependence of Google's two sides, which I refer to innumerable times in these pages.

Rather than merely document the features, screens, and processes of activating Google's business services, I strive in this book to engage your mind in a thorough reconsideration of marketing in the online space. In this conceptual rethink, Google is a sun by which light you see things differently. Costly mistakes are being made, even by companies determined to Google their way to success. Online marketing is difficult and barbarously competitive. Perhaps the biggest mistake of all is believing that Google AdWords, AdSense, or its shopping engine, Froogle, ensure your success and prosperity simply by flipping on their respective switches.

Google marketing rewards patience, detail, and persistence. Most of all, success comes from a penetrating understanding of the organic nature of Google's business innovations. I want every reader to understand the connection between ordinary searches and sales at your site. Understanding keyword patterns on the front end lends a competitive advantage on the back end. Your site, your product, your brand, and your positioning are parts of the Google whole, as are consumer impulses, search keywords, and destination choices. The key to building your business with Google is matching up to your fair share of the consumer ebb and flow, and success is maximized when you operate with an awareness of the entire Googling ocean. (Damn that persistent metaphor!)

The goal of this book is to think big, in every sense. Big ambition. Big understanding. Be assured that this isn't physics, though, and I'm not Stephen Hawking. (He doesn't even return my phone calls.) This book proceeds to higher levels of Google awareness one step at a time, with attention to easily mastered details.

Conventions Used in This Book

In the course of writing many *For Dummies* books, I have exhausted the planetary supply of wretched jokes and foolish puns that fit in this section. Most of them play on the double meaning of the word "convention," and feature hilarious riffs on bad food, crowds, and Trekkies. Although demand remains high for the priceless wit that enlivens such classic *For Dummies* farce, and with full recognition of the painful disappointment this announcement will cause, I have decided to forego any further whimsy in this space. The genre has been plumbed, and I must move on to new artistic horizons. (Previous first paragraphs of this section can be found in my collected writings, currently housed at the Smithsonian.)

As to conventions on the page, certain types of text are set off in special ways to increase recognition, enhance understanding, and allow the production department to show off. These bits of text include URL Web addresses:

```
www.google.com
```

Several chapters ask you to examine, alter, and optimize the HTML tags of your Web site. Additionally, Google sometimes requires you to cut and paste small chunks of HTML. All HTML code is presented like this:

```
<meta title="The Coin Trader">
<meta description="All for Coins and Coins for All">
<meta keywords="coin, coins, trade, trader, trading, historic
            coins, ancient coins, collecting, collections,
            collect, hobby, coin trader, coin trading">
```

In the chapters ahead, I discuss keywords many times. In the normal flow of a paragraph, I italicize keywords, like this: *imported chocolate dark "desperate author."* However, when you enter keywords into Google, do not italicize them.

What You're Not to Read

Although this book presents a lot of detail, very little of it is technical or superfluous. In fact, I urge you to pay special attention to the detailed instructions in coding your pages and administering your Google campaigns. Online marketing success depends on little things done correctly. To Google, tiny details loom large and have a big effect on your visibility within Google.

Some chapters might not apply to you. If you're a sole proprietor or small business, the chapter about premium services, while interesting, is not required reading for your business. Certainly, you shouldn't feel as though you must read this book from start to finish. Feel free to skip chapters, with the understanding that even chapters that seem too elementary or don't directly apply to your immediate goals might contain tips or insights that could be useful and are worth reading at some point.

Foolish Assumptions

This section of the Introduction usually starts with *de rigeur* reassurances that you're not really a dummy, that everyone feels stupid when tackling something new, and other homilies designed to distance the author from the insulting *For Dummies* title. Nowhere have such reassurances been more apt than here. This is a business book, and its readers are angling into a brave new world of search-engine marketing with sharply opportunistic instincts, some degree of acquired online skill, and plenty of smarts.

Now, about that online skill. This book is forced to make certain assumptions about your abilities to deliver important knowledge without spending too much space on background. I start from square one with the marketing concepts and Google's tools. But in certain areas that must precede square one, you're on your own. To wit:

- ✔ **Business startup.** I discuss conceptual issues as they relate to positioning a business in Google, but in general I regard your overall field of enterprise and product development to be outside this book's scope. Likewise, issues of customer service, inventory and fulfillment of product, merchant accounts, and all other aspects of your business transactions are out of bounds. Only in the case of purely online businesses (affiliate-based portals or sites enrolled in the AdSense program, for example) does this book touch on every link in the transaction chain. Otherwise, this book is about augmenting an existing business, not starting a new business.

- ✔ **Site creation.** I need to distinguish here between site *creation* and site *optimization.* The latter is a major subject in this book. The former I describe nowhere. I assume you can create a Web page. I assume you can register a domain. I assume you can upload new material to your server or domain host. However, I do walk you through the alteration of certain HTML tags.

- ✔ **Basic Google searching and Web navigation.** I assume that readers are newcomers neither to the online realm nor to Google's search engine. You need to understand the principle of linking and have a conception of the Web as an interconnected network of links. You need to understand Google as a keyword processor and be familiar (or get familiar) with its many different search results pages.

To summarize: if you know Google from the front end (searching) and have owned and updated a Web page, you'll be fine.

How This Book Is Organized

First I print the manuscript. Then I throw it in the air. Then I gather up all the pages and stack them in a pile. It works for me, but my editor is an organizational freak, and that method doesn't satisfy her refined sensibilities. Fine. Rather than endure her nagging, I put everything into parts and chapters.

Part I: Meeting the Other Side of Google

More than just an overview (though Chapter 1 *is* an overview of Google's business services), Part I delves into three of the most important aspects of Google marketing: getting into Google's Web index, building a network of incoming links, and optimizing your site. Those three subjects are closely related, and each is geared to enhancing your PageRank in Google — the holy grail of online marketing. PageRank is explained in Chapter 2, where you can also find out how to get a toehold in Google if your site doesn't yet appear on search results pages. Chapter 3 is about networking your way to higher visibility. Chapter 4 concentrates on fine-tuning your site (or completely redesigning it, depending on the state of its optimization) to attain higher stature in Google. Site optimization is detailed, finicky, necessary, invaluable work.

Part II: Creating and Managing an AdWords Campaign

Part II contains the juice for many people. AdWords is Google's innovative implementation of search advertising — or more precisely, cost-per-click advertising. This type of marketing is turning the traditional online advertising field upside down, shaking it, and throwing it into the corner to consider its shortcomings. Google did not invent cost-per-click payment for ad placement. But Google's overwhelming volume of traffic, outstanding administrative tools, democratically level playing field, and superbly streamlined process of bidding for position have combined to take the leadership role. Other cost-per-click programs exist, and full-time marketers do them all. But *everybody* who advertises in this manner uses Google.

The chapters in this part are thorough. They assume you know nothing about search advertising, cost-per-click advertising, or Google advertising. Chapter 6 starts with the theory of it all, and Chapter 7 helps you design a campaign. It's important to move slowly at first because, in truth, most AdWords campaigns undergo a few false starts. So, even though Chapter 8 assumes that you're operating an activated campaign, you might want to read that chapter and the next one (which illustrates and explains all the administrative screens) before actually putting your ads in play. Chapter 10 is for ambitious advertisers running multiple campaigns but also contains strategy insights for everyone.

Part III: Creating Site Revenue with AdSense

Part III is about AdSense, Google's inventive program that allows any professional-level site to publish AdWords ads. This syndication is accomplished with little effort on the Webmaster's part — joining is a simple matter of pasting a bit of code into an approved site. When visitors click the ads, the host site splits the revenue (the cost per click of that ad) with Google. The payout is pennies, usually, so this is a high-volume business or a sideline that puts a little revenue icing on the main enterprise.

AdSense has developed a user and optimization community nearly as intense as the groups surrounding AdWords, which has a head start on the younger AdSense. I don't assume that you have any knowledge about the AdSense program or advertising syndication. It's a good idea, though, to be familiar with AdWords before embarking on an AdSense campaign. That doesn't mean you must run an AdWords campaign first, but I suggest reading Chapters 6 and 7 in Part II.

Part III is a soup-to-nuts rundown of AdSense, from theory to design to optimization. One chapter contains rare directions for modifying AdSense placement and HTML code to integrate the ads on your page, avoiding the ugly displays that have become commonplace. Plenty of examples address design concerns while the text hammers home optimization principles that generate the most effective ads for your site.

Part IV: Google Business for the Larger Company

Google is about grass-roots adoption of its various services, but the company doesn't ignore major corporate advertisers and search partners. Large companies are valuable customers for Google, and you've probably noticed some of its high-profile partners: AOL, Netscape, Forbes.com, and many others. Big players don't hesitate to hunker down with masses swarming to AdWords and AdSense. The slick efficiencies of those services cuts the fat from corporate balance sheets. Google supplies premium versions of those two services for large firms that fulfill certain traffic requirements, and this part covers those augmented, personalized services.

Beyond AdWords and AdSense, Google offers back-end access to Froogle, Google's shopping search engine, and Google Catalogs, a service for mail-order businesses. (See *Google For Dummies* for a complete description of how those Google spinoffs work.)

Part V: The Part of Tens

The "Part of Tens" is a *For Dummies* tradition. The chapters here round up resources and services that don't fit easily into the rest of the book and are valuable reading in spare moments. You should feel free to jump around here. (I mean jump around within these chapters, not jump around while reading the chapters. But hey — whatever.)

Icons Used in This Book

I wanted to use an icon of a steaming mug to indicate paragraphs I wrote while under the influence of thick espresso residue. Once again, my editor thwarted me with her "sensible" approach. So, I've used a few more useful icons to set off certain paragraphs:

In the spirit of Johnny Appleseed, I scatter these things all over the place. Each one flags a particularly useful bit of knowledge or process.

Gentle, soothing reminders are best. So . . . TAKE YOUR MUFFINS OUT OF THE OVEN!! That's the sort of thing that deserves one of these icons. I also use them to drive home an important point that, if forgotten, might cause hassle or wasted effort down the road.

I rarely devolve into a techno-mumbling, chip-eating, basement-dwelling, glazed-eyeball geek. My inner nerd doesn't slip out in this book much because the focus is mostly business issues. However, when I feel like spewing technical information that doesn't directly apply to the forward movement of your business, I slap on this icon. Feel free to ignore such paragraphs.

Very few mistakes will cause your computer to melt down. However, it's definitely possible to waste time, money, and effort, run afoul of Google's guidelines, lose ground, and otherwise set back your business goals. When discussing dire consequences, I tag paragraphs with the Warning icon.

Where to Go from Here

To the cash register, perhaps? If you're already at home with this book, get some coffee. That's what I'm going to do.

Although it's not necessary to read this book in order, I urge you to get your head around Chapters 2, 3, and 4 at some point. Everyone has their eyes on AdWords and AdSense, and you might want to get started with them quickly. You might be tempted to skip these chapters entirely. Go ahead, break my spirit. Seriously, AdWords and AdSense don't work well when the target site is poorly optimized, for a number of reasons fully discussed throughout the book. AdWords, in particular, is tricky at first, and impatience usually results in wasted money.

So, if you have a rough plan for building your business with Google, read Chapters 2, 3, and 4, and then head for whichever parts apply to your plan (AdWords, AdSense, or premium-level programs). If you're a newcomer to Google's business side and want the grand tour, start with Chapter 1. If you're already operating Google campaigns and are familiar with site-optimization issues, head for the inner chapters in the AdWords or AdSense sections.

Part I

Meeting the Other Side of Google

The 5th Wave   By Rich Tennant

"For 30 years I've put a hat and coat on to make sales calls and I'm not changing now just because I'm doing it on the Web from my living room."

In this part . . .

This part is an introductory survey of Google's business services and a launching pad to preparing for those services. Plus a few other things. Everyone is familiar with Google's consumer face — the front end, which is the search engine. But Google is more than a search company; it's a technology company defined by its advertising services and other business programs.

Chapter 1 provides an overview of Google's entire slate of business services. Without documenting the details — a task left for the book's other chapters — Chapter 1 paints a picture of Google behind the scenes. Chapter 2 discusses getting into the Google index, the first essential step in leveraging Google's clout in building your business.

Chapter 3 is more intense, following up on a site's entry into Google with a full tutorial on improving your site's PageRank by networking. In this context, *networking* means creating incoming links from other sites to your site. Building a competitive PageRank is the prime task in Google marketing, and Chapter 4 continues this quest by tackling the thorny but rewarding topic of site optimization. Chapter 5 rounds out the section with an explanation of why and how to put free Google searches on your site.

Some people relegate Google's entire business story to its AdWords program (covered in Part II). As important as the AdWords program admittedly has become, the site optimization and link-networking information in Part I is the bedrock of any Google-oriented business plan. Any AdWords campaign sits on a shaky foundation without that bedrock.

Chapter 1

Meeting the Business Side of Google

*L*ike Yahoo! and eBay before it, Google came on the scene with good technology and then needed to work out a way to make money. Fortunately, that's where you come in. To put it simply, Google makes money when you do. That's the ideal, anyway. Google's revenue model is based largely on increasing the visibility and traffic of its thousands of small-business partners, streamlining their marketing costs, qualifying their leads, and helping track returns on investment.

There's genius in Google's method — and fortunate timing. The typical revenue path of online media companies is lined on one side with advertising and on the other side with special services. Consider Yahoo!. While gaining a huge "eyeball share" with its Web directory and building its empire on free services to its users, Yahoo! began serving up advertisements. Although this was an old-media approach, it occurred when demand for Yahoo's ad space exceeded supply. So the company could easily charge premium prices for the privilege of placing an ad on its pages. This happy advertising era reached its height, unsurprisingly, during the greatest inflation of the Internet bubble.

When the bubble was pricked, and the demand for banner ads cooled, Yahoo! started enhancing its free services (for example, Yahoo! Mail) and charging for them. This method of supplementing revenue has worked. Yahoo! is a robust media company which, by the way, owns serious search assets that might yet constitute a challenge to Google's dominance. (See the next section.)

Google's business isn't just advertising

In the beginning of this chapter, I emphasize advertising as the revenue model that drives Google's growth as a business-services company. My accent on advertising is not meant to diminish Google's great success in licensing its basic search technology to Yahoo!, AOL, Netscape, and many other high-profile Internet portals. This licensing activity has generated strong revenue flows for Google, matured the company's business standing, and extended its brand to near-ubiquity. But most readers of this book are interested less in licensing Google's search engine than in using AdWords and AdSense as business tools.

It's difficult to predict how far AdWords and AdSense will take Google, and what their effect on Internet culture will be. It's not a stretch to imagine that search advertising, using the cost-per-click model that Google popularized, could alter the Web landscape by reducing advertisers' reliance on flashing banners and those heinous pop-ups.

Certainly, the business side of Google is revolutionizing online marketing, changing it from an art to a science, from guesswork to measurement, from blind spending to targeted cost-per-lead.

Now consider Google's contrasting situation and how it navigated its own infancy as a media company. Yahoo! surrounded its core directory with information pages, but Google concentrated all its resources in the search engine. Google paired exceptional keyword matching with *cost-per-click advertising* to build an advertising business that paired advertisers with customers through matched keywords.

Google and Its Competition

Google's dominance of consumer searching is awesome. There has been no such near-monopoly since Yahoo! was the only important search-and-find Web destination in 1994. The numbers have become a familiar mantra: more than 200 million searches a day, constituting about 50 percent of global search queries. Alongside those numbers looms Google's activity as a business partner to businesses of all sizes. In that arena, Google also dominates, though its clout varies depending on the service.

But our focus is on business services whose influence and effectiveness are tied to Google's preeminence as a consumer search engine. Google's command of the majority of eyeballs in the Internet population makes it the one site in which online businesses must be visible, either in the search result listings or through advertising on search results pages. Will this situation persist? Is marketing in Google a long-term strategy?

The answer to both questions is yes, but Google might not retain its consumer dominance forever. Google stunned the Internet's foundation companies (Yahoo!, Microsoft, and AOL) by reviving search as a viable industry. Google didn't just improve searching; it brought it back from the dead, after Microsoft, for one, had mostly written it off. Competition always pursues pioneers, and now that Google has shone new light on the search industry, its would-be vanquishers loom.

Yahoo! acquired important search assets Inktomi (an engine technology company of long standing) and Overture (a pioneer of placing advertisement on search pages). Now Yahoo!, which once powered its search results and ads with Google's engines, has launched its own consumer engine and pay-per-click advertising program. This development is the start of a rearrangement of the competitive landscape, and Google's vaunted 80-percent share dropped when it no longer provided search results for Yahoo! searches.

Yahoo!'s separation doesn't affect Google's licensing provision with Netscape and AOL, two other major partners. Both receive search results from Google when their members enter keyword queries. But future changes in that quarter would likewise reduce Google's supremacy in processing consumer searches.

Microsoft is famous for coming late to the party and then drinking everyone's punch. Microsoft's Web portal, MSN.com, powers its search results with the Inktomi engine (owned by Yahoo!) and receives its advertising from Overture (likewise owned by Yahoo!). Microsoft is actively working on proprietary alternatives to these licensing deals while publicly and explicitly targeting Google's standing in the field.

All eyes are on this imminent battle of search and related advertising technologies. There seems little doubt that Google's consumer dominance will be cut down. But the ongoing story rests in the hands of consumers. New search engines might not satisfy users who have grown accustomed to Google's ranking style and speed. Those users might migrate from the interfaces that once hosted Google results to Google itself.

Furthermore, Google isn't exactly spending its days at the beach — it's a restless company staffed by high-octane brainpower. Google owns a stunning array of popular search services (fully described in *Google For Dummies*) that buffers it against lost market share in the flagship search engine. It is continually innovating and improving its revenue programs. And its extended advertising network (AdSense and premium-level AdSense partners such as USAToday.com and Discovery.com) creates an important platform for advertisers that will last a long time.

In the next two years, online businesses might want to diversify their marketing efforts, reaching for recognition on other platforms besides Google's advertising network. But even if Google doesn't remain the only essential staging area for Internet marketing, it will remain a crucial one.

Two Sides of the Google Coin

Google is really two companies: Google the search engine and Google the business-services company. Together, the two sides form Google the media company. Along the same lines, Google is employed by two breeds of user: consumers who are searching and business partners of all sizes who seek online visibility.

Google's two sides can't be separated like an Oreo cookie; they're stuck together by keywords. Keywords typed into the search engine are used also to determine the ads placed next to the user's search results, because advertisers bid for the right to launch ads on those keywords. Those same ads are launched to thousands of partner sites in Google's expanded advertising network. Even sites that don't advertise but appear prominently on the search results page probably built their content and HTML coding around the very same keywords. As you can see, the consumer experience (finding destinations) and the business experience (finding customers) are inextricably linked by shared keywords.

But make no mistake: We business users do not enjoy the same weight in the Google equation as consumer users. (Of course, most of us use Google's front end as consumers, too.) Google's first concern is the search experience, and the primary relationship is between Google and the consumer. Without satisfied searchers, the business side has no value. Consumers may freely focus on the search experience, with no awareness of the business forces competing in the background. But business users who ignore consumer-search priorities court their own downfall.

Google's Empowerment Model

At the top of this chapter, I stated that Google's business model makes money when you do. But as I also mentioned, Google makes money even if you don't. That's not a situation Google likes, and it tries to help you correct it, as I discuss in Part II. Google wants you to succeed.

This reciprocity is built into Google's advertising services in three ways:

- ✔ **They are democratic.** Anyone can get involved, from a first-time entrepreneur with a new Web site to a billion-dollar corporation. As in any great democracy, ingenuity, knowledge, and persistence can compete with, and sometimes triumph over, incumbency and deep pockets.

- ✔ **They are reciprocal.** Google's success is good for you, and your success is good for Google. Google's consumer users win, too, when you work effectively in Google's advertising programs. This three-way reciprocity is difficult to establish (and even measure) in traditional media advertising.

- ✔ **They are efficient.** And that's an understatement. Google's innovations in search advertising strive for an ideal match of advertiser to customer, hinged on a keyword. You pay only for reasonably good matches recognized by your potential customers. Google's AdSense program, in which participating sites share ad revenue with Google, doesn't cost the participant a dime — now *that's* efficiency.

eBay, the most successful dot-com venture through the collapse of the Internet bubble, was founded on the same three principles: democracy (anybody could get involved), reciprocity (eBay and its users benefited when its participants succeeded), and efficiency (participants controlled their costs and tracked their returns). In time, the advantages of eBay's system got the attention of midsize brick-and-mortar stores, which now operate eBay outlets as an essential part of their business plan. Much larger corporations routinely use eBay to dispose of inventory. The playing field is level and the economics are equally favorable, whether you are selling computers or a lamp in your attic.

Google's two prime-time revenue programs, AdWords and AdSense, have followed an adoption curve similar to eBay's. Fashioned for universal participation, both programs were adopted first by small players — single Webmasters, entrepreneurs, and one-product companies. Word spread, and now both programs are in far-flung use by the Internet's largest publishers, manufacturers, and e-tailers. As with eBay, small and large participants enjoy the same benefits.

The Three Goals of Every Webmaster

Innumerable business plans operate side by side on the Web. But all these sites — online stores, travel agencies, virtual magazines, community portals, even modest personal sites — share three fundamental goals:

✔ **Increase presence.** Putting up a Web site is like mounting a billboard in a desert: Nobody sees it. Chapter 3 explains how to network your site to greater visibility by getting other sites to link to it. In the context of Google, increasing Web presence means increasing presence in Google's *Web index* — the gigantic collection of Web pages from which Google derives its search results. And that means raising the site's PageRank, which I discuss in Chapter 3.

✔ **Drive traffic.** Traffic is the natural extension of presence. For our purposes, presence is visibility in Google, but that presence, by itself, doesn't do a Webmaster much good. Google visibility must be turned into traffic, which happens when Google searchers click your link.

✔ **Convert visitors.** Traffic is enough for some Webmastering purposes. In nonrevenue sites, the goal might be just to get eyeballs on the home page. But that simple ambition is rarely the objective of a site. Almost every Webmaster wants to get visitors to do something — visit a certain page, fill out a form, join a mailing list, travel across an opt-out page, buy a product, click an ad. Whatever the aim, the conversion of traffic from unproductive visits to productive visits is the final step that nearly all Webmasters seek.

Google is a powerful ally in the first two goals. Nothing increases presence like a high listing on a Google search results page. If high positioning isn't enough to drive traffic or isn't possible in certain searches, Google's advertising program (AdWords) can help divert the flow of traffic in your direction. Google can't magically convert visitors, but it does help its AdWords users track visitors who do convert.

Google and Your Web Site

Google's come-one, come-all advertising programs (AdWords and AdSense) are enticing to every Webmaster with entrepreneurial inclinations. "The main Google index — a marketing venue in itself — presents you with three significant opportunities for business growth:"

✔ **Google search listings.** Getting into the listings (see Chapter 2) is the first major step. As you work your way in, concentrate on building up your PageRank (see Chapter 3). Many Webmasters attain ongoing success without any advertising by fighting for and retaining a high search-page position for important keywords (see Chapter 4).

✔ **AdWords.** Google's search advertising program, AdWords increases presence and drives traffic. And the first part — increasing presence — is free. AdWords ads appear on the right side (and sometimes at the top) of Google search pages. Advertisers pay for their ad only when a Google user clicks on it. The AdWords program offers a quick way to place your site on a search results page without necessarily being in the Google index. (Part II explores AdWords in detail.)

✔ **AdSense.** Google's ad-syndication program, AdSense is a method of making money on your site. Webmasters in the AdSense program display AdWords ads on their pages and share advertiser payments with Google. The goal of an AdSense page is to get visitors to scoot *off* the page by clicking an ad. The ads are supplied by Google, and in fact are the same AdWords you see on Google search results pages. When a visitor clicks one, the AdSense publisher shares the cost-per-click ad revenue with Google. Participating in the AdSense program is free to any qualifying page or site. (Part III fully describes the AdSense program.)

The three marketing venues just described — search listings, AdWords, and AdSense — roughly correspond to three business activities. Understanding how and to what degree to approach these three activities helps guide you toward the best Google marketing service for your talent and taste:

✔ **Optimize.** Site optimization is ongoing, detail-minded work that asks for writing talent, organizational skill, a willingness to update and tweak daily, and an eagerness to stay on top of an evolving field. Optimization is the foremost activity for those aspiring to climb upwards to greater visibility in Google's search results listings. Don't forget, though, that certain optimization tasks are necessary in all aspects of online marketing. To some extent, site optimization is integral to every site's greater success. If you love to optimize, climbing the listings is your marketing arena. (Chapter 4 is all about optimization.)

✔ **Publicize.** If your site has the goods — by which I mean great information, saleable products, interactive features, or an essential service — the slow grind of optimization might be too gradual a path for you. If you're ready to transact business now and are confident in your site's ability to convert visitors without an optimization overhaul, advertising might be your bet. AdWords offers a cost-efficient method of sending qualified leads to your domain. You pay by the click — which means you're buying actual visitors, not ad displays — so your *return on investment (ROI)* depends on your site's ability to convert. As you learn in Part II, you can strictly control your costs in AdWords by placing a ceiling on the amount you pay per click and on your overall expenditures.

✔ **Monetize.** If you don't sell products, and want your site itself to generate revenue, AdSense is a program made for your entrepreneurial needs. AdSense is a free way to join Google's advertising network and display AdWords ads. Revenue earned in this manner — by publishing ads that generate income — is called *passive revenue.* Unlike the busy lifestyle of fulfilling orders taken through a Web site, the passive-revenue lifestyle lets the site do the work, not you.

Google and Your Product

E-tailers whose catalogs range from one product to thousands can be represented in Google's two shopping portals: Google Catalogs and Froogle. Google Catalogs is a search engine dedicated to displaying printed catalogs and linking to their sites. It's available only to companies that publish such catalogs. Froogle is available to any business that sells a product through a Web site.

There is no downside to being represented in Froogle and Google Catalogs. Participation in both is free. By themselves, however, these two services should not comprise a total online marketing plan for your site and its products. Many e-tailers and offline retailers also use AdWords; a quick glance in the Google search page for *books*, *furniture*, or *2004 autos* shows you the caliber of advertiser using Google advertising.

Chapter 2

Getting into Google

This chapter is about getting your site to appear on Google search pages. I'm not talking about the Google Directory, submission to which is a simple matter also covered here. The challenge is to appear in search results based on keywords related to your site. Chapters 3 and 4 focus on becoming more prominently placed on those search results pages; this chapter is more elementary but no less crucial for new sites.

The Three-Step Process

Many of the suggestions, tactics, and concepts discussed in this chapter and Chapter 3 and 4 apply to both getting into Google (the first step) and improving a site's status in Google (an ongoing project). Understanding the Google crawl (this chapter), networking your site (Chapter 3), and site optimization (Chapter 4) are important topics for newcomers and veterans alike. There's no proper order in which to tackle these subjects — they are presented here in a certain order, but the topics in these three chapters add up to a single process that maximizes your site's exposure in Google.

Here is a summary of the ground covered in these three chapters:

✔ **Getting into Google (Chapter 2).** Understand how the Google spider crawls the Web and what the spider looks at. Judge whether to submit a new page manually to the index or let the spider find it. Find out how to keep material *out* of Google.

✔ **Networking your site (Chapter 3).** Develop a matrix of incoming links, which is crucial for building a higher status in Google and effective for getting into the index at the start.

✔ **Optimizing your site for Google (Chapter 4).** Create content, optimize your page's meta tags, and introduce keywords as the fundamental building blocks of a highly ranked site. These are golden topics for the serious Webmaster at all stages of business development, from conception to customer interaction.

First things first. New sites must get into Google and then work to raise their profiles. Getting into Google really means getting into the Google *index*, which is a database of Web content. Google builds the index by crawling through the Web collecting pages. When a user searches for keywords, Google doesn't actually search the Web — it searches its index.

If your site already appears in Google search results, you might feel tempted to skip this chapter and head straight for Chapter 3. However, the next two sections contain useful information about Google's behavior and ways for both new and existing sites to leverage its quirks.

Meet Google's Pet Spider

All search engines operate in the same basic way: they *crawl* the Web with automatic software robots called *spiders* or *crawlers*, which create searchable indexes of Web content. Every engine allows visitors to search its index for keywords and groups of keywords. Search results come in a variety of list formats, but most display a bit of information about each Web page in the list and a link to that page.

Each engine's index is unique, thanks to the programming of its spider. The main element of that programming is the engine's *algorithm*, which ranks pages in an index. This ranking determines the order in which search results are presented.

Google's central technology asset is its algorithm — the complex ranking formula that gives people good search results and often seems to be reading people's minds when they Google something. The results of Google's algorithm are summarized in a single ranking statistic called *PageRank*. Google is secretive about the software formula from which PageRank is derived, but the company does promote the importance of PageRank, and offers Webmasters broad hints for improving a site's PageRank. Google displays a general approximation of any page's rank (on a 0-to-10 scale) in the Google Toolbar, which is shown in Figure 2-1. Although the exact formulation of PageRank is a well-protected secret, its basic ingredients are well-known (and discussed in Chapter 3).

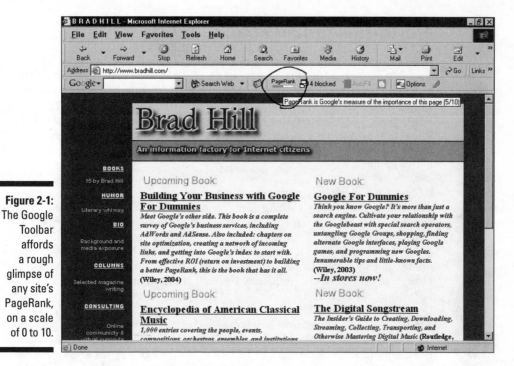

Figure 2-1:
The Google
Toolbar
affords
a rough
glimpse of
any site's
PageRank,
on a scale
of 0 to 10.

The Google PageRank is like a carrot dangled before the ambitious gaze of Webmasters, who devote considerable energy to inching their pages up to a higher PageRank, thereby moving them up the search results list. Chapter 3 is devoted to improving your site's ranking and position on search results pages.

Search engine integrity

One reason pre-Google search engines declined in usefulness and popularity as Web-content portals was the emergence of paid listings. Hungry for revenue, some engines sold positions on the search results page to advertisers. This dilution of objectivity polluted search results and undermined the essential democracy of the Web. The distinction blurred between search engines, which supposedly located what *you* wanted, and browser channels, which sent you to the browser's business affiliates. Even though many search engines did not accept paid placement, distrust grew among users.

Google started a renaissance of utility and trust. Google's integrity is symbolized by its gunk-free home page, the spartan design of which lures the user with the promise of search, and nothing but search. To be sure, Google accepts advertising, and Parts II and III of this book are all about Google ads. But Google's paid content is clearly separated from search listings. Not everyone agrees with the ranking of search results in Google, but nobody thinks that a high rank can be bought.

Timing Google's crawl

Google crawls the Web at varying depths and on more than one schedule. The so-called *deep crawl* occurs roughly once a month. This extensive reconnaissance of Web content requires more than a week to complete and an undisclosed length of time after completion to build the results into the index. For this reason, it can take up to six weeks for a new page to appear in Google. Brand new sites at new domain addresses that have never been crawled before might not even be indexed at first, depending on considerations explained later in this chapter.

If Google relied entirely on the deep crawl, its index would quickly become outdated in the rapidly shifting Web. To stay current, Google launches various supplemental *fresh crawls* that skim the Web more shallowly and frequently than the deep crawl. These supplementary spiders do not update the entire index, but they freshen it by updating the content of some sites. Google does not divulge its fresh-crawling schedules or targets, but Webmasters can get an indication of the crawl's frequency through sharp observance.

Google has no obligation to touch any particular URL with a fresh crawl. Sites can increase their chance of being crawled often, however, by changing their content and adding pages frequently. Remember the shallowness aspect of the fresh crawl; Google might dip into the home page of your site (the front page, or index page) but not dive into a deep exploration of the site's inner pages. (More than once I've observed a new index page of my site in Google within a day of my updating it, while a new inner page added at the same time was missing.) But Google's spider can compare previous crawl results with the current crawl, and if it learns from the top navigation page that new content is added regularly, it might start crawling the entire site during its frequent visits.

The deep crawl is more automatic and mindlessly thorough than the fresh crawl. Chances are good that in a deep crawl cycle, any URL already in the main index will be reassessed down to its last page. However, Google does not necessarily include every page of a site. As usual, the reasons and formulas involved in excluding certain pages are not divulged. The main fact to remember is that Google applies PageRank considerations to every single page, not just to domains and top pages. If a specific page is important to you and is not appearing in Google search results, your task is to apply every networking and optimization tactic described in Chapter 3 to that page. You may also manually submit that specific page to Google (see the next section).

The terms *deep crawl* and *fresh crawl* are widely used in the online marketing community to distinguish between the thorough spidering of the Web that Google launches approximately monthly and various intermediate crawls run at Google's discretion. Google itself acknowledges both levels of spider activity, but is secretive about exact schedules, crawl depths, and formulas by which the company chooses crawl targets. To a large extent, targets are determined by automatic processes built into the spider's programming, but humans at Google also direct the spider to specific destinations for various reasons, some of which are discussed in this chapter.

Earlier, I said that the Google index remains static between crawls. Technically, that's true. Google matches keywords against the index, not against live Web content, so any pages put online (or modified) between visits from Google's spider remain excluded from (or out of date in) the search results until they are crawled again. But two factors work against the index remaining unchanged for long. First, the frequency of fresh crawls keeps the index evolving in a state that Google-watchers call *everflux*. Second, some time is required to put crawl results into the index on Google's thousands of servers. The irregular heaving and churning of the index that results from these two factors is called the *Google dance*.

To submit or not to submit

You can get your site into the Google index in two simple ways:

- ✔ Submit the site manually
- ✔ Let the crawl find it

Neither method offers a guarantee. Google accepts URL submissions, but it doesn't respond to them nor assure Webmasters that their submissions will be added to the index. When Google decides to manually add a site, it does so by sending the spider crawling to the submitted URL to take stock of the site's various pages. Characteristically, Google doesn't inform the Webmaster that the site has been accepted, and it doesn't provide a schedule for crawling accepted sites.

Google's hands-off operation

Google is a reasonably communicative company in certain departments, such as AdWords, AdSense, and enterprise solutions. And Google accepts URL submissions for the index, though it doesn't acknowledge them. But asking humans at Google to interfere with the construction of its index is an exercise in futility.

Google builds its index through robotic interaction, for the most part, and prides itself on these sophisticated automated processes. Google does not correct a Webmaster's outdated listings or make any custom change to the index. The company counts on time and thorough crawling to solve problems. Google doesn't want to hear from you about your index issues.

The key to attracting Google's spider is getting your page linked on other sites. Google finds your content by following links to your pages. With no *incoming links* (also called *backlinks*), you are an unreachable island as far as the Google crawl is concerned. This isolated condition is the natural state of any new site. Of course, anybody can reach you directly by entering the URL, but you won't pluck the spider's web until you get some other sites to link to you. See Chapter 3 for a detailed tutorial in creating a backlink network.

Submitting a site might not be a ticket to instant success, but at least it's easy. Enter your submitted URL at this address:

```
www.google.com/addurl.html
```

Fill in the form (see Figure 2-2) and click the Add URL button, keeping in mind that the button is misnamed. You are not *adding* the URL, you are *submitting* it. Only the spider can add your site, and only a Google human can tell it to.

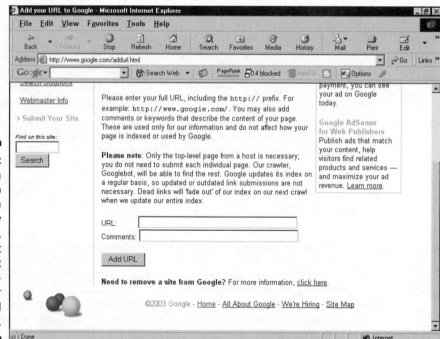

Figure 2-2: Submitting a URL to Google could hardly be easier, but don't expect acknowledgment or guaranteed results.

If you add a page to a URL already in the Google index, there's no need to submit the new page. Under most circumstances, Google will find the new page the next time your site is crawled in its entirety.

You don't have to choose between submitting and not submitting; do both if you're impatient. Submitting doesn't stop the spider from visiting you in the normal course of events, but it doesn't encourage the spider, either. Conversely, the spider's failure to find you doesn't affect the disposition of your submitted request. Are you getting the idea that gaining admission to Google's index is a crapshoot? Not really. In fact, Google's spider is so thorough that entering the index is practically inevitable if you follow the networking suggestions in the next chapter. Submitting a URL manually *is* a crapshoot, though. My best suggestion is to submit if you must, but don't *only* submit. Get to work networking your site and implementing other optimization tactics in Chapter 3, which will get you inside the index more quickly and push your site to a higher PageRank.

The directory route

If submitting a URL seems too uncertain and networking seems too difficult, you can get into the Web index by getting your site listed in the Google Directory. The Google Directory is a categorized list of Web sites, built by hand. Google does not build its own directory — a fact that surprises many people. Instead, Google repurposes the large Web directory created by the Open Directory Project. The Open Directory Project (ODP) is a non-profit organization staffed by thousands of volunteer editors who accept URL submissions for their respective subject niches. Google applies a PageRank to the Open Directory (see the bars on the left in Figure 2-3), thereby reordering the directory listings, and presents the whole thing in familiar Google style.

Naturally, the Google spider crawls the directory, so any new directory listing is automatically added to Google's main Web index. Submit a URL to the Open Directory Project at this address:

```
www.dmoz.org/add.html
```

When it comes to accepting submissions, the Open Directory Project does not guarantee your entry any more than Google does. With ODP, you are at the mercy of whichever editor is in charge of your most relevant category, and the chance of developing a companionable dialogue with that person is slim. Furthermore, the ODP URL-submission process is much more complicated than at Google. Finally, you can usually count on a long and indeterminate wait before your site is added. Keep checking by searching for your site in the Google Directory.

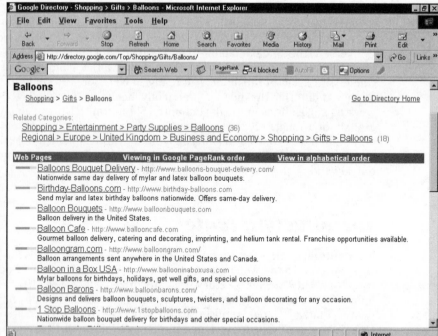

Figure 2-3:
Listing in the
Google
Directory
assures
being
crawled for
the Web
index.

Checking your site's status in Google

During the sometimes-long wait to be included in Google, you naturally want to know when you've succeeded. (So you can run through the streets yelling, "Google me! Google me!")

How do you know whether your site is in the Google index? Don't try searching for it with general keywords — that method is hit-or-miss. You could search for an exact phrase located in your site's text (by putting quotes around the phrase), but if the phrase is not unique you could get tons of other matches.

The best bet is to simply search for your URL, as shown in Figure 2-4. Make it exact, and include the *www* prefix. If you're searching for an inner page of the site, precision is likewise necessary, so remember to include the *.htm* or *.html* file extension if it exists.

When adding a page to a site already in Google, be prepared for a long wait for it to appear, especially if you don't change your content often. If Google's spider checks your site during only its deep crawl and the timing is off, you could tap your fingers for about six weeks before seeing the new page in search results.

Indexing frustrations

Moving is hell, on land and in cyberspace. Moving your site from one URL to another — and especially from one domain to another — presents a vexing indexing problem. There's a good chance that Google will continue to list your old site after you move, and even after it begins to list your new site. The Google spider is not dense. It trusts incoming links, many of which probably still point to your old location. From Google's perspective, you haven't really moved until you update your entire network of incoming links (which, if you take Chapter 3 seriously, you worked hard to establish), pointing them to your new location. Your PageRank will drop considerably, too, until you get those backlinks up to speed. Moving is a serious consideration for any site that depends on stature in Google, and it shouldn't be undertaken lightly or without planning.

Partial listings can also spark frustration, for example, when Google's spider locates your site and files the address but does not crawl all of its content. Because Google's descriptions are quoted from the pages, your listing on any search page is bereft of a description. This situation bodes ill, for descriptions often provide the motivation to click on search results. Your only recourse is to build up your PageRank to the level at which Google sniffs out all your content and provides descriptions of your pages. See Chapter 3.

Figure 2-4:
Search for your page or site address to see whether you're in the Google index.

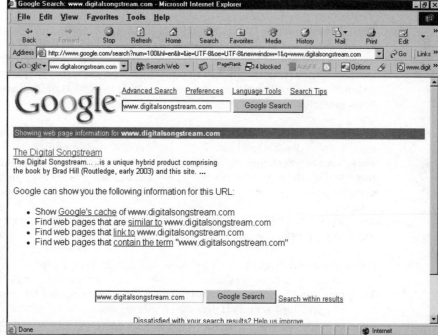

Keeping Google Out

This book is about partnering with Google: getting into the index, improving your PageRank, advertising on Google, distributing other people's Google ads on your site, and other ways of building your online business through Google. So a section about rebuffing Google might seem counterproductive. But in the interest of covering all bases, here it is.

Sometimes even publicity-hungry Webmasters want to keep Google away from certain parts of their business. Private pages designed for friends and semiprivate pages created for select visitors shouldn't be indexed for the world at large. Entire sites that are still under development while existing on the Web in a live state might best be excluded from Google.

It's fairly easy to prevent Google from indexing an entire site or selected pages of a site even if the spider crawls your URL. You can prevent Google also from *caching* pages of your site, a process by which Google stores each indexed page on its servers. This section explains how to prevent Google from crawling and caching your site.

Deflecting the crawl

The key to deflecting Google's spider is the *robots.txt file,* also known as the Robots Exclusion Protocol. Google's spider understands and obeys this protocol. The robots.txt file is a short, simple text file that you place in the top-level directory (root directory) of your domain server. (If you lease your Web space from your ISP, not from a dedicated Web host, you probably need administrative help in placing the robots.txt file.)

Create the robots.txt file in Notepad or another text editor, and transfer it as an ASCII text file. It's best not to use Microsoft Word or another word processor to create the robots.txt file. But if you do, remember to save it as a plain text file with the *.txt* file extension. Then make sure you transfer it to your server as a binary file, which is the default setting of many FTP (file transfer protocol) programs.

The robots.txt file contains two instructions:

- **User-agent.** This instruction specifies which search engine crawler must follow the robots.txt instructions. You may specify Google's spider, multiple specific spiders, or all spiders. (The command works for all spiders that seek and acknowledge the robots.txt file.)

- **Disallow.** This line specifies which directories (Web page folders) or specific pages at your site are off-limits to the search engine. You must include a separate `Disallow` line for each excluded directory.

The robots.txt resource site

The information in this chapter gives you everything you need to construct an effective robots.txt file. If you want to know more, such as a list of spider names and general information about crawlers, go to the Web Robots Page here:

`www.robotstxt.org`

The FAQ (frequently asked questions) section at this site is particularly useful:

`www.robotstxt.org/wc/faq.html`

A sample robots.txt file looks like this:

```
User-agent: *
Disallow: /
```

This example is the most common and simplest robots.txt file. The asterisk after `User-agent` means all spiders are excluded. The forward slash after `Disallow` means all site directories are off-limits.

The name of Google's spider is Googlebot. (I would have preferred Charlotte.) If you want to exclude only Google and no other search engines, use this robots.txt file:

```
User-agent: Googlebot
Disallow: /
```

You may identify certain directories as out-of-bounds, either to Google or all spiders. For example:

```
User-agent: *
Disallow: /cgi-bin/
Disallow: /family/
Disallow: /photos/
```

Notice the forward slashes at both ends of the directory strings in the preceding example. Google understands that the first slash implies your domain address before it. So, on the first `Disallow` line, if that line were found at the `bradhill.com` site, would be shorthand for `http://www.bradhill.com/cgi-bin/`, and Google would know to exclude that directory from the crawl. The second forward slash means you're excluding an entire directory.

To exclude individual pages, type the page address following the first forward slash, and leave off the second forward slash, like this:

```
User-agent: *
Disallow: /family/reunion-notes.htm
Disallow: /blog/archive00082.htm
```

Each excluded directory and page must be listed on its own `Disallow` line. Do not group multiple items on one line.

To exclude a certain type of file, use the asterisk followed by the file extension on the `Disallow` line, like this:

```
User-agent: *
Disallow: /family/*.jpg
```

This example tells all spiders to exclude *.jpg* files (a certain type of picture file) from indexing. In Google's case, this sort of command is apt because Google devotes an entire search engine to images (`www.google.com/images`). If you want to exclude *all* images on your site from the Google Images index, use a robots.txt file with the name of Google's Image spider, which is Googlebot-Image:

```
User-agent: Googlebot-Image
Disallow: /
```

Remember that your graphic logos are also included in this broad exclusion, and therefore won't turn up in Google's image search. That omission is normally not a problem and doesn't affect the display of your images when people visit your site.

Use the asterisk-plus-extension technique to exclude any type of file from the crawl, such as *.doc* and *.pdf* files.

Effects of the robots.txt file are not immediate in many cases, especially when you're trying to exclude a page that's currently included. First, you must wait for the spider to crawl your site again, and your site's crawl cycle could be daily, monthly, or sometime in between, depending on its PageRank. Second, the page you want excluded, if previously included, will live on in Google's cache for some time. (See the next section for information about requesting removal from the cache and avoiding the cache from the start of a page's life.)

You may adjust the robots.txt file as often as you'd like. It's a good tool when building fresh pages that you don't want indexed while still under construction. When they're finished, take them out of the robots.txt file.

Excluding pages with the meta tag

In some situations, using a `meta` tag to deflect spiders is easier than constructing a robots.txt file. If you code your HTML by hand, as opposed to using graphic design programs such as Dreamweaver or Front Page, throwing in the `meta` tag is a piece of cake. Also, if you want to exclude only one page, or the occasional page here and there, the `meta` tag option could be easier.

Using both `meta` tags and the robots.txt file is fine. Not all spiders understand the `meta` tag described here, but Google does.

Note: See Chapter 3 for the effective use of other `meta` tags that are part of the site optimization process.

You place `meta` tags after the `<head>` tag at the top of an HTML document. (Note that `meta` tags can be uppercase or lowercase.) To dissuade the Google spider from indexing any individual page of your site, put this tag among your other `meta` tags in that page's HTML:

```
<meta name="robots" content="noindex, nofollow">
```

Note the two commands, `noindex` and `nofollow`. The first prevents Google from indexing your page, and the second prevents Google from following links on that page. If you want the page to be excluded from the index but would like Google to follow its outgoing links, leave off the `nofollow` command, like this:

```
<meta name="robots" content="noindex">
```

Make your command Google-specific by using the name of Google's spider, Googlebot:

```
<meta name="googlebot" content="noindex, nofollow">
```

Avoiding the cache

Other `meta` commands prevent pages from being copied into Google's cache. The *cache* is a storehouse of Web pages copied by Google. Clicking the Cached link on a search results page quickly brings up the page as it appeared when last crawled, which might be different than it appears now, live on the Web.

This feature is great for Google's consumer users. I used it recently after watching David Letterman complain about the CBS.com site, which hosted a photo of archrival Jay Leno. By the time Letterman's rant aired, late at night, CBS had already changed the site by replacing Leno's picture with Letterman's. I wanted to see the original gaffe, so I hit the Cached link in Google, and there it was. Frequently crawled sites that make major updates daily, such as Slate.com, generally run about a day behind in the Google cache.

Site owners are not universally happy about the Google cache. For one thing, the cache treads upon a gray area of copyright infringement, since Google does not obtain authorization to make copies of the sites it crawls. (Google does remove cached links upon request.) Second, when Webmasters change a page, they want it *changed!* Often, as in the CBS example, the site's owner does not want people like me dredging up old mistakes.

Prevent any page from entering the Google archive with the following `meta` tag:

```
<meta name="googlebot" content="noarchive">
```

Extend the command to all spiders fluent in `meta` tag commands by replacing `googlebot` with `robots`:

```
<meta name="robots" content="noarchive">
```

The invisibility problem

Deflecting Google's spider when it reaches your site is easy enough, as the previous sections explain. A bigger problem is when Google reaches your site, but can't see it. The spider is well equipped to make fine distinctions about your content, HTML tags, and link network, but it is a creature of simple tastes. Creating a site using certain technologies stumps the Google arachnid and sends it scurrying away empty-handed. In particular, three factors are apt to frustrate or displease Google:

✔ **Frames.** Frames have been generally loathed since their introduction in the HTML specification early in the Web's history. They wreak havoc with the Back button, and they confuse the fundamental format of Web addresses (one page per address) by dividing one page address into multiple portions that operate like little, independent Web pages. However, frames do have legitimate uses. Google itself uses frames to display threads in Google Groups (see Chapter 4). But the Google spider turns up its nose when it encounters frames. Framed pages are not necessarily excluded from the index. But errors can ensue hurting both the index and your visitors — either your framed pages won't be included, or searchers are sent to the wrong page because of addressing confusion. If you do use frames, make your site Google-friendly (and human-friendly) by providing links to unframed versions of the same content, as Google does in Google Groups. These links give Google's diligent spider another route to your valuable content, and your visitors get a choice of viewing modes — everybody wins.

✔ **Splash pages.** Splash pages (not to be confused with doorway pages) are content-empty entry pages to Web sites. You've probably seen them. Some splash pages employ cool multimedia introductions to the content within — useless and invisible to Google. Others are mere static welcome mats that force users to click again before getting into the site. Google does not like pointing its searchers to splash pages. In fact, these tedious welcome mats are bad site design by any standard, even if you don't care about Google indexing, and I recommend getting rid of them. Give your visitors, and Google, meaningful content from the first click, and you'll be rewarded with happier visitors and better placement in Google's index.

✔ **Dynamically generated pages.** A *dynamic page* is one that is created on the fly based on choices made by the site visitor. Sites that pull their content from databases (XML sites provide a good example) generate dynamic pages. When Google crawls such a site, it can generate huge numbers of pages, sometimes crashing the site or its server. The Google spider picks up some dynamically generated pages, but generally backs off when it encounters dynamic content. As a result, the site's content, hidden in its database, remains invisible to Google. The spider can't collect it, evaluate it, index it, or apply PageRank to it. (Weblog pages do not fall into this category — they are dynamically generated by *you,* the Webmaster, but not by your visitors.)

Inadvertent invisibility is a good segue to the next chapter, which deals with design issues of all sorts in the quest to optimize pages for Google's spider.

Chapter 3

Building Your PageRank Through Networking

Google's PageRank is probably the most observed, mysterious, important, and craved statistic in the entire online marketing field. This might be especially true among the vast numbers of entrepreneurs, Webmasters, small businesses, medium businesses, thriving businesses, struggling businesses, online stores, service sites, and other enterprises not up to the level of clout enjoyed by Amazon.com, eBay, Yahoo!, and other Internet juggernauts. For nearly all online ventures, visibility in Google is a marketing imperative — and PageRank determines a site's visibility.

As described in Chapter 2, PageRank is the result of Google's internal ranking algorithm. (You can view a crude version of any site's PageRank by calling up that site while running the Google Toolbar.) Although PageRank's formulas and specific results aren't publicized, enough is known about it — partly through trial and error, and partly through Google's sparse proclamations — to catalyze entire marketing niches devoted to raising a site's PageRank.

The value of improving a site's PageRank lies in positioning: Highly ranked pages appear close to the top of Google's search results lists. Positioning is determined also by *which* search page is being displayed, and there are as many unique search pages as there are keyword combinations. The goal is to place your site high on search results pages that closely correlate with your site's subject. A high PageRank always boosts a site's position relative to similar sites.

Jockeying for position in search engines is not a new sport. To the contrary, Webmasters have engaged in the contest for high search-result positions for years. Google's increasing dominance in the field has concentrated the most meaningful screen real estate onto a single engine's result pages, and competition for that space has become ferocious. Winning techniques have become more demanding, precise, and artful. The field of *search engine optimization (SEO)* covers other engines besides Google, but much more attention is paid to Google's search results than to those of any other single engine.

Competition for Googlespace is cruel. Broad subject areas such as music, news, or baseball are jammed with major industrial sites, and breaking into the rarefied atmosphere clotted with corporate behemoths such as MTV.com, CNN.com, and MLB.com is, for the most part, impossible. Google's default display setting shows only 10 results on the user's search page. (This setting can be extended to 100 listings, but many people don't bother.) Google's reputation for delivering the best sites, fast, discourages casual searching beyond the first page. So the pressure is on to break into the top 10.

The good news is that getting near the top of the list is doable for narrower, precisely targeted subjects. It's not unusual for sole proprietors of commercial sites to score the top position in a Google search of targeted keyword phrases.

Google strives to be, and largely is, democratic. The ranking of Google search results is based on merit and popularity. Any Web site, large or small, can gain favorable positioning by leveraging good content, diligent networking, and smart optimizing.

Incoming Links and PageRank

One key to higher PageRank is getting linked on other sites. PageRank is a complicated algorithm, and largely a secret one, but Google acknowledges that the number of links pointing to a site is the largest single factor of that site's PageRank. The two major marketing efforts to undertake when building your business with Google are creating incoming links and optimizing your site. This chapter is devoted to incoming links, and Chapter 4 is about optimization; each contributes enormously to a site's PageRank, overall visibility, and marketing success.

In theory, any single page currently crawled by Google (that is, currently in the index) that links to your page or site is enough to send Google's spider crawling toward you. In practice, you want as many incoming links as possible, both to increase your site's chance of being crawled (which sounds a little creepy) and to improve your site's PageRank once in the index.

The dual role of networking

Links from one site to another not only help Google find a target site when it is new but also contribute to the target site's PageRank. Among other considerations, Google's ranking algorithm measures each page's popularity based on the number of other pages that link to it. The theory is that if Page A puts up a link to Page B, there must be something worthwhile on Page B. If 100 sites link to Page B, the target page becomes more worthy in Google's eyes. If 100,000 links to Page B are scattered around the Web, Page B must really have something going for it. From Google's viewpoint, Page B must have special value to Google's users, and therefore deserves higher positioning on the search results page when it matches the search keywords.

Google doesn't rely totally on counting backlinks, by any means. Many other page-analysis calculations take place when determining PageRank. Even the counting of backlinks is more complex than it seems at first, because Google also evaluates the worthiness of the referring pages (the pages linking to Page B) to determine how important those backlinks are.

The outcome of all this evaluation, from the user's viewpoint, is a sense of the living network underlying all Web pages and sites. No single page in the Google index exists in isolation — they're all embedded in a deeply complex matrix of connectivity.

For the Webmaster and online marketer, Google offers a glimpse into the effectiveness of any site's networking, and the status it enjoys among its peers.

Developing incoming links (from other pages to yours) is a major part of the Google optimization process. Online entrepreneurs seeking to drive traffic to their sites through Google spend immense portions of their development time networking. This networking is accomplished the old-fashioned way — by introducing oneself and talking to other Webmasters — and also through more impersonal means. The following section discusses human networking; I cover link exchanges, which are less personal, in the section after that.

Human Networking

Building a link network by hand, as it were, involves contacting other sites, introducing yourself, and asking to be linked — it's as simple as that. Offering to link back in return smoothes the way to a reciprocal agreement in many cases, but the willingness to trade links doesn't mean you should approach other sites indiscriminately. Keeping your network relevant to the topic of your site has two benefits:

✔ First, you are more likely to succeed when you have something of value to offer — namely, the relevance of your site. Other Webmasters are more interested in trading links with sites likely to send traffic their way, and that sort of traffic-sharing happens mostly among related sites.

✔ Second, placing irrelevant outgoing links on your pages devalues your own site. Diluting the editorial focus of your page (and yes, even a single link undermines that focus) is always a poor optimization move. Google notices, too; the spider examines outgoing and incoming links with remarkable fastidiousness. Irrelevant links tend to lower the PageRank of your page and the pages you link to.

Exchanging links is sometimes a simple and courteous agreement. More substantial alliances might include sharing content. If you run a site about dogs and come across a great article about how to train garden-trampling Labradors, you could offer to trade an article of your own in exchange for the right to post the lab article. Each article would contain a link to the originating page.

Broadly speaking, you want incoming links to point to your top page, or index page. The danger of requesting that incoming links point to inner pages that exactly match the topical focus of the other site is that you could end up with an unfocused network of incoming links aimed at various pages all over your site. From the PageRank-building perspective, such a diverse backlink situation does you little good. There's nothing wrong with putting attention on an important inner page and cultivating its individual PageRank. The point is to gather your efforts into a PageRank campaign likely to raise the stature of your most important business content in Google. In most cases, that means getting your main page, the one with navigation links to all your other pages, as high as possible in Google's search results for relevant keywords.

Working the Link Exchanges

Link exchange sites offer a formal method of exchanging links, with an emphasis on raising Google PageRank. The best of these clearinghouses function also as topical directories built by participating sites that submit their links (see Figure 3-1).

In a nutshell, link exchange sites work by supplying an outgoing link to your site (an incoming link, or backlink, from your perspective) and asking for an incoming link from you in return. There is sometimes no standard of acceptance, application process, or human communication between you and the link exchange. You simply type your site information into a form (see Figure 3-2), and within a short time the link to your site is created. You have an informal obligation to return the favor at your site, which, when multiplied by the many participants in the exchange, helps raise the PageRank of the link exchange site. Most link exchanges operate free of charge to the participants.

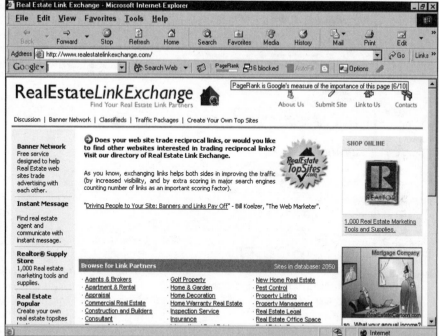

Figure 3-1:
A link
exchange
site that
offers a
real estate
directory.

Although the preceding description covers many bases, the link exchange field is complicated. Two major variations are prevalent:

✔ **Paid link building.** Certain online marketing companies specialize in building incoming link networks for their clients. Ideally, they approach high-quality sites with strong relevance to the client site (in other words, similar sites with high PageRank), and request placement of a link to the client site. Content exchange is usually not involved. These services act as agents on your behalf and work best when your site is good enough to benefit other sites by linking to you.

✔ **Link farms.** These exchanges build vast numbers of outgoing links with indiscriminate disregard for topicality or any sort of editorial policy. Only a fine line distinguishes legitimate link exchanges that accept site information automatically and link farms. Google doesn't like link farms. Remember that Google's spider has an inclusive robotic eye with great peripheral vision. It sees the truth about link connections and their honesty. Building your backlink network around link farms can do you little good and might penalize your PageRank.

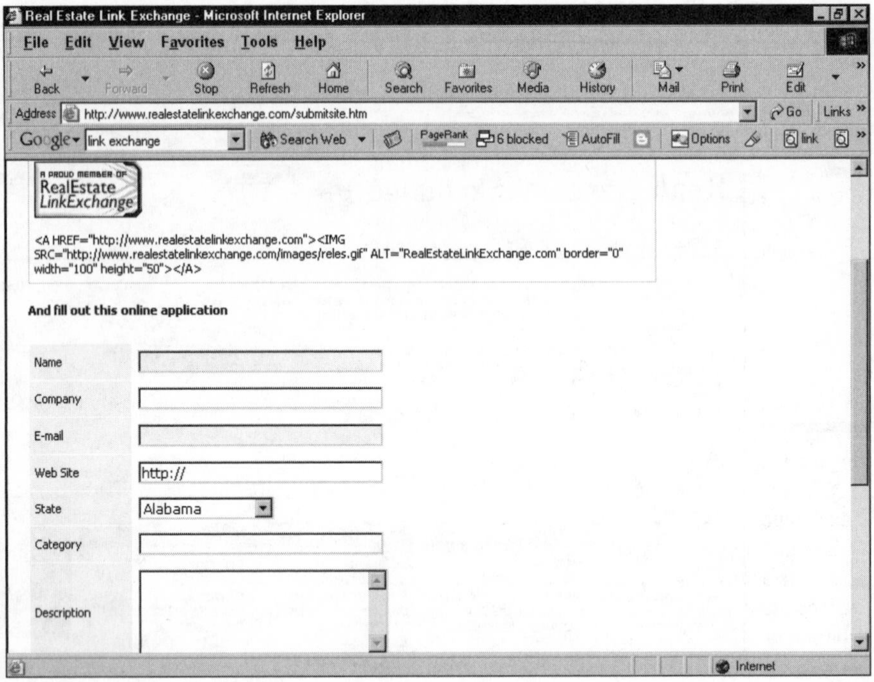

Figure 3-2:
A standard
link-
submission
form at
a link
exchange.
HTML code
is provided
for the
reciprocal
link.

Google claims to distinguish link farms from meaningful link exchanges, and generally discourages using any kind of link exchange site that contains no content besides the links to build PageRank. Choose carefully. The more editorial discretion exercised by the site, the more legitimate it probably is. Use exchanges that maintain a tight topical focus in your field. A general rule is: The more personal the link exchange, the more valuable the incoming link.

Link exchanges work on the principle that a rising tide lifts all boats. If the exchange site benefits from a high PageRank (thanks to dozens of incoming links from participating sites), its enhanced stature in Google bolsters the PageRank of each participating site. The best and most honorable link exchanges concentrate their networks in one certain field, in which case the rising tide is lifting the boats of sites that naturally are in competition. The mutual benefit is well and good, but the challenge remains to distinguish oneself from the high-floating crowd and keep ascending on the search results page. Site optimization techniques described in Chapter 4 can help with that.

When assessing link exchanges, select sites with a reasonably high PageRank — say, 4 or higher. The higher PageRank benefits your own PageRank when Google evaluates the backlink. A high PageRank also provides a kind of Google "stamp of approval," which might not be forthcoming at a less reputable link farm. (To easily see a site's PageRank, use the Google Toolbar. For example, in Figure 3-1, the Google Toolbar lists a PageRank of 6.)

Coding Effective Link Exchanges

Links are simple to use — one click sends the surfer to another page — but more complex behind the scenes. Rudimentary knowledge of HTML link code is needed to optimize your incoming links, and that's what this section gives you.

In most link exchanges, you either provide the complete HTML code for your link or fill in a form that's then used to construct the code. When personally trading links with another site, you might not need to provide complete code for your partner's use, but doing so maximizes the value of that backlink.

The following information might seem excessively detailed, but it meets the Google spider at its own level. Do not ignore this stuff. Google optimization is all about detail.

The underlying code of any incoming link consists of three parts:

- ✔ **URL of the link's target page.** This is the link's destination address.
- ✔ **Link title.** This text appears when a visitor hovers the mouse over the link.
- ✔ **Anchor text.** This is the (usually underlined) link itself, seen and clicked by visitors.

```
<a> </a>
```

As with most other HTML tags, the opening tag (`<a>`) indicates the presence of some content that is influenced by the tag, and the closing tag (`</a>`) indicates that the tag is finished and its influence has ended. Between these two tags, you place your anchor text. (Remember, the anchor text is what the visitor sees and clicks.)

When creating the three parts of a link, the keys are relevance and consistency. Let's say your hobby is trading old coins. You operate a trading site called The Coin Trader, and the site URL is `www.the-coin-trader.com`. (No such site exists as of this writing.) The simplest way to create a powerfully consistent link that Google will respect is to use the words "the coin trader" in all three parts, like this:

```
<a href="http://www.the-coin-trader.com" title="The Coin
         Trader">The Coin Trader</a>
```

Google looks at that link with approval, because its topicality is crystal clear. (Figure 3-3 illustrates this link as it appears on a Web page.)

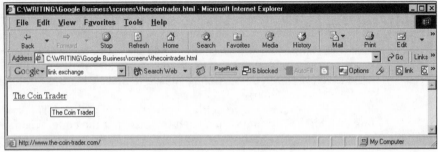

A few important points about this basic link code:

✔ Notice that the first `<a>` tag is considerably extended by two elements: `href`, which stands for *hypertext reference* and is a signpost for the destination URL, and the `title` indicator followed by the title. These two elements — the URL and the title — are contained in the opening anchor tag.

✔ Notice also the quotation marks surrounding the URL and the title. They are necessary; don't leave them off.

✔ Capitalization is not necessary but is a good idea in those portions visible to the visitor: the title and the anchor text.

✔ Take special note of spaces between elements. A space between `a` and `href` *is* necessary. *Do not* separate the anchor text from the tag brackets (before and after) with a space. *Do* leave a space between the closing quote of the URL and the `title` indicator.

To review, these are the tag elements of link code (see Figure 3-4):

✔ `<a>` and `</a>`. The opening and closing anchor tags.

✔ `href`, placed within the opening anchor tag. Identifies the target URL.

✔ The **target URL,** placed within quotation marks. Google looks at this.

✔ `title`, placed within the opening anchor tag. Describes the link title when a user hovers the mouse cursor over the link.

✔ The **link title itself,** placed within quotation marks. This is what appears when a visitor hovers the mouse over a link. Google looks at this.

✔ The **anchor text,** which appears right before the closing anchor tag. This is the link that visitors see and click. Google looks at this.

The quest for consistency needn't eliminate imagination. You have no choice about the URL. And the anchor text is most effective when it simply relates the site name, without devolving into advertising *about* the site. But the link title offers some latitude, and it's not uncommon to see a bit of advertising when you hover your mouse over links on tightly optimized pages. In our example, the title might read, "The Coin Trader: A clearinghouse for ancient and exotic coins." Or "The Coin Trader. Browse, trade, learn! All types of coins; all trade offers welcome." (See Figure 3-5.) The latter title is on the wordy side, but it conforms to the optimization rule of consistency by repeating key words (*coin, coins, trader,* and *trade*). I'll harangue you more about keywords later in Chapter 4.

Figure 3-4:
The tag elements of optimized link code. Provide code like this when supplying links to your site.

Target URL

```
<a href="http://www.civil-war-site.com" title= "The
Civil War Site: An online community for recreationists">
The Civil War Site</a>
```

Anchor text   Link title

Don't confuse the link title with the page title. These two types of titles belong to different HTML tags. I cover proper coding of the page title later in this chapter.

Figure 3-5:
A highly optimized link with a descriptive link title.

Distributing Bylines and Link Sigs

Up to here, this chapter offers ways to market links to your site. Personal link trades and less personal link exchange sites help you build an incoming link network that gets you into the Google index or, if already inside, builds up your site's PageRank. Now it's time to consider a less explicit type of backlink networking, one that requires sharing and publishing content. Of course, you publish content on your own site. But putting your words on other sites is a meaningful, spider-approved way to develop incoming links from sites in your field.

Publishing articles

Everybody needs content. If you're in the process of building a site or even optimizing an existing site, you know how difficult it can be to generate sufficient focused editorial content to make your pages interesting. Even hardcore transactional sites, such as online bookstores, surround their product descriptions with a good deal of editorial content. So whatever you have, somebody else probably wants to use it. By the same token, you might be casting a greedy eye on articles you spotted on competing sites.

Article trading is a sophisticated type of link exchange. Each article has several potential links that might or might not target the same destination:

- ✔ First, the article's byline (which tells the reader who wrote the article) may be presented in the form of a link to your site.

- ✔ Second, an attribution link (which describes who the author is and where the author's site is located) usually contains a link to your site.

- ✔ Third, you may embed links to your site directly in the article text — but don't do so gratuitously. Link to pages in your site that enhance the article.

Even if you don't have articles to trade, nothing is stopping you from asking to use articles you spot elsewhere. If the other site's Webmaster is concerned with Google PageRank (and who isn't?), he or she might be very glad to give you access to get the backlink.

Article submission sites provide another venue in which your content can easily be published outside your own site, creating backlinks. Some of these sites are article farms, which accept every article posted to them and freely redistribute all articles it publishes. Check out the terms of submission, if you don't want your article being reused elsewhere. Some submission sites exist for the main purpose of making posted articles available to other visitors; they are sites you visit to *get* content as well as give it. (See Figure 3-6.) Another type of submission site presents articles as information, not as available content.

Keep a log of your article submissions. Submitting the same article to one location twice is frowned upon, even if done unintentionally. If you're branded a spammer at a submission site, you might be barred from submitting to that site again.

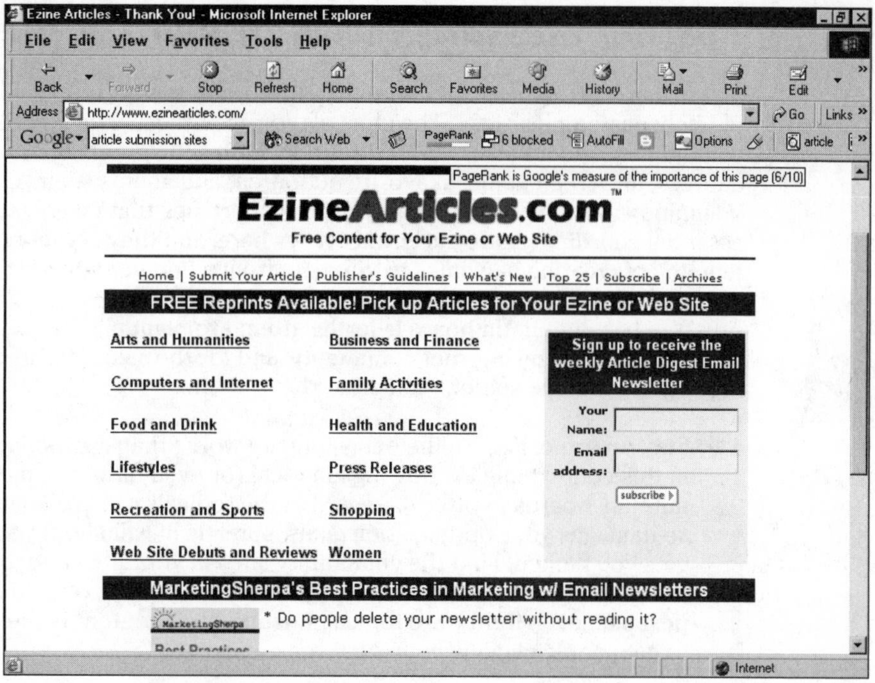

Figure 3-6:
An article
submission
site in
which all
articles are
available to
other sites.

E-zines are fertile ground, too. Don't count on getting paid for an e-zine acceptance; that's not your purpose, anyway. Most e-zines are published as Web pages, even if they're also produced in alternative, non-HTML formats. So your published article would most likely get crawled, and your attribution link and byline would add to your backlink network.

E-zines do not generally offer automated submission and acceptance. They are human-run publications for the most part, with editorial guidelines and standards.

Human-run sites are always the best bet. The more prestigious the site in its field, the greater value there is in being published on that site. Shoot for the top, even if multiple submissions and rewrites are required to get an article accepted. Improving your articles makes your own site better, and when your site improves, high-quality sites are more willing to link to it. Nothing stops you from submitting rejected articles to less demanding sites while you continue to strive for prestigious publication.

Posting messages with linked sig files

A *sig file* is an enhanced signature that appears at the bottom of e-mails and publicly posted messages. The most elaborate of these digital calling cards contain the sender's name, e-mail address, Web URL, phone numbers, postal address, IM screen name, a favorite quotation, and some clever ASCII art. Voluminous sigs are frankly annoying. But short sigs that convey the sender's essential coordinates are accepted everywhere, and they serve the added function of creating backlinks to your site from wherever you post them.

Any Web-based bulletin board is fertile ground to plant a linked sig. But for the well-being of the Internet community, and for the sake of your good standing with the Google spider, remember these points:

- ✔ **Stay on topic.** Few online behaviors are worse than spamming, which, in this context, means posting identical (or even differing) messages to multiple boards in utter disregard of the topicality of the boards. Doing so damages your optimization goals, spreads ill will about your site, and gets you flamed. Find the community sites in your field and join them — not just to plant links but to engage in the flow of conversation. Don't post ads, even if they are topical. Posting good content is the best way to get people clicking your sig link.

- ✔ **Usenet doesn't count.** Usenet newsgroups, the native bulletin-board structure of the Internet, can be fun, informative, and good builders of traffic. But they are not part of the World Wide Web, and Google's Web spider does not crawl them. There's nothing wrong with spreading your link sig around Usenet, but it's not a PageRank strategy. True, Google maintains a Web-based archive of Usenet newsgroups (called Google Groups), but current wisdom has it that Google doesn't crawl its own Google Groups for the Web index.

- ✔ **Check the host's PageRank.** One consideration when choosing communities in which to get involved is PageRank. (Use the Google Toolbar to see any page's rank on a 0-to-10 scale.) Of course, low-ranked message boards might offer other values that appeal to you.

- ✔ **Don't submit message pages to Google.** Google accepts URL submissions for inclusion in the index, as described earlier in this chapter. Some marketing professionals suggest submitting every single message-board page that contains your link, in an effort to hasten the inclusion of your entire backlink network. Don't do this. You'll drive Google crazy, and you'll drive yourself to the grave.

Meaningless backlinks

Ideally, a link from one site to another is an endorsement. This ideal harks back to the Web in its infancy, when most pages (created by college students, naturally) were simple link lists — personal bookmarks shared with the world. Google's PageRank algorithm starts with this ideal. The formula supposes that if Page A links to Page B, Webmaster A endorses the content of Page B.

This ideal is alive and well on millions of sites but has also degraded to the point of becoming meaningless on other sites. Even when an endorsement is genuine, new page-generating technologies have challenged Google's algorithm through massive replication of linked endorsements.

One example is found in Weblogs (blogs). Blogs often carry suggested links to other blogs, which in turn link back, and all blog sites in this mutual admiration network generate new pages at astonishing rates. Gigantic, incestuous backlink networks result from blog exchanges. This situation has caused Google to tweak its algorithm, and it now weighs Weblog backlinks with a sensitivity to the automated technology involved. (Google owns Blogger.com, one of the most popular Weblog hosts, so the company is clearly not anti-blog.)

Meaningless backlinking can be seen also in sites that generate their own backlinks. This tactic is accomplished by creating hundreds of content-poor pages that link to the site's main pages. Naturally, standard navigation design creates ingrown backlink structures, as inner pages link back to top pages, and vice versa. Google's spider tackles this phenomenon by using sophisticated content analysis and can identify in-house link farms fairly easily. Google takes PageRank integrity seriously and does not hesitate to ban a site from the index if it tries to cheat the honest link-building process.

Assessing Your Incoming Link Network

After all the work outlined up to this point, you might want to pause and take stock. How are your incoming links shaping up? This section explains how to find out, but remember the time lag involved. Depending on the timing of Google's crawl and the status of sites linking to you, it can take as long as six weeks for a page with your link on it to refresh in Google's index. This section also includes three methods of viewing and assessing your backlink network.

Using the Google link: operator

The Google search engine accepts certain *operators* that define how Google matches keywords against the index. You can use universal Boolean operators, such as AND, OR, and NOT. In addition, Google has devised special operators to manipulate Google search results and fine-tune a search. One of these special constructs is the link: operator, which displays a list of pages that link to a specified page. This and other Google operators are used with a colon punctuation mark followed by a keyword. When using the `link:` operator, the keyword is always a page URL. Here's an example:

```
link: www.nytimes.com
```

The result is a list of pages that link to the *New York Times* home page (see Figure 3-7). You may check backlinks to inner pages of a site, too, like this:

```
link: www.nytimes.com/pages/world/index.html
```

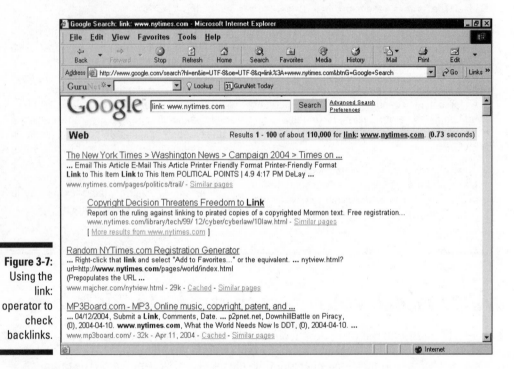

Figure 3-7:
Using the
link:
operator to
check
backlinks.

Google's `link:` operator does not deliver complete results — by a long shot. Google itself admits that the results of a `link:` operator search are not indicative of the entire backlink structure used by Google's spider to formulate a site's PageRank. Lycos (`www.lycos.com`) also uses the `link:` operator, and its results are far more comprehensive than Google's. (However, I've also uncovered errors in Lycos results.) Both Google and Lycos are valuable venues for `link:` operator testing.

Using the Theme Link Reputation Tool

The Theme Link Reputation Tool, is a little-known and brilliant gadget that measures the PageRank worthiness of sites that link to you. Remember,

Google cares about the PageRank of referring sites. A referring site's PageRank contributes to *your* PageRank. Figure 3-8 shows the Theme Link Reputation Tool waiting to be used.

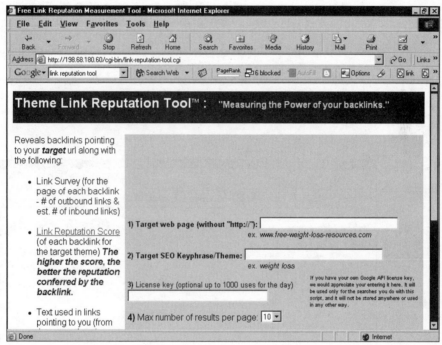

Figure 3-8: The tool is ready to accept your site address and keywords.

The Theme Link Reputation Tool is located here:

```
http://198.68.180.60/cgi-bin/link-reputation-tool.cgi
```

Follow these steps to use the Theme Link Reputation Tool:

1. **In the first field, enter your site address.**

   That's the URL without the `http://` prefix.

2. **In the second field, enter your site's core keywords.**

   This chapter's involvement in optimization keywords gets more intense in the next chapter. For now, determine a single keyword or two-word phrase that best describes your page's content. In our fictional example from earlier, `www.the-coin-trader.com`, the optimization key phrase might be "coin trading" or "coin collecting." A good single keyword would be "coins" or "collecting."

3. **Using the drop-down menu, select the number of results per page.**

   The third field is optional; I discuss Google license keys in a moment.

4. **Click the Submit button.**

The results page (see Figure 3-9) presents a table with information about your backlinks, including the pages on which they're located and a Reputation Score for each one. The Reputation Score quantifies the factors that Google's spider takes into consideration when evaluating the worth of links from one page to another. Of course, the Theme Link Reputation Tool is not a Google site, and it's not privy to the Google algorithm. But the general parameters of backlink evaluation are well-known, and this tool can give you some idea of whether your backlink network is benefiting you as much as it should.

Click the Reputation Score column to sort your results from highest reputation to lowest.

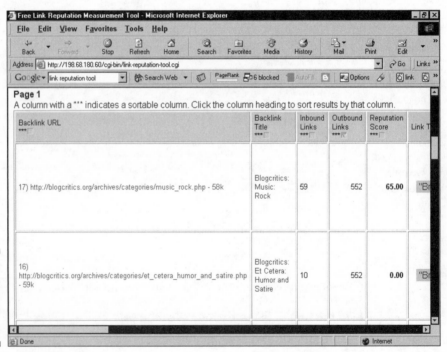

Figure 3-9:
The pages that link to your site are ranked.

You can call up only 50 backlink results at a time. This means you won't see your entire network if you've been working hard. Another thing to remember: If you use the Theme Link Reputation Tool often, go to Chapter 5 and discover how to obtain a Google license key. It's free. You can run tools such as the LRMT 1000 times each day without a key, but then they stop functioning. The free license key is good for 1000 daily searches at any site that accesses the Google index, like this one. To discover more about such sites, some of which are more fun than Google itself, please read *Google For Dummies*.

Using Alexa

Alexa is a search and data site that presents information about site traffic and backlinks in an Amazon-like format. (It's owned by Amazon.com.) This interface is less daunting than that of the Theme Link Reputation Tool, described in the preceding section. Alexa displays basic traffic statistics, traffic rankings, links to related sites, backlink statistics, information about backlisting sites, and a smattering of other measurements.

Alexa compiles its data from the users of the Alexa Toolbar, a browser enhancement similar to the Google Toolbar. In fact, Alexa is a Google partner, and uses the Google index for its searches. The Alexa Toolbar, like the Google Toolbar, allows keyword searching from any site on the Web and blocks pop-ups. Unlike the Google Toolbar, however, the Alexa Toolbar is an incontrovertible spy on your Web movements. Alexa tracks the surfing of its users to gather information for its Related Sites feature, which is really a recommendation engine similar to Amazon's. Related sites, in part, are sites visited sequentially by groups of users.

The best way to experience Alexa's measurement of backlinks is to visit and enter your site's address. Alexa is located here:

```
www.alexa.com
```

Since I don't know your site's address, let's use BlogCritics again (`www.blog critics.org`) as an example. Simply enter that address (or any other URL) into the keyword box at the top of the page, and click the Web Search button. As you can see in Figure 3-10, the resulting display page at Alexa looks a little like an Amazon catalogue page. Scroll down until you see *Other sites that link to this site*. That, of course, is the backlink metric. The number of backlinking sites is represented as a link; click it to see the identity of those sites.

The backlinks page (see Figure 3-11) is an enhanced version of a Google results page when using the `link:` operator. Clicking the <u>Site info</u> link next to any backlist site displays the Alexa page for that site. Be careful about clicking the main link for any item — that takes you out of Alexa to the item's site.

Alexa reveals a more deeply informed view of your backlinks and their sphere of influence than the `link:` operator in Google. Clicking the <u>Site info</u> link yields possible new locations for backlinks. The related sites (under *People who visit this page also visit*) can be harvested for ideas; these sites also tell you something about where your visitors go before and after viewing your site.

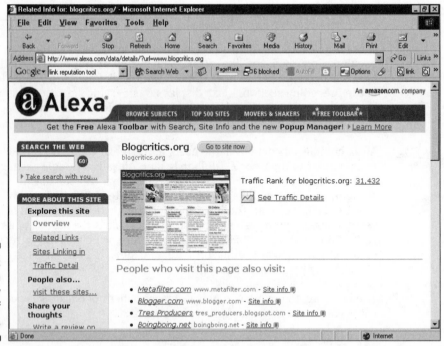

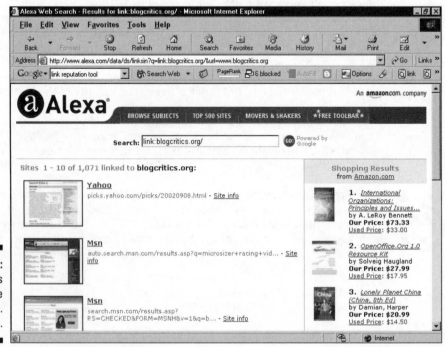

Chapter 4

Optimizing a Site for Google

The field of search engine optimization (SEO) is both simple and complex. It's simple in that the principles of preparing your site for beneficial crawling are a lot easier than SEO companies (who want you as a client) might have you believe. It's also complex because ideal SEO goes beyond tweaking a site's tags or page structure to a deeper consideration of a site's purpose, who it wants to attract, and how it wants visitors to behave.

SEO might or might not be connected to making money. (For low-revenue and no-revenue sites that want more traffic, the main investment is time.) Improving a site's placement on Google's search pages is a generally desirable goal for any Webmaster, even those not selling products or trying to convert free visitors into paying customers. So this chapter concentrates on site optimization for its own sake. I sometimes refer to revenue priorities, but the focus is raising a site's visibility for the sake of visibility.

To that end, search engine optimization — which, in the context of this book, means Google optimization — is about creating Web pages that are ranked highly in search engines. Optimization is not about tricking the Google spider, though some disreputable SEO companies have based their services on just that — a risky game, in Google's case. Optimization is a win-win-win strategy that results in a site that's more coherent to visitors, ranked higher in the search index, and more prosperous for the owner. In a well-optimized site, the goals of everyone involved converge.

Optimizing before Building

A fully optimized site is not built from the outside in — in other words, as a visitor conceives it. Instead, you build an optimized site from key concepts and keywords, and its pages never stray from a tight connection to those concepts and their related keywords. Furthermore, business-oriented Web designers are always focused on their target audience — the people who search for the key concepts and keywords embedded in the Web page. This circular thinking — the relentless integration of design with result, of keyword with content — distinguishes a finely optimized site.

In theory, you would construct a perfectly optimized site in roughly this order:

1. **Conceive the site.**

   Conception means determining the site's purpose in specific terms. An optimized site can have more than one purpose (information publishing and Amazon affiliation, for example), but those purposes should be tightly related. Conception means also identifying your target audience.

2. **Identify keywords.**

   Boiling down the site's mission to key concepts and keywords is essential. Keywords can be single words or phrases, but keep phrases short for now — three words at most. For example, using the fictional The Coin Trader site (from Chapter 3), the keywords and phrases might be *coins, coin trader, coin trading, trading, collecting, coin collecting,* and so on.

   Eventually, you need keywords for every page of your site, and they might differ from the core words used to distill the subject matter of your entire site. During the entire keyword process, think about your target audience — not only as a topical demographic, but as searchers going into Google with certain keywords. When you identify keywords, you identify your customers.

3. **Register a domain.**

   Choose a domain name that incorporates core keywords.

4. **Design the site.**

   Use spider-friendly principles explained in this chapter, Chapter 3, and the final section of Chapter 2.

5. **Write and acquire content.**

   Content development is an ongoing process that starts while you design the site.

6. **Optimize content by keyword.**

   Embedding keywords in your page's text helps visitors and Google understand the content quickly.

7. Tag the site.

Tagging means embedding keywords into important HTML tags that Google's spider observes.

So much for theory, you're probably thinking. Few Webmasters deal with optimization issues from the very start. Most people optimize after the fact, which is why SEO professionals stay in business: It's harder to fix problems than avoid them. But no matter how you approach it, improving your optimization isn't hard at all. And the knowledge it provides about sound page design, content development, concise communication, and smart tagging translates to invaluable online marketing technique.

The steps just provided merely sketch a process. The following sections get down to the nuts and bolts.

Keywords, Keywords, Keywords

If you're not dreaming of keywords at night, you're not optimizing enough. Keywords are the thread that runs through the entire SEO process from start to finish.

Your keywords are the kernels of your site's content. They're embedded in your site's important headers and HTML tags. If your domain name is apt, keywords are drilled into every incoming link because the domain name is spelled out in each link to your site. An appropriate domain name spreads the identity and purpose of your site through the Web.

Your content should be densely saturated with keywords. Your keywords are carried into Google's search engine by your future customers and visitors, who are searching for your site as well as similar sites that might contain links to your site — links that spell out your site domain, which, ideally, contains core keywords. If you're an AdWords advertiser, your site's keywords probably form the basis of your ads and determine on which results pages your ads appear. In that case, Google users searching for your keywords find your site through your ads, further driving to your site visitors who are thinking about the same keywords you are.

Keywords are the battleground of Google marketing. You and your competitors are fighting for position on search pages resulting from keywords you have in common. Remember, Google is all about keywords, so your site should be all about keywords. As I described in the preceding section, keywords can actually form the basis of a business plan and even help determine the nature of a business, if that business will be marketed online. This concept might seem far-fetched — doesn't the business come first, then the keywords which define it? Often, yes. But keyword-based marketing has become an imperative in the online space, especially for small businesses, and I am seeing sites and business plans created on a foundation of keywords.

Keywords are not purchased — not even in Google AdWords, where the advertiser purchases a position, not a keyword. Keywords can be shared but a position cannot be shared. When you select keywords around which to build and market a site, you're attempting to secure position on the search page, in competition with other "owners" of the same keywords. All this notwithstanding, you should *feel* as if you own your keywords and that they will propel you to dominance in your field.

This section deals with selecting keywords. Later, I discus how to embed them in your content and HTML tags.

Going for the edge

When it comes to building business, you don't just optimize — you optimize *for something*. More accurately, you optimize *for somebody*, and that somebody is the customer or visitor you seek.

Accordingly, define your site in terms of specific keywords, not general ones. If you operate a courier service in Chicago, for example, you might not want to optimize for the keyword *couriers*. Your potential customers probably reside in Chicago and are searching more specifically, by location. Optimizing for *chicago couriers* makes more sense. Check both searches in Google to see the competitive difference of the two key phrases. A recent check of *couriers* brought up 441,000 results, the top 10 of which were large companies offering nationwide service. A search of *chicago couriers* resulted in about 19,000 hits, including an undefined smattering of companies in the top 10. There was room to make noise on the *chicago couriers* results page. Interestingly, a search for *chicago couriers same day* turned up 50,000 hits, with mostly small companies near the top — only 4 of which operated strictly in Chicago. That page presented a tightly contested field, but with plenty of room for a same-day courier site dedicated to Chicago deliveries.

This type of experimentation and keyword research is part of the keyword selection process. Read on to find out about other keyword research tips.

Checking out Wordtracker

Wordtracker is one of the most popular keyword assessment tools on the Web. Nearly everybody who optimizes has used Wordtracker at least once. This interactive gadget looks at your keywords, shows related keywords, and displays a table displaying the relative popularity of keywords. This much technology brought to bear on simple keywords might seem like overkill, but keywords are too important to treat casually. In addition to choosing keywords (which, by itself, is not necessarily easy), you should assess their competitive value — and that's exactly what Wordtracker does.

Evaluating keywords means assessing two factors: *popularity,* or the frequency with which they appear, and *competition,* or the number of sites using them. (By "using them," I mean using the keywords in any fashion and any context, not just in the site's `meta` tags.)

Wordtracker covers both bases by suggesting keywords related to your core terms and by evaluating the suggested keywords you select. (In Wordtracker, a *keyword* means either a word or a phrase.) Wordtracker is a paid service, charging by the day, the week, the month, a 3-month period, or a year. You can concentrate your keyword research into a 1-day or 7-day blitz, without committing to an ongoing subscription.

Wordtracker offers a free trial of 15 keyword suggestions, using just one search engine (Alta Vista as of this writing) instead of the multiple search engines that paying customers get. The free trial is a good opportunity to walk through Wordtracker's screens and tools. Start here:

```
www.wordtracker.com
```

Click the icon for the free trial and surf through whatever opening screens Wordtracker throws at you before getting down to business. The Wordtracker process comprises four steps:

- ✔ **Enter keywords.** On the Step 1 page, enter one or more keywords. Keep your list short for now. One word works well because it gives Wordtracker a relatively open field to find related words. As you can see in Figure 4-1, you can opt in and out of two settings: Lateral and Thesaurus. I find the Lateral search more helpful because it investigates hundreds of Web pages related to the keyword topic. The Thesaurus just finds synonyms, which doesn't turn up much with new terms such as *mp3*. You may choose both types of search, but because the free trial delivers truncated results, I'd stick with Lateral. Click the Proceed button.

- ✔ **Select keywords.** Step 2 displays a preliminary list of related keywords, with your original at the top. Click a keyword for more detail. When you do, the right side of the screen displays a table containing the selected word and a list of related words. (See Figure 4-2.) On this screen, any clicked keyword from the left-hand list is added to a basket in which Wordtracker performs its keyword analysis and comparison in Step 4.

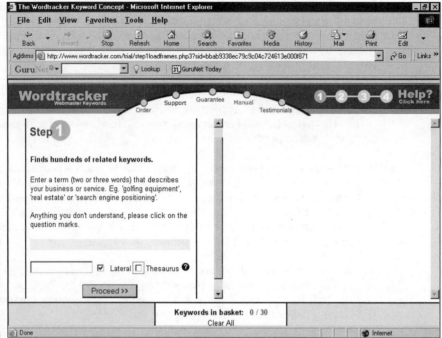

Figure 4-1:
Entering
a keyword
in Word-
tracker.

Try the shovel icons; they dig into the corresponding keyword and find related words to *it*. (Clicking the shovel icon next to your original keyword merely replicates Step 1, so try the shovel icon next to a different word.) The number in the Count column indicates the number of times that keyword appears in Wordtracker's index. The Predict column is Wordtracker's estimate of search queries for that keyword in major search engines over the next 60 days. (Click the <u>Predict</u> link to see which engines are currently represented.) When you're finished, click the arrow icon for Step 3.

✔ **Export or e-mail your keywords.** Wordtracker creates a tab-delimited text file of your selected keywords and an e-mail link (both in the paid version). In the trial version, simply move through this step by clicking the Step 4: Competition link.

✔ **View your competition results.** If you select all 15 keywords in Step 2, this step takes a minute to load. What you finally see is a table listing your keywords and their total instances in Wordtracker's index, this time ranked by the Keyword Effectiveness Index (KEI), as shown in Figure 4-3.

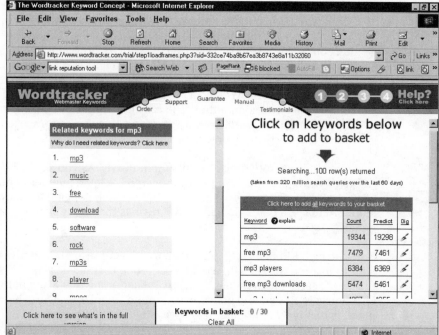

Figure 4-2:
Word-
tracker
displays
related
keywords
and their
popularity.

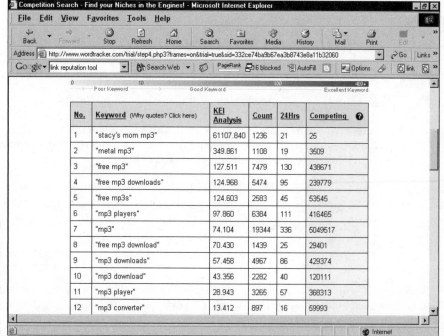

Figure 4-3:
Measure of
the potential
marketabil-
ity of your
words.

KEI is a measure of each keyword's competitive power and is constructed from two other statistics: the keyword's *count* (frequency of appearance) and its *breadth* (the number of sites containing it). The idea here is that by comparing a keyword's frequency with its prevalence, you can gauge its effectiveness. When a high count is concentrated in only a few sites, there's less competition among sites optimizing for that word than there could be. Conversely, when a lower count is distributed among a large number of sites, competition is fierce among sites optimizing for a relatively unpopular word. Broadly speaking, it makes more sense to optimize your site for the first scenario than for the second.

Don't use KEI as a rote tool, obeying it mindlessly. As you see in Figure 4-3, KEI gives the highest rank to *stacy's mom mp3.* A large number of hits are concentrated in 25 pages — possibly on a single site belonging to Stacy or her mom. (Actually, a quick Google search reveals that Stacy's Mom is a music group.)

Note the high KEI of *metal mp3,* which might inspire an imaginative entrepreneur to test the waters with a page devoted to that music genre. Note also that *mp3* scores much higher than *mp3s,* suggesting that a site optimized for MP3 music topics should concentrate on the singular keyword, because the plural is relatively unpopular and spread among many sites.

Read on to discover a free means of comparing the popularity of keywords as search terms.

Trying the Overture Search Suggestion Tool

Overture, a search technology company owned by Yahoo!, provides some services similar to Google's searching and AdWords programs. Overture offers front-end searching at its main site, as Google does, but the company's main businesses involve licensing its search engine to other companies and providing a search-engine advertising service.

The Overture Search Suggestion Tool reports the number of times your keyword (or phrase) was entered in Overture keyword boxes as a search term during the previous month. The report is easy, fast, free, and available for unlimited use. Try it here:

```
inventory.overture.com
```

As you can see in Figure 4-4, Overture tells you about your term and delivers a list (often a long one) of related keywords. The list is ranked by frequency of search use in the previous month.

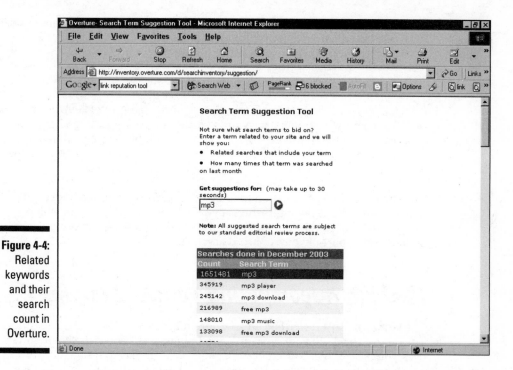

Figure 4-4:
Related
keywords
and their
search
count in
Overture.

The Overture Search Suggestion Tool is valuable on two counts: It suggests keywords and phrases that are in active play among searchers, and it ranks keywords according to popularity. The Overture list gives you a good idea of the competitive landscape surrounding your keywords and offers ideas for niche subjects.

Remember the connection between keywords as search queries and keywords as linchpins of optimization? Roughly, if a keyword is in heavy rotation as a search term, it is in rampant use as an optimization point. That means (again, speaking broadly) when you optimize a page or site for a popular keyword, you're competing in a thick field of sites. These popular keywords are the "hot" keywords that SEO consultants speak about. The broader the subject of your page, and the more general your keywords, the harder it is to make your mark — a lesson I repeat in the chapters about AdWords. The more likely path to success lies in niche subject categories, where you can create uniquely powerful content, fine-tune your optimization, and climb toward the top of that category's search page.

Keeping this in mind, use Overture to find keyword niches that apply to your content (if you have content at this point) and to give you new keyword ideas. Then take these new ideas to Wordtracker (described in the preceding section) to discover their position in the Keyword Effectiveness Index.

Google also provides a Keyword Suggestion Tool in the suite of online products associated with AdWords. Anyone can use this keyword machine, even nonadvertisers, by going to this page:

```
Adwords.google.com/select/KeywordSandbox
```

Google's Keyword Suggestion Tool delivers unranked lists of keyword suggestions based on your original keywords. Without any supporting information (popularity or competitiveness), the lists are arguably less useful than those in Wordtracker and Overture. But Google does an exemplary job on the suggestion part, with deep, wide-ranging, and imaginative lists of keywords.

Nobody beats Google at understanding context throughout its index, and you'll be amazed at the interesting keyword suggestions, many of which manage to be both relevant and unexpected. Google's suggestion tool is an indispensable part of your keyword arsenal.

Peeking at competing keyword groups

The keyword tools described so far afford a broad view of your competition. The degree to which your keywords are hot is a measure of the competitiveness you face. You can also check the keywords in play at a specific site easily by looking at its meta-tag keywords. (I get into optimizing meta tags later in this chapter.) The snooping described here isn't unethical; the Web is engineered to make code-specified keywords accessible to anyone. All modern Web browsers display a page's HTML code in two clicks.

Checking the keywords of successful sites in your field is instructive, revealing, and sometimes disillusioning. You can get a tutorial in smart keywording this way; you can also get a cold-water lesson in the apparent irrelevancy of tagged keywords in some cases. When a poorly tagged site lands in Google's top ten results for certain keywords, you know that optimization isn't everything, and that good content on its own can work wonders. However, smart optimization always helps promote good content.

Checking a site's meta tags is a simple, three-step process:

1. **Go to any site.**

2. **Click the View menu of your browser.**

3. **Choose Page Source, Source, or Page Info.**

   The Page Source and Source views display that page's entire HTML code, either in a text processor such as Notepad or a special browser window, depending on your browser and its settings. There is no way to change the code of another site in your browser, even inadvertently. The Page Info view (in Netscape) summarizes the page's feature in several categories, such as tags, graphics, and links.

With the page's source code on your screen (see Figure 4-5 for an example), look near the top for the `meta` tags. One `meta` tag probably starts this way:

```
<meta name="keywords" content=
```

followed by a string of keywords and keyword phrases. If the page's code doesn't contain the `meta` tag like this, it simply means that the page's owner has not coded keywords into the `meta` tag. But he or she might have optimized the page for certain keywords in other ways.

The influence of `meta` keywords on search engine crawlers has diminished during the last few years, so it's increasingly common to see pages without them. At any rate, you're peeking at the `meta` tag to gain keyword ideas and better understand a competing site's success, not to critique that site's optimization.

You can also check out the page's link text — an important area of page optimization, as described in the Chapter 3. It's easy to simply look at the site's outgoing links and view how they are worded. The easiest way to do this, if you use the Netscape browser, is to click the Page Info selection of the View menu, then click the Links tab to see a summary of all the site's links and link text.

```
www.digitalsongstream[1] - Notepad                                    _ 8 X
File   Edit   Search   Help
<html>

<head>
<title>The Digital Songstream</title>
<meta name="generator" content="Namo WebEditor v5.0">
<meta name="keywords" content="digital music, online music, review, reviews, mp3, rip, burn,
ripping, burning, download, music, p2p, file-share, file-sharing, riaa">
</head>


<p style="line-height:100%; margin-top:0; margin-bottom:0;"><body bgcolor="#000000" text="black"
link="#660000" vlink="#660000" alink="#CC0000">
<table border="0" width="751" align="center" cellspacing="1">
    <tr>
        <td width="751" colspan="6">
            <p><img src="http://www.digitalsongstream.com/sitelogo-14.gif" border="0"
usemap="#ImageMap1"></p>
        </td>
    </tr>
    <tr bgcolor="#000000">
        <td width="123"><p align="center"><b><span style="font-size:9pt;"><a
href="http://www.digitalsongstream.com"><font color="#FFFFFF"
face="verdana">HOME</font></a></span></b></p>
        </td>
        <td width="123"><p align="center"><b><span style="font-size:9pt;"><a
href="http://www.digitalsongstream.com/newslog"><font color="#FFFFFF"
face="verdana">NEWSLOG</font></a></span></b></p>
        </td>
        <td width="123"><p align="center"><b><span style="font-size:9pt;"><a
href="http://www.digitalsongstream.com/book"><font color="#FFFFFF"
face="verdana">BOOK</font></a></span></b></p>
        </td>
        <td width="123"><p align="center"><b><span style="font-size:9pt;"><a
href="http://www.digitalsongstream.com/reviews"><font color="#FFFFFF"
face="verdana">REVIEWS</font></a></span></b></p>
        </td>
        <td width="123"><p align="center"><b><span style="font-size:9pt;"><a
```

Figure 4-5:
A page's source code, with the meta keyword tag highlighted.

On the other hand, eBay (www.ebay.com) isn't above optimizing for keywords in the meta space, even though it has virtually no competition in the auction field. However, eBay does compete ferociously in the broader e-tailing space, and its keywords reflect its desire to promote wide-ranging product categories: "ebay, electronics, cars, clothing, apparel, collectibles, sporting goods, ebay, digital cameras, antiques, tickets, jewelry, online shopping, auction, online auction." See Figure 4-6.

Some major media sites, such as the New York Times site (www.nytimes.com), do not contain meta keywords. Likewise, Google itself does not optimize its home page in this fashion, as you can see in Figure 4-7. (I understand that google.com has a rather high PageRank in Google.)

A recent Google search for *picnic baskets hand-woven* brought up www.basketville.com as the number-one site. Checking its meta keywords turned up: "Basketville, Baskets, Shaker baskets, Nantucket baskets, Ash splint baskets, Black ash baskets, Basket weaving, Putney, Vermont, Antique reproduction baskets, Shaker style reproductions, Nantucket style reproductions, Picnic baskets, Gardening baskets, Laundry baskets, Country baskets, Spoke bottom baskets, Scrimshaw, Gift baskets, Basket store." Note that *hand-woven* is not a meta keyword; the site is optimized for that keyword in other ways.

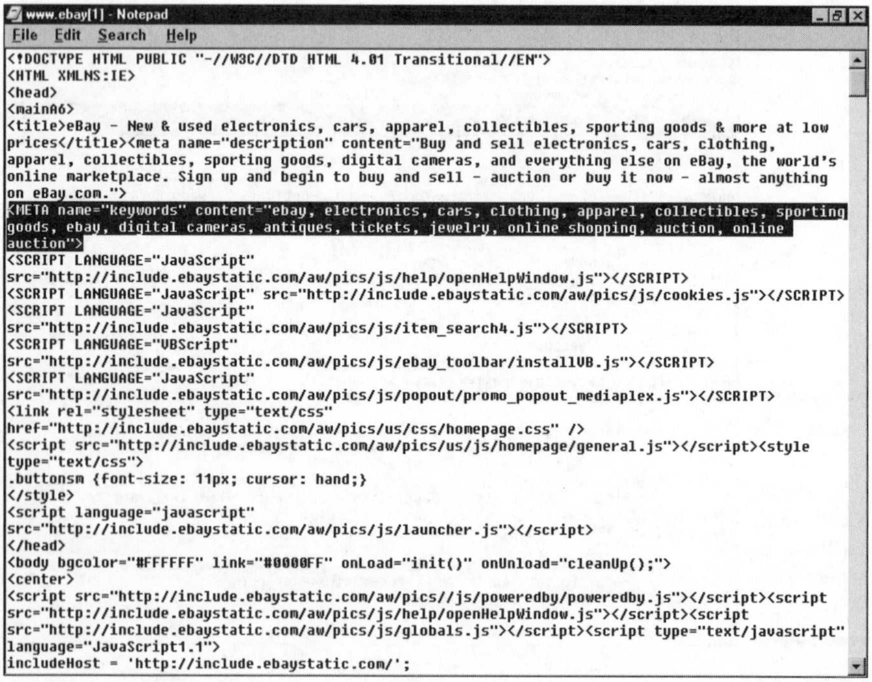


```
<!DOCTYPE HTML PUBLIC "-//W3C//DTD HTML 4.01 Transitional//EN">
<HTML XMLNS:IE>
<head>
<mainA6>
<title>eBay - New & used electronics, cars, apparel, collectibles, sporting goods & more at low
prices</title><meta name="description" content="Buy and sell electronics, cars, clothing,
apparel, collectibles, sporting goods, digital cameras, and everything else on eBay, the world's
online marketplace. Sign up and begin to buy and sell - auction or buy it now - almost anything
on eBay.com.">
<META name="keywords" content="ebay, electronics, cars, clothing, apparel, collectibles, sporting
goods, ebay, digital cameras, antiques, tickets, jewelry, online shopping, auction, online
auction">
<SCRIPT LANGUAGE="JavaScript"
src="http://include.ebaystatic.com/aw/pics/js/help/openHelpWindow.js"></SCRIPT>
<SCRIPT LANGUAGE="JavaScript" src="http://include.ebaystatic.com/aw/pics/js/cookies.js"></SCRIPT>
<SCRIPT LANGUAGE="JavaScript"
src="http://include.ebaystatic.com/aw/pics/js/item_search4.js"></SCRIPT>
<SCRIPT LANGUAGE="VBScript"
src="http://include.ebaystatic.com/aw/pics/js/ebay_toolbar/installVB.js"></SCRIPT>
<SCRIPT LANGUAGE="JavaScript"
src="http://include.ebaystatic.com/aw/pics/js/popout/promo_popout_mediaplex.js"></SCRIPT>
<link rel="stylesheet" type="text/css"
href="http://include.ebaystatic.com/aw/pics/us/css/homepage.css" />
<script src="http://include.ebaystatic.com/aw/pics/us/js/homepage/general.js"></script><style
type="text/css">
.buttonsm {font-size: 11px; cursor: hand;}
</style>
<script language="javascript"
src="http://include.ebaystatic.com/aw/pics/js/launcher.js"></script>
</head>
<body bgcolor="#FFFFFF" link="#0000FF" onLoad="init()" onUnload="cleanUp();">
<center>
<script src="http://include.ebaystatic.com/aw/pics//js/poweredby/poweredby.js"></script><script
src="http://include.ebaystatic.com/aw/pics/js/help/openHelpWindow.js"></script><script
src="http://include.ebaystatic.com/aw/pics/js/globals.js"></script><script type="text/javascript"
language="JavaScript1.1">
includeHost = 'http://include.ebaystatic.com/';
```

Figure 4-6: The meta keyword tag, highlighted in the source code of eBay's home page.

Figure 4-7:
Source code of Google's home page. It doesn't use the meta keyword tag, which would appear in the highlighted part.

Determining great keywords

The tools described in this section help you brainstorm and evaluate keywords. Eventually choices need to be made, and they are business-plan choices as much as optimization choices.

Everyone wants to succeed in the businesses represented by hot keywords — the most-searched words — because that's where the highest traffic flows. If you're not on that first page of search results, you're not visible. However, rising to the top of competitive search pages is sometimes impossible.

Success is less about meeting the competitive standard of hot keywords than it is about becoming a hot site in a smaller niche. There is a lot of traffic out there. Google fulfills over 55 billion searches a year. A small niche in Google still represents thousands or millions of searches, and that many potential visitors and customers. So, refine your keyword choices to specific, tightly defined concepts around which you can build a high-quality, optimized page. Better to focus your ambition on quality and precision than grapple with Goliath.

The only meaningful test of keywords and your page's optimization is performance. Fortunately, Google makes performance easy to track through the PageRank display in the Google browser window and, of course, the search results pages. However, remember that it can take six weeks for PageRank changes to affect your place in the index. Your traffic logs also serve as indicators of the success of your optimization efforts.

Selecting a Domain

Carrying through the idea that site optimization begins at the beginning, the first SEO step is to register your site's domain. The domain name should be chosen with an eye to the keywords around which your site is, or will be, constructed. Ideally, the domain actually contains core keywords.

Searching for *.com* domain names can be discouraging. With the Web 10 years old, most of the obvious *.com* names have been long taken. But as an obsessive domain-checker, I can tell you that imagination and brain-wracking persistence can locate that elusive name.

The best domain from an optimization viewpoint is one that incorporates your chosen keywords. You should probably ignore gigantic success stories Yahoo!, eBay, Amazon, and Google, whose domain names (and company names) have little contextual meaning. If you own technology or a business model as groundbreaking and earth-shaking as each of these companies deploys, you can get cute with the domain name, too.

For most businesses, the domain name should convey the subject at hand. The relevance factor in the domain name isn't about making it easy for visitors to remember you, although that doesn't hurt. You should choose a domain name that contains your keyword(s) for the Google spider, which looks hard at domains as indicators of relevance.

The spider's needs in this matter outweigh your visitors' needs. Accordingly, throw out the old-school optimizing rule that *.com* is a more valuable extension than *.net*, *.biz*, or the others. Although it's better to have a perfect domain name as a *.com* than another extension, Google's spider treats *.net*, *.org*, *.biz*, and other domain extensions the same as the *.com* extension. As little as it cares about the domain extension, Googlebot does care about domain names matching page content, and it rewards that correlation.

The average person remembers the *.com* extension more readily than others, and usually assumes that a site address uses that extension. In that sense, *.com* is preferable for business cards and conversations. But when visitors find your site through a search engine and then bookmark it in the browser, the extension type is irrelevant. And from the viewpoint of search engine optimization, the extension doesn't matter. So your job is to optimize with a spider-friendly domain name, and then provide your visitors such great content and site organization that they bookmark you.

It's not difficult to find small businesses competing effectively on Google's search pages with big industrial sites by using keyword-inspired domain names in niche categories. For example a search for *special education news* shows www.educationnews.com and www.specialednews.com rising above powerhouses BBC, CNN, USNews, and others which have special education sections in their mammoth sites. Of course, it takes optimization in all ways, not just in the domain name, to crack the top ten.

Google recommends against registering domains containing misspellings of popular Web destinations, such as goggle.com, ebray.com, or yagoo.com. In fact, Google threatens expulsion from the index for attempting to lure visitors in this manner.

Just about any domain registrar can report the availability of names, but some are faster and more flexible than others. Network Solutions (www.network solutions.com) allows you to search multiple domain names simultaneously (see Figure 4-8).

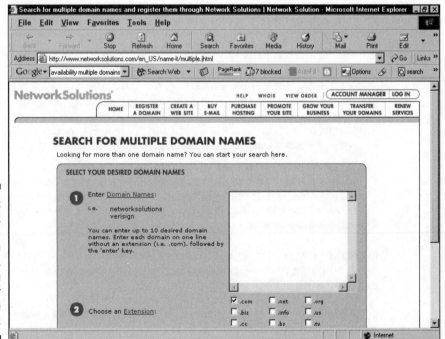

Figure 4-8: Network Solutions, a domain registrar, lets you search for multiple domains.

Effective Site Design

There is site design, and there is page and content design:

- ✔ **Site design** refers to overall structure, link navigation, distribution of text, and effective tagging.
- ✔ **Page and content design** refers to layout, content choices, keyword density, and tagging.

This section and the next discuss site design and page design, respectively.

The first lessons in site design are about what *not* to do. Here, it is enough to touch down on the points discussed at the end of Chapter 2 (in "The invisibility problem" section). Google's spider either doesn't like or can't understand these design features:

- ✔ **Splash pages.** These are the content-free entry pages to Web sites. Splash pages often exist for no purpose other than to display a big graphic or present some multimedia. They can be fun, but Google gets nothing from graphics and multimedia, and a splash page is located at your most important address, the location at which Google expects to find a strongly optimized indication of what the site is about. This is not the place to disappoint Google. Serious business sites never use empty splash pages. Many visitors think they're a pain in the neck, too.

- ✔ **Dynamic pages.** Some sites can't avoid these delivery structures, which pull page content from a database. A site that displays MLS real estate listings, for example, must create those pages on the fly from visitor input. Google doesn't penalize for dynamic generation, but the spider usually backs off from these portions of a site, for fear of generating huge numbers of pages. Google assesses static pages much better than dynamic ones.

- ✔ **Frames.** Frames are easier to eliminate than dynamic pages. Frames confuse spiders, because each frame on a page behaves like a separate page in some ways. For optimization purposes, rip down your frames and recast your site as a collection of unframed pages. Try using HTML tables instead of frames.

In creating the overall page structure of your site, the question isn't so much how long your pages should be, but how focused. The answer is, "Very focused." Keep each page on-topic and move related, differently focused content to new pages. Topical divisions are easier for Google to get a handle on, and clearer for your human visitors — plus they give you a chance to develop a robust network of navigational links.

When text is not text

The imperative to stage your content and keywords as text, not graphics, is plain enough. But occasionally, site-designing software can fool you into thinking that a graphic is text. The figure is an example of an all-graphics page that appears to be text. Google can't index this page because it can't read the words. (In this case, the page is an information source for local members of a dance troupe and is not intended to attract a wider audience.) Even if the page had a strong backlink network, it would never get into the Web index because Google would be unable to assess its content or assign a PageRank.

This page was created with ImageReady, an Adobe program that creates and slices images for deployment on a Web page. Although most sophisticated graphics programs allow placement of text in the graphic image, *it stops being text* when you do so. As information, graphical words are invisible to Google.

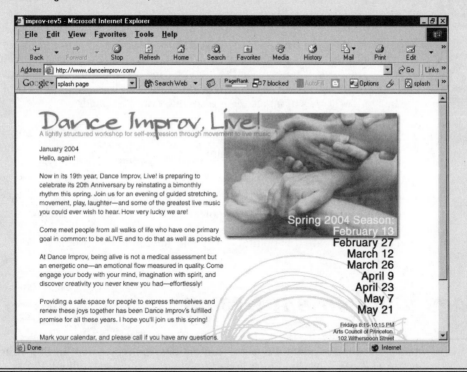

Each separate and topically focused page has its own name and location, so your navigation links act as incoming links to those pages, helping establish them in Google. And the text in those navigation links (which I discuss shortly) helps Google understand what the pages are about.

Through all this site planning, never forget keywords. Your site should be optimized according to overall concepts, and each page should have its own specially targeted keywords. Ideally, these niched keywords are reflected in each page's title, `meta` tags, and the text of incoming navigation links.

Keep life simple for the Google spider and your visitors. Avoid creating wild-goose chases in which visitors chase links down dead ends. A tidy link structure in which each main group of pages is reachable from one link on the home page helps Google assess the entire site and get the maximum number of pages into the index. Google can sweep through a well-organized site in a flash and gain an extraordinary amount of understanding about it.

The golden rule of optimization is this: Do unto Google as your visitors would have you do unto them. The Google spider responds well to the same site qualities that visitors value. Keep it simple, organized, and on-topic. Don't be subtle. Eliminate unnecessary clicks. Don't waste the visitor's time.

Another great rule of thumb: Convey your information in text, not graphics. Google loves text. It understands text. When Google's spider encounters an image on the page, it recognizes the filetype (*.jpg* or *.gif* in most cases), but it can't see the image, interpret it, or recognize any text that might be part of the image. Two types of image file are common on Web pages:

- ✔ **Logos.** Graphic logos are perfectly fine to use. But be aware that any supporting text built into the graphic, such as the site's tagline ("Coins for All and All for Coins!") serves no optimization value and is wasted as a PageRank asset.
- ✔ **Links.** Graphic buttons can be used for links, but doing so wastes an optimization opportunity to incorporate a keyword in the anchor text.

Don't underestimate this point: Convey information in text, not images.

Page and Content Design

It might be strange to think of "content design." Content authorship, certainly, but what is content design? Content design involves optimizing your editorial content by dividing it in certain ways on the page, tying it to key concepts, and embedding it with keywords. As such, content design is closely associated with page design, which is likewise concerned with layout, the division of content, and the density of keywords per page.

Page design is a broader consideration, including the overall look-and-feel of the page on which your content sits. Colors, tables, navigation menus, and links — these are all page design elements. Your content elements consist of the information on the page, all of which, ideally, is textual.

Design your pages as if you were serving an information meal to your visitors (and to Google's spider). Don't overfeed. Don't create wild mixtures of incompatible foods. Divide the meal into well-defined courses.

Optimize each page according to the following principles:

- **Focus.** Don't let any single page divert from its topic. Move extraneous information to another page.

- **Size.** In the eye of Google's spider, the length of a page doesn't matter much. To a certain extent, the amount of content per page is a matter of design and anticipating the needs of your visitors. Breaking up a long article into two or three pages lends a compact quality to the site, but makes your readers click more. Page length should be determined by keyword density — see the next point.

- **Keyword density.** This important optimization factor is a measure of how many keywords exist on the page relative to overall text. If your page contains 500 words, and 50 of them are your keywords, the keyword density is 10 percent. Online tools can quickly measure the density of any page. One such gadget is provided by Search Engine World (see Figure 4-9) at the following address:

```
www.searchengineworld.com/cgi-bin/kwda.cgi
```

Figure 4-10 is a results page of the Keyword Density Analyzer at Search Engine World. You want a density neither too high nor too low; most optimization pros think 15 percent is a top limit for an article page. On the other hand, Search Engine world's own home page sports a density of 45 percent for the keywords *search engine*. The danger of loading up too heavily with keywords lies in making Google think you're stuffing the page with keywords to artificially inflate its PageRank.

- **Keyword distribution.** You might think that distributing keywords evenly across the page is the right idea, but concentrating them near the top is better optimization. And repeating your main concepts at the start of a page of text is good writing.

- **Optimized headings.** Google's spider gives headings a little more weight than ordinary text. So, without distorting the meaning of your content, try to place your key concepts and words in larger-font headlines. Again, this is both good writing and good optimizing.

- **Link creation.** Think of ways to make keywords into links. For example, if you have a glossary in your page, link keywords to their glossary entries.

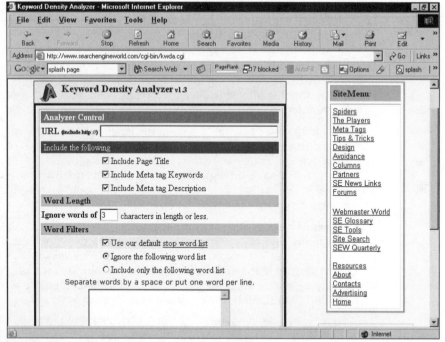

Figure 4-9:
The
Keyword
Density
Analyzer at
Search
Engine
World.

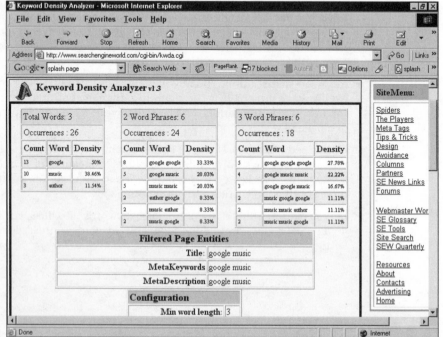

Figure 4-10:
Results
of the
Keyword
Density
Analyzer,
which seeks
instances
of your
keywords in
all combina-
tions.

Tag Design

Tagging is the hidden optimization of a Web page. Hidden from your visitors, that is, but not from Google. The Google spider examines certain HTML tags and feeds them into the PageRank equation. I've described proper coding of link tags in Chapter 3. In addition to links, four other tags are significant:

- ✔ title tag
- ✔ description tag
- ✔ keywords tag
- ✔ alt tag

The description and keywords tags are meta tags, and are placed near the top of your page's HTML code (between the <head> and </head> tags). The title tag goes between the head tags, too, but isn't a meta tag. Each is a separate tag, so the entire meta array might look like this:

```
<title="The Coin Trader">
<meta description="All for Coins and Coins for All">
<meta keywords="coin, coins, trade, trader, trading, historic
        coins, ancient coins, collecting, collections,
        collect, hobby, coin trader, coin trading">
```

Figure 4-11 illustrates the meta and title portion of a real page's source code.

Creating a title tag

The title tag conveys the page title, which should certainly contain a keyword or two. This one isn't rocket science — just put in your page title. The worst mistake you can make is to forget to assign the page a title. Every Web surfer has seen pages like this. Pages missing the title tag fail to display a title in the browser's title bar and the Windows taskbar, and are frowned on by Google's spider. Leaving out the page title is a blow to any page's optimization and PageRank.

```
www.bradhill[1] - Notepad                                                    _ 5 X
File   Edit   Search   Help
<html>

<head>
<meta http-equiv="content-type" content="text/html; charset=Windows-1252">
<meta name="keywords" content="brad hill, book author, author, internet, online services, google,
google for dummies, digital music, adwords, adsense, dummies, for dummies, idiots quide, piano,
music">
<meta name="description" content="Author: Google, digital music, For Dummies books">
<title>BRAD HILL</title>
<meta name="generator" content="Namo WebEditor v5.0">
</head>

<body bgcolor="maroon" text="black" link="#FFFFCC" vlink="#FFFFCC" alink="white">
<table border="0" width="731" cellpadding="3" cellspacing="2">
    <tr>
        <td width="127" height="59" bordercolorlight="silver">
            <p> </p>
        </td>
        <td width="586" height="59" bgcolor="#C8CCC8" bordercolorlight="silver">
<p style="line-height:100%; margin-top:0; margin-bottom:0;"><img src="name-logo-05.gif"
border="0" width="244" height="60" alt="Brad Hill: Music, Net culture, online destinations"></p>
        </td>
    </tr>
    <tr>
        <td width="127" height="25">
            <p> </p>
        </td>
        <td width="586" height="25" bgcolor="#888488">
            <p><font face="Lucida Sans Unicode" color="#C8CCC8"><span
style="font-size:10pt;"><b>An
            Information Factory for Internet Citizens</b></span></font></p>
        </td>
    </tr>
    <tr>
        <td width="127" height="419" align="left" valign="top">
            <div align="left">
```

Figure 4-11:
The description, keyword, and title tags are highlighted.

Creating a description tag

Google does still look at the `description` tag, though, and some people regard it as an important optimization point. Karyn Greenstreet, owner of the Passion for Business site (`www.passionforbusiness.com`), goes so far as to say, "In my opinion, the primary reason why a site is ranked number one on a search engine is that the keyword phrase people use to find the site is listed in the 'description' metatag." Indeed, Greenstreet notes that a business coaching site named for its owner (`www.annstrong.com`) appears in the number-one slot when searching for the keywords *small business coaching*. Those words do not appear on the home page but do appear in the `description` tag. However, they also appear in her `keywords` tag.

The upshot of all this speculation is this: Optimize everything. These tags are so easy to tweak that there's no point in leaving one out of your process. Greenstreet concurs: "The SEO tricks are so easy, I can't understand why everyone doesn't do them. What works with one search engine won't work with another, but if you cover all your bases, you're better off."

In the page description, you can get a little more imaginative than in the `title` tag. At the same time, don't be wordy and definitely don't stuff keywords indiscriminately into this tag. Devise a brief, one-line description of the site that uses a keyword or two.

Creating a keywords tag

Earlier in this chapter I described how to look at the `meta` keywords of other pages. Now it's time to create your own. Unlike the `description` tag, the `keywords` tag *is* important to Google — though, admittedly, less than it used to be. The `meta keywords` tag has been devalued as an optimization point for all engines, thanks to the abuse it suffered for years. Stuffing this tag with keywords is the easiest of all optimization tricks, so Googlebot now takes the tag with a grain of salt. Still, the spider does take it.

Pour your keywords into the `meta` tag, but don't spam it. Do not place more than three instances of a word in this tag, including instances in which the word is part of a key phrase. Look again at the sample keywords I contrived for the fictional site The Coin Trader:

```
<meta keywords="coin, coins, trade, trader, trading, historic
          coins, ancient coins, collecting, collections,
          collect, hobby, coin trader, coin trading">
```

Use keywords that might be missing from the page's content, such as specific product names, geographical locations relevant to the business, and common misspellings of your core keywords. The `keywords` tag can fill in gaps that potentially clarify details of your page's targeting or give it an edge over competing pages. Merely duplicating the keywords embedded in your content is futile because search crawlers (including Google) are increasingly harvesting your page's topical information from page text.

Although I didn't include three-word key phrases in the example, don't hesitate to use them in the `meta` tag. (Separate them from other words and phrases by commas.) According to a research report in mid-2003, 45 percent of all searches are for keyword phrases of three words or more. Never forget the point of this tag and the obsessive keyword focus throughout your site: You're trying to match keyword queries entered by Google users.

Creating alt tags

The `alt` tag is the HTML tag that displays a floating caption when a visitor hovers the mouse over an image. (See Figure 4-12.) The image could be your logo, an illustration in an article, or anything at all. (Remember: Try to use only text links. If you do use graphic links, use an `alt` tag on each one.) The `alt` tag is embedded in the HTML `image` tag, and looks like this:

```
<img src="name-sitelogo.gif" alt="The Coin Trader: All for
                Coins and Coins for All">
```

You can include other tag elements in the `image` tag, such as dimension elements that size the image. I excluded such elements for simplicity in the example. For convenience and consistency, place the `alt` tag as the final element in the `image` tag.

The content of the `alt` tag varies according to the graphic it's captioning. In the case of a site logo, be sure to use keywords. This is where you can place the site description that Google ignores when it resides in the `description` tag.

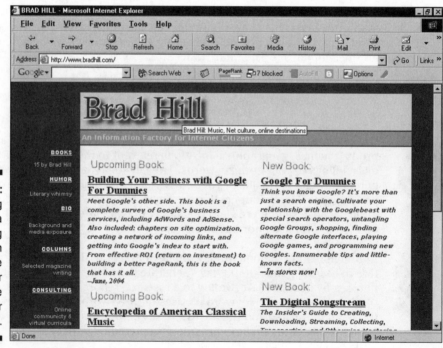

Figure 4-12:
The alt tag creates a floating caption when the visitor hovers the mouse over a graphic.

Poisoning the Google Spider

This section is about risky optimization tactics intended to artificially inflate PageRank, manipulate the ordering of search result pages in Google, and gain an unfair advantage in the index. Google, with a superb reputation to protect, is harsh in dealing with the techniques described here. The company resorts to only one remedy when a site violates its guidelines: expulsion from the Web index.

No guarantees or even policies are published concerning when or how an eliminated site can work its way back into the index. Google doesn't even explain *why* a site was removed. Being blacklisted from Google is a serious — one might even say catastrophic — business consequence. This section is here not to give anyone ideas but to inform readers of unscrupulous tricks to avoid.

Most outlawed optimization tricks concentrate on one of two angles:

✔ Loading up on keywords

✔ Hiding the site's identity or location

Keyword stuffing, as it's called, is usually attempted in a fashion that remains invisible to visitors, although occasionally you run across a site that fla-grantly plasters its pages with visible keywords. Keywords can be hidden in two ways: in the HTML `meta` tags and on the visible page using a font color that matches the page's background color. Sometimes the color is different but a tiny typeface makes the stuffed words inconspicuous. To a crawler, all this is glaringly visible.

More diabolical is hiding an entire site, either from the search engine or from visitors. Actually, the hiding always goes both ways; both the engine and the visitors are deceived. This bait-and-switch tactic is usually called *cloaking* and is accomplished in a couple of ways.

First, an underhanded Webmaster or SEO specialist can create a page, let it be indexed by Google, and then switch out the content of that page for new content. It can be quite a surprise to click a site about butterfly migration pat-terns and land on a pornography page. This type of cloaking provides only temporary joy to the deceiving Webmaster, of course, because Google's spider sees the change at the next crawl, and nobody can anticipate Google's crawl schedule well enough to continue the deception for months on end.

Second, *redirection* can create enduring confusion. Here, a *doorway page* is designed to rank high in Google and then used to redirect traffic (usually quickly and invisibly) to a different site. Visitors never see the indexed page at all. Not all doorway pages are illicit; the term is also used to describe legitimate entrances to Web sites.

I don't want to moralize. Suffice to say that these artificial optimization schemes degrade the online culture and risk getting your site tossed from its most important online portal.

A Glossary of SEO Terms

Search engine optimization (SEO) is an ongoing and continually refining process. This chapter provides a good start, but if you're bitten by the optimization bug, you'll certainly explore the subject online. SEO sites abound and are better understood if you know the major buzzwords. The Glossary, at the back of the book, rounds up the terms used in this chapter and other words and abbreviations you might run into while researching.

Considering SEO Services

Site optimization doesn't take a degree in rocket science, but it does take time plus near-obsessive attention to detail. You can hire a professional to shoulder some of the burden, on a consulting level or through hands-on control of the site and its relationship with Google. (Most SEO companies widen the focus to include other search engines as well.)

For a discussion of specific SEO resources, see Chapter 16. Here, I provide an overview of SEO services and, in particular, explain what to avoid.

Unfortunately, you must approach the field of search engine optimization with caution. Search engine manipulation was rampant during the 1990s, because search engine results could be easily manipulated. Over time, the major search engines caught on. But some of them didn't help their own integrity by selling listings on results pages. The entire value of the search experience was degraded. Google entered the scene with more interest in pure search results and less vulnerability to trickery.

Google probably *can* be fooled some of the time, at least temporarily. (And many other search engines don't deploy the effort needed to effectively police their search results.) But with its pristine reputation at stake, Google spares no effort in keeping its results clean. The aura of integrity emanating from Google has largely seeped into the SEO field, but chicanery persists in some quarters. Google still publicizes the dire story of a company called Website Results, which enjoyed a wild dot-com ride until its shady SEO practices were uncovered, and warns Webmasters even more stringently than I'm doing about SEO companies.

Plenty of good SEO help is available, and the best criterion for finding good help is knowing what to avoid:

- ✔ **The spam approach.** Avoid companies that contact you in a spammy way. Nearly everyone owning a domain has received a truckload of e-mail from companies claiming that they've already researched your site; your search results are pathetic; and they can yank you from oblivion to the top ten. Outlandish claims notwithstanding, you should know that if a company uses spam to get customers, it would probably use unsavory techniques to get *you* customers.

- ✔ **Guarantees.** Speaking of outlandish claims, avoid any guarantee. In fact, be wary of any sort of performance-oriented assurance. An SEO company should be specific about the *tasks* it intends to accomplish, not the *results* it intends to deliver. Everyone knows what the goals are — higher placement on search pages and more visitors — but predicting exact results is impossible. Certainly, any promise to deliver your site into the top ten of its keywords should be treated skeptically. Great success is possible, but a promise of great success is unprofessional.

- ✔ **Vagueness.** Don't be double-talked or swayed by results-oriented pitches. A good SEO consultant tells you every detail of the plan of action. If you've read this chapter and still don't understand what the SEO company is proposing, the company is probably being intentionally vague.

- ✔ **Automated solutions.** Avoid getting involved with companies that use automated, bulk submissions to search engines. In Google's case, automated submissions violate its Terms of Service and can result in exclusion from the index.

- ✔ **Confusion between ads and listings.** If an SEO company has promised you placement on the first results page (the promise itself is a bad sign), one easy way to fulfill the promise is to purchase AdWords on your behalf and then send you the bill. AdWords is a terrific program, but it's a separate marketing campaign than basic site optimization. Certain online marketing companies specialize in consulting or operating AdWords campaigns, and they are discussed elsewhere in this book. If an SEO company places AdWords on your behalf instead of working on your PageRank, dump it.

✔ **New software.** Be skeptical of any SEO professional who suggests that you implement any tactic that requires you to install any software.

✔ **Poisoning the spider.** Be careful of any recommendation that violates the guidelines I lay out in the "Poisoning the Google Spider" section. I am not the final authority of Google's policies, but my guidelines are broad and well recognized in the legitimate optimization industry. Remember the consequences: Google *does* expel sites that try to manipulate the index, and working with SEO consultants who cut corners could cost you months of work.

Most above-board SEO companies these days are defensive in their self-promotion. ("We never use unethical techniques!") That's a good start. Before signing on, find out explicitly what the company will be doing. The best SEO services determine what your site is about (that alone can be invaluable if you are putting out vague or mixed content) and focus its mission. When a site is improved for visitors, its PageRank usually improves in short order.

Chapter 5

Putting Google Search on Your Site

*T*he simplest and most identifiable method of partnering with Google is to incorporate Google searching on your site. You may offer Google search to your visitors free of charge (to them and to you), and you may customize the search to a reasonable degree. Giving your users options to search the Web or your site (or other specific sites) is fairly easy.

Google offers four free search services and three paid services:

- ✔ **Google Free.** A Google-branded search box that delivers Web results.

- ✔ **Google Free SafeSearch.** Same as Google Free, but delivers edited search results free of adult content.

- ✔ **Google Free Web and Site Search.** An enhanced version of Google Free with an added option to search only your site or only another site selected by you.

- ✔ **Customized Free Web (and Site) Search.** With or without the Site Search option, free customization is available to registered users, enabling them to display search results under their site's logo and with their site's colors.

- ✔ **Silver and Gold Search.** Two paid search service plans for sites conducting millions of searches per year.

- ✔ **Custom Web Search.** The highest level of paid search, for extremely high-traffic sites. ISPs and publishers such as EarthLink and the Washington Post are two clients of Custom Web Search.

This chapter describes the free services. See Chapter 15 for information about Google's premium services.

Offering Google searches from your site doesn't build business in the sense of directly increasing revenue. Any financial benefit derives indirectly from making your site more attractive and useful to your visitors.

By the same token, adding a Google search box on your site doesn't make your site more likely to be crawled (or more thoroughly crawled), and it doesn't improve your PageRank. However, adding Google Free indirectly enhances your site and makes it more magnetic, if searching is of value to your users. In particular, using Web and Site Search might be the simplest way to offer a search engine for your own content.

Terms and Restrictions

Most public Web sites are eligible to host a Google search box. Remember, though, that you're hosting only the search box, not the search results. The box resides on your page, but when visitors launch their searches, they're taken to Google to see the results. In the uncustomized version of Google Free, the results look just as they do when you start a search from Google, because they *are* the same. Even fully customized searches are not displayed on your site, even though they're designed to look as though they are.

In using Google Free, you're giving your visitors an easy way to *leave your site*. The search results page doesn't provide a link back to your site, and there's no way to place such a link. You can, however, force the results page to open in a new browser window, leaving your visitor anchored at your site in the first window. (I explain how later.) Of course, if a visitor restricts the search to your domain (with the Web and Site Search), the search results are filled with links back to your site. Indeed, this scenario is one of the most attractive aspects of using Google Free.

Right now you might be thinking, "Ah, well, I'll strip out the Web search and just offer in-site search." It's a clever thought, but you would find the HTML code uncooperative. The Web search option can't be removed.

Despite all these considerations, offering Google search is an attractive option to many sites for many reasons. Nearly all types of sites, from personal to commercial, are eligible. Terms of Service (TOS) do apply to Google Free, but Google doesn't insist on a digital agreement from you before getting started. The TOS is far less compelling than a *Harry Potter* book, and to save you the trouble of perusing it, the following items summarize its main points:

✔ **No frames, mirrors, or cache.** Google doesn't want you appropriating the search process technically or prohibiting the results from being displayed on a Google-served page. You also are not allowed to capture the results, store them in a database, or otherwise take ownership of them. The ban against mirror sites (replicated site at various locations) is an extension of Google's identical stricture against them in the Web index.

✔ **Monogamy, please.** Google is a demanding partner. You may not place another company's search box on the same page with Google's. This requirement is widely ignored.

✔ **Accept Google, accept its ads.** Google displays advertisements on nearly ever search results page, including the ones appearing on your site. That's because these results aren't on your pages. So don't think that you're going to provide your visitors with an ad-free experience.

✔ **Keep it clean.** Google doesn't want to be associated with illegal sites, domains that propagate copyright infringement, adult sites, or sites that sell alcohol or tobacco to minors.

✔ **Be nice to Google.** Don't say mean things about the company that's providing free use of its logo and search engine.

✔ **Google doesn't know you.** Don't pretend that Google is affiliated with or endorses your site's content.

✔ **Obey logo laws.** Several bylaws apply to the Google logo. Don't draw on it, even though Google does. Likewise, don't take archived logo variations from Google's site and use them with your search box. Don't distort the logo by squishing it or stretching it. (You may choose from a selection of sanctioned sizes and colors, though.) Surprisingly, you must not allow Google's logo to be larger or more prominent than the site logo — Google doesn't want anyone to mistake your dog-and-pony show for the true, majestic Google site.

✔ **Google can cut you off.** As with all TOS agreements, the provider (Google in this case) can end this collaboration at any time.

The ads Google serves on search pages launched from your site aren't published by you, and they're not AdSense ads. There's no benefit to you if one of your visitors clicks them, because that person is no longer your visitor. Once that person is off your site, he or she is Google's visitor, and Google receives the full benefit of ad clickthroughs. Offering Google Free shouldn't inhibit you from considering becoming an AdSense publisher (as described in Part III). By working both sides of the fence, you get the benefit of users clicking through ads placed on your pages, while offering visitors the convenience of Googling from your site.

I strongly suggest that if you add Google Free to your site, you go the whole route with Web and Site Search, fully customized for your site. The ability to search your own domain and present search results in the color scheme of your site (complete with logo) distinguishes Google Free from other ways of initiating a Web search from your site. Without those features, Google Free is a less compelling way of searching than using the Google Toolbar, which offers your visitors one-click searching from your site and any non-Google site.

Getting Your Code

With a bit of HTML savvy (just the ability to cut, paste, and upload HTML documents to your site's server), you can be hosting Google searches in minutes. Registration is not required for basic Google Free, but if you want to customize the search results, Google needs to know who you are and where your domain is.

Google Free is installed on your page by means of a small chunk of HTML code. No JavaScript is involved. The snippet is a simple form, comprising the Google logo (which is called from a Google server, not stored on yours), a keyword entry box, a search button, and (in the case of Web and Site Search) radio buttons that toggle between search domains. (See Figure 5-1.)

Figure 5-1:
Google's Web and Site Search is free and easy to install.

1. **Go to the search code page here:**

   ```
   www.google.com/searchcode.html
   ```

2. **Scroll down the page to the first code sample, and copy the entire sample to the Clipboard.**

   Highlight the sample with your mouse, and then press Ctrl+C. Figure 5-2 shows the code after it is highlighted.

3. **Paste the code into the HTML document representing your Web page.**

   Methods differ widely at this point. You can use any text processor, such as Windows Notepad, to paste the code. Or you can use an HTML text generator, which highlights different types of HTML tags, making the code easier to navigate. Or use the HTML portion of a graphic Web-page editor such as Dreamweaver. However you do it, you need to choose where you want the search box to appear on your page, and position the code to make that happen.

4. **Upload the new HTML document for your page to its place on your site server.**

5. **Visit your page to see the results.**

   Depending on your software, you might be able to view the result before uploading and make adjustments.

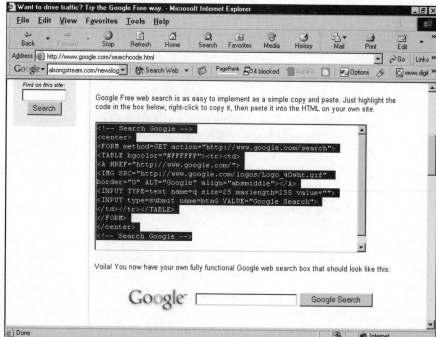

Figure 5-2: Highlight, copy, and paste Google's free HTML code to install Google Free search.

SafeSearch is a Google searching option that blocks Web pages containing explicit sexual content from appearing in search results. To install a SafeSearch box, follow the same steps but in Step 2 scroll further down the code page to the SafeSearch HTML. The search box appears on your page with the Google SafeSearch logo attached (as shown in Figure 5-3).

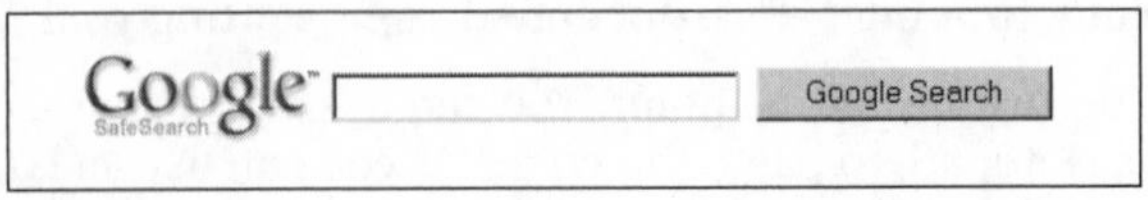

Figure 5-3:
A Google
SafeSearch
form.

Free Web and Site Search

If you choose Web and Site Search, you need to alter the preset HTML code a bit, tailoring it to your Web site. The basic appearance doesn't change much, but you need to plug in your site's domain information. Otherwise, Google won't know how to offer visitors the option of limiting a search to your site. Follow these steps:

1. **Go to the search code page:**

   ```
   www.google.com/searchcode.html
   ```

2. **Scroll down the page to the last code sample, and copy the entire sample to the Clipboard.**

3. **Paste the code into the HTML document representing your Web page.** You may paste it anywhere in your HTML document. Google allows the search box to appear anywhere on the page.

4. **Change the first two instances of YOUR DOMAIN NAME to your actual domain address, including the *http://* prefix.**

   There are three instances of YOUR DOMAIN NAME. In the first two, type your Web address, as in *http://www.bradhill.com.* (That one's mine. Type in yours.)

5. **Change the third instance of YOUR DOMAIN NAME, to the name you want to appear on your page.**

   In Figure 5-1, note that instead of typing *www.digitalsongstream.com,* I typed *Digital Songstream.* I preferred using the name of the site, rather than the address of the site. Type whatever you want your visitors to see.

6. **Upload the new HTML document for your page to its place on your site server.**

You can specify more than one site in which to constrain searches. However, you must always include a search option for the entire Web. In addition to the entire Web and your own site, you may include any other public Web site. I cover multiple domains in the "Customizing Search Results" section of this chapter.

Tweaking the search form

Before moving on to customizing the search results, you might want to make small changes to the display of the Google search box and the elements surrounding it. Doing so requires a bit of HTML familiarity, but some tricks are downright easy. Remember the Terms of Service, summarized previously in the chapter. You may not distort the Google logo, and you may not add disparaging comments about Google. Beyond those innocuous guidelines, nothing is stopping you from elongating or shortening the search box, stacking the elements vertically instead of horizontally, changing the font type and size, and forcing searches to appear in a new browser window.

Stretching and shrinking the search box

Google's code automatically wraps the search button to below the search form if your page doesn't have enough room for the natural horizontal layout shown in Figure 5-1. You can maintain the horizontal layout in a narrower space by shrinking the search box. In the HTML code, look for this line:

```
<INPUT TYPE=text name=q size=25 maxlength=255 value="">
```

The `size` variable determines the horizontal size of the keyword box; a smaller number narrows the entry box. Figure 5-4 shows a keyword box at size 14.

Also in Figure 5-4, note that the elements are stacked vertically to fit into a narrow table column. To create this stacking, you use the break tag, `br`. Placed after a line of code, the break tag forces the next code element below the previous one, instead of next to it. Here is what the modified code looks like. The `br` tags are in boldface for emphasis:

```
<INPUT TYPE=text name=q size=25 maxlength=255 value=""><br>
<INPUT type=submit name=btnG VALUE="Search"><br>
<A HREF="http://www.google.com/">
<IMG SRC="http://www.google.com/logos/Logo_40wht.gif"
border="0" ALT="Google" align="absmiddle"></A>
```

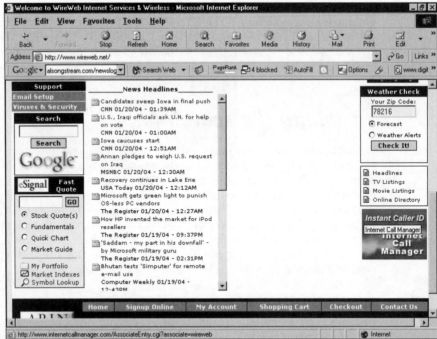

Figure 5-4:
This
Webmaster
shrank the
keyword
box and also
stacked the
elements.

The first line represents the keyword box. The second line is the Search button (the text of which the Webmaster easily changed from Google Search to Search, thereby shrinking the button to a narrower fit). The last three lines refer to the Google logo.

Changing typeface and font size

As long as you're getting creative, you should know how easy it is to change the font type and font size of the search options. You can perform this trick only in the Web and Site Search, because it's the only type of search that has a search-option type to alter. Find the following lines of code:

```
<INPUT type=submit name=btnG VALUE="Google Search">
<font size=-1>
```

The first line refers to the Google Search button, and I included it just to help you find the second line, which is the one that counts. Looks fairly self-explanatory, doesn't it? To make a larger font, change the default setting (-1) to 0 or a positive number, using a plus sign before the positive number. Figure 5-5 illustrates an altered version of Figure 5-1, with the font size boosted to +2.

Figure 5-5:
Eeek!
Large font!
Probably too
large.
Experiment
with the font
tag setting
to find the
perfect size.

Notice that in Figure 5-5 I also changed the typeface from the default (which, on the host page, was Times Roman) to Arial. I did this by adding the `face` variable to the `font` tag like this:

```
<font size=-1 face="arial">
```

Don't forget to put quotation marks around the typeface.

Forcing results to a new browser window

When visitors use your free Google search, they click right out of your site. Providing a convenience shouldn't necessarily mean that you lose your visitors. Forcing the search results to display in a new browser window keeps your site alive in the old browser window. Google encourages this code tweak, and it's easy to do. You just need to add a `target` variable with a `blank` page value to the first line of the code sample. Here's that line, unaltered:

```
<form method=GET action="http://www.google.com/search">
```

The blank-page variable is written like this: _blank. Yes, that's a single under-line followed by the word *blank*. Precede this with the target command. The whole thing looks like this:

```
<form method=GET action="http://www.google.com/search"
          target=_blank>
```

Now when your visitors launch a search, the results pop open in a new window. If you continue to the next section and follow the customization sug-gestions, that new window looks a lot like (but isn't!) a page on your site.

Using a different logo

Google offers several stickers from which to choose an official logo. You can see the selection here:

```
http://www.google.com/stickers.html
```

Figures 5-1 and 5-5 both use the 40-percent logo on a white background — that's the default logo used in all the code samples. To switch logos, follow these steps:

1. **Right-click any logo and choose Copy Image Location.**

2. **In the code sample, find this line:**

   ```
   <IMG SRC="http://www.google.com/logos/Logo_40wht.gif"
             border="0" ALT="Google">
   ```

3. **Highlight the location of the image, which is the following part:**

   ```
   http://www.google.com/logos/Logo_40wht.gif
   ```

4. **Paste the copied image location in place of the original.**

   To simplify, you're copying one image location and pasting it over the previous image location. Make sure the final image location is sur-rounded by quotation marks.

5. **Paste the altered code into your Web page.**

   Your server now pulls the correct logo from Google's server.

6. **Upload the new HTML document for your page to its place on your site server.**

HTML jockeys, go wild

Every element of the HTML code sample is up for grabs. Google doesn't much care how you arrange the elements, as long as you follow these two important guidelines: Don't distort the logo, and don't trash Google.

Customizing Search Results

Satisfyingly, Google encourages you to customize search results pages so that they look (more or less) like your site pages. This customization puts your site logo and color scheme on the search result pages.

To customize, you must register as a Google Free user. Google gets you customizing first, and then collects your basic information. Registration is free and painless:

1. **Go to the start page:**

   ```
   services.google.com/cobrand/free_select
   ```

2. **Choose the Free WebSearch plus SiteSearch option or the Free WebSearch option.**

   In Figure 5-6, I'm choosing WebSearch plus SiteSearch.

Figure 5-6: Start your customization by choosing a search option and filling in domains to be searched from your page.

3. **Enter the domain address or addresses that you want as search options.**

Separate multiple domains with semicolons. You are free to offer your visitors searches constrained to any public domain. Think about which site searches might benefit your visitors. A local news site might offer searches of the New York Times (`www.nytimes.com`). A search optimization specialist might offer searches of the article database at `www.seotoday.com`. Your choice is not etched in stone; you may sign in anytime to change your selections.

4. **Click the Continue button.**

On the Step 2 of 4 page, Google tells you how many pages of your selected domains currently reside in Google's Web index. (See Figure 5-7.) These statistics give you some idea of the depth of the search you're making available to your visitors. Google *doesn't* crawl domains you selected if they're not in the index, and it doesn't make a special crawl through them if they're in the index. These statistics are presented to help you judge whether the domains are worth searching.

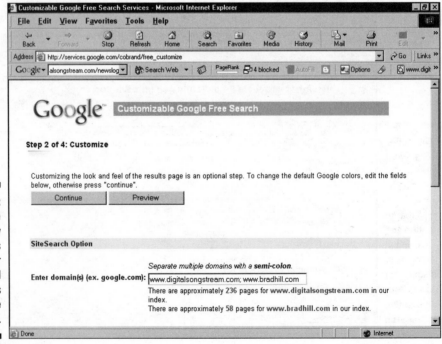

Figure 5-7: Google reports how many pages of your selected domains reside in the Web index.

5. On the Step 2 of 4 page, scroll down to fill in the customization fields.

This is where the fun starts. The first cluster of settings (see Figure 5-8) relates to your site logo, which can appear at the top of your visitors' search results pages. Despite the presence of Width and Height boxes, you needn't fill them in if you don't know your logo's dimension in pixels. But you must enter the location of your graphics logo file, if you have one, including the *http://* prefix.

As you experiment with the fields, click the Preview button whenever you want to see how your search results page would look if you saved the current settings. The Preview window stays open as you continue fiddling, and updates when you next click the Preview button. Figure 5-9 shows a somewhat jarring work in progress. Figure 5-10 illustrates a nicely integrated color scheme.

6. Click the Continue button.

7. On the Step 3 of 4 page, fill in your name, e-mail address, and a password. Click the Continue button.

8. On the Step 4 of 4 page, copy the entire HTML code sample and paste it into your Web page.

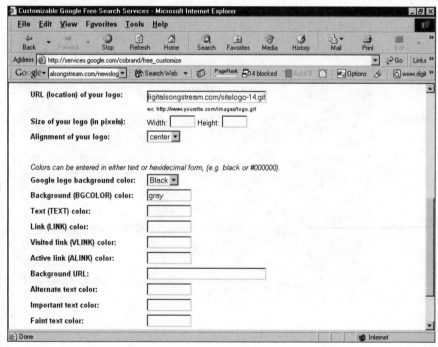

Figure 5-8:
Fill in the customiza-tion fields to create a distinctive search results page.

Figure 5-9:
Black logo,
gray search
table, and
a white
background.
It doesn't
work.

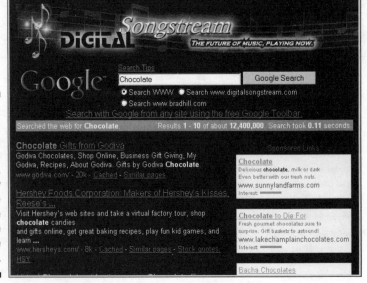

Figure 5-10:
A custom-
ized search
results
page,
served by
Google
with the
appearance
of the
original site.

The colors you use in customizations can be determined by hexadecimal values understood in HTML. You're not limited to black, blue, red, and other basic hues. If you want to exactly match backgrounds and other elements in your pages, look in your HTML to find the hexadecimal values you need, and enter them in the customization fields.

Figure 5-11 illustrates what happens without a fully integrated color scheme. The result is hardly hideous, but it looks thrown together rather than blended in. (And here, as in many sites, the Google-only guideline is ignored.)

By contrast, Figure 5-12 shows a nicely integrated search box. Note the custom Search button, replacing Google's default button.

You can't use the Site Search feature as an enterprise solution, tempting though it might be. Google searches only public Web sites, not corporate intranets.

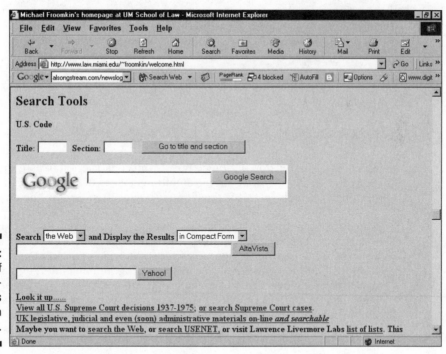

Figure 5-11: A lack of customization results in a rough look.

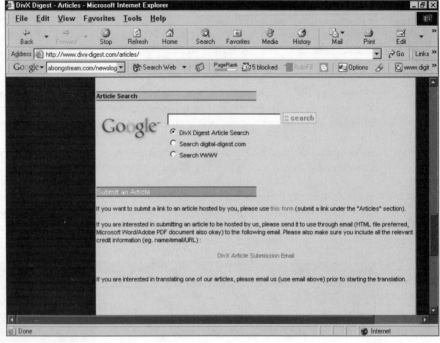

Figure 5-12:
Nice design integration and a custom Search button, to boot.

Building Your Own Google Site

The ultimate extension of Google Free is the construction of an entire site dedicated to Google search. This ambitious task is best accomplished as a third-party Google interface developer, an avocation Google encourages.

Google offers software developers a free license to access the Google Web index. This license enables alternate Google sites to deliver Google search results through new interfaces. Developers download a software kit that includes the Google Web API (Application Programming Interface). An API is necessary whenever one program or Web site hooks into a necessary underlying system, such as Google or the Windows operating system. If your computer runs Windows, every application program you have uses the Windows API. Similarly, every alternate Google interface uses the Google API.

Entrepreneurial developers can use Google's Application Programming Interface (API) to query the Google index from their own programs. The details of doing so are beyond the scope of this book. For more information, go here:

```
http://www.google.com/apis/index.html
```

On that page, you can download a developer's kit and Google license key.

Anyone can get a license key, even those without ambitions to run a Google-like site. Getting a key is a good idea if you use some of those non-Google interfaces. Each license key allows you 1000 searches per day. Many alternate Google sites invite users to plug in their license keys instead of relying on the site's key. Doing so shares the load and makes it less likely that the site will freeze because it has used up its allowed number of searches.

An example of an effective alternate Google is the Google Ultimate Interface, shown in Figure 5-13. Go here:

```
www.faganfinder.com/google.html
```

For two entire chapters of alternate Google sites, see *Google For Dummies*.

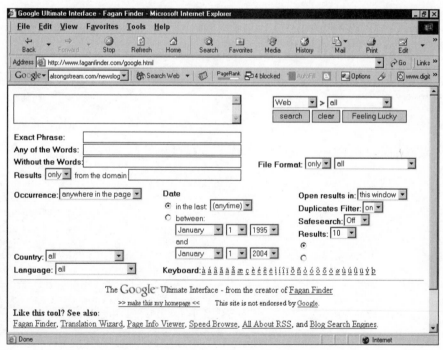

Figure 5-13:
One of the best alternatives to Google, the Google Ultimate Interface.

Part II
Creating and Managing an AdWords Campaign

The 5th Wave   By Rich Tennant

"We have no problem funding your web site, Frank. Of all the chicken farmers operating web sites, yours has the most impressive cluck-through rate."

In this part . . .

*P*art II, the fattest part of this book, is dedicated to the AdWords program. AdWords enjoyed most of the press as Google's advertising revenue emerged as an important business story. As the leading brand of cost-per-click (CPC) advertising, Google is sparking the explosion in Search Engine Marketing (SEM), a business strategy that is attracting individual entrepreneurs and massive corporations alike. Indeed, the profoundly democratic character of CPC advertising and Google's sophisticated bidding model level the playing field for small players. Chapter 6 provides an overview of the AdWords program, and Chapter 7 tells you how to get started.

Another aspect of AdWords that keeps Google in the lead is its ever-improving suite of reporting tools. New conversion-tracking tools emphasize Google's commitment to return on investment (ROI), and its keyword-matching technology and instant implementation of changes lend advantages to the most nimble advertisers. Chapter 8 covers the reporting tools. Chapters 9 and 10 discuss slightly more advanced aspects of advertising on Google, from selecting keywords to bidding on them, from constructing a campaign to recovering from false starts.

The chapters in this part take apart every aspect of AdWords, from theory to practice, conception to execution.

Chapter 6

Introducing Search Advertising and Google AdWords

*T*his first chapter on AdWords is an overview of both search advertising in theory and AdWords in practice. I sketch the main points of Google's service here, and get into the details in later chapters.

Search advertising brings new marketing propositions to the table. This is not to say that search advertising is brand new, but it is reaching a *tipping point* (to borrow author Malcolm Gladwell's phrase). Nobody knows what we are tipping into. But there's no question that search advertising, with its revolutionary pay-for-performance model, precise targeting, and client control, is rocking the advertising world.

This chapter argues the revolutionary benefits of search advertising, and then proceeds to an overview of the preeminent search advertising venue: the Google AdWords program. Be sure to reference the glossary at the back of the book, which includes all important search advertising and AdWords terms you're likely to encounter.

Old Advertising in an Old Media

Let's watch TV. I like *Late Show with David Letterman, 24,* and — even though I'm so far beyond my teen years I can barely remember them — *Smallville.* The two prime-time shows are presented in six acts broken up by commercials. *Letterman* usually has six or seven segments separated by increasingly longer breaks as the hour proceeds. Commercials take up nearly a third of the shows' time slots. Ads run the gamut: cars, beer, movies, insurance, and medications for aging Boomers, computers, drugstores. They're entertaining or banal; long or short; punchy or pedestrian. And they're almost all irrelevant to my desires and needs.

I'm not the only one complaining. Most TV ads are irrelevant to almost everyone who sees them. Indeed, the irrelevancy is part of the plan in blanket advertising. Blanket ads are shown indiscriminately to an entire audience, with the idea that for every 20 (or 30, or 100) people who see the ad, 1 person finds it relevant. Advertisers pay to reach that 1 person multiplied by huge audience groups, and simply don't care about the rest.

This sort of TV promotion was started in an earlier era, when both the medium and society were more consolidated. In the 1950s and 1960s, television for most people offered between three and six channels. Huge audiences watched popular shows. (If you don't remember watching *The Ed Sullivan Show* every Sunday night, you're younger than I am.) Furthermore, nothing like today's product diversity existed. So, in that simpler time, more people gathered in bigger groups with more shared desires. Blanket advertising was a reasonably cost-efficient way to get a message out to a great number of people who would find it relevant.

Blanket ads still work, but finer targeting is now necessary. In the past, only the most rudimentary sort of targeting was put into play — matching a product to the type of audience likely to be watching a program. Now advertisers match a product to age and lifestyle categories supplied by audience measurement services. With the advent of TiVo and other personal video recorders (PVRs), these services are becoming quite specific about the viewing and surfing habits of the TV audience. Nevertheless, blanket advertising still works according to an old-media principle: Show the ad to everyone in the target group, and hope it's relevant to at least a few.

How often are TV ads relevant and interesting to you? Not often, I'm guessing, even if you match the demographic targeted by a show's sponsors. The irrelevancy of ads is why ad-skipping technology built into TiVo, ReplayTV, and the other PVRs has become so popular. In fact, the TV industry is alarmed about the ease with which the audience can time-shift its viewing and avoid ads entirely. If the ads were precisely targeted to each of us, individually, we probably wouldn't want to skip them. At least, not as much.

Old Advertising in a New Medium

Relevance is the quality that makes an advertisement effective. This golden rule is as true online as it is offline. We live in an ad-saturated age, but our problem isn't too many ads — it's too many irrelevant ads.

If ads could be targeted more specifically to what individuals want, the total number of sponsored messages might not be reduced. But irrelevant advertising systems that blanket us from billboards, airwaves, and all other media would erode as advertisers flocked to promotional systems that didn't waste their money. This is where the Internet comes in.

But the Net hasn't completely saved us from irrelevant ads. The online equivalent of TV's blanket advertising started with static banner ads and evolved to video pop-ups. The latter format obscures the content of Web pages to play commercials that, in the glitziest examples, look just like TV ads. These distractions are even pushier than a TV commercial because their style of interruption is more invasive. Whereas television schedules its commercials in planned breaks, Web pop-ups fly right into your face *while* you're trying to read a page. They're more intrusive than television, radio, or magazine advertising.

Pushy Internet ads are more galling than pushy TV ads because the Internet is inherently a medium in which content is pulled, not pushed. Television is more passive; the audience settles on its couches and lets content be pushed at it. Changing to another station is traditionally the limit of a viewer's control, or *pull,* over TV. (PVRs give the viewer more control, but that's when ads are skipped entirely.)

On the Internet, content appears on the screen when the viewer pulls it to the screen, usually by clicking a link or bookmark. Some slightly pushy experiences can occur online, as when somebody instant-messages you and the IM window pops open on your screen. Even then, though, the pushy IM can't happen unless you give the messaging person your IM coordinates — a type of pull. With e-mail, letters are pushed into your mailbox, but they don't fully appear on your screen until you click (pull) them.

Pushy advertising in a pull medium is bound to result in conflict. Sure enough, banners, pop-ups, and spam are all extremely ineffective. They result in such built-up consumer resentment and miniscule response rates that they survive only because of economies of scale. Because they can be distributed in massive numbers at low cost, even their dismal effectiveness pays out. Generally, the least effective ad types (such as e-mail spam) are the cheapest, making them the most pervasive and the most persistent. Spam is the Internet's most aggressive type of blanket advertising, with the least degree of relevance. In principle, though, spam is no less pushy, broadly targeted, irrelevant, and inappropriate to the medium than a video pop-up at a respected Web site.

New Advertising in a New Medium

Now, finally, the Internet is poised to save us from irrelevant advertising. Search advertising offers better response rates and better ways to track whether ads are reaching the right people. Search advertising is revolutionary in that it discards blanket advertising in favor of precise targets, controlled costs, and meeting a pull medium on its own terms.

All Internet advertising, even the blanket type, contains an advantage over advertising in most other media: It invites the viewer to take action immediately. Clicking an ad takes consumers to the next step in their relationship with the advertiser. At that next step, some type of conversion is possible — a sale, a registration, a bookmarked site, or some other behavior that "captures" the customer in a sense. Besides this dynamic quality of online ads, search advertising makes four distinct and earth-shaking improvements on blanket advertising:

- ✔ **Search advertising is positioned on results pages of search engines, where the customer is looking for the advertiser.** Well, perhaps the customer is not literally looking for *you,* but he or she is looking for *something.* The searcher is in a pulling mood — in the mood to consume information, products, and services. If the advertiser provides relevancy to that person's search, the heavenly marketing match is made. And the chance of a response is much greater than when a blanket ad wrenches a viewer out of a passive state.

- ✔ **Search ads are aligned with keywords and appear on results pages for those keywords.** So, as long as the advertiser chooses keywords appropriate to the message, and the searcher uses keywords appropriate to the search goal, relevancy is guaranteed. Compared to the built-in irrelevancy of blanket advertising, this degree of match-up between advertiser and consumer is groundbreaking.

- ✔ **Search advertisers pay only for responses.** The advertiser pays each time a searcher clicks the ad. When that treasured click happens, the advertiser receives a qualified lead — somebody who searched for some combination of keywords and chose to click an advertisement that promised relevancy as good (or better) than nonsponsored search results. Contrast this method with the old-media system in which the advertiser pays for sheer exposure. In the online universe, exposure means paying for *impressions* — the number of times the ad is displayed, even if nobody clicks it.

- ✔ **Search advertising offers detailed, multifaceted, hands-on control of the advertising campaign.** Google is particularly strong in this department. Advertisers can micromanage their accounts, measuring performance and enhancing their efficiency on a minute-by-minute basis. I hasten to add that such obsessive management is not necessary in search advertising. But the ability to control the campaign as it proceeds represents one of the great advantages over broadcast and traditional print advertising, in which you purchase a campaign and either it works or it doesn't. Tweaking, adjusting, and resculpting the campaign in midstream to *make* it work is part of the search advertising system.

Let me be clear. Google didn't invent search advertising. Google didn't even invent *pay-per-click (PPC) advertising,* which has supplanted pay-per-impression sponsored links on Google's pages. But Google has refined the game considerably, improving the basic parameters of search advertising.

Google is involved in PPC competition with other search engines, and to some extent they leapfrog, one improvement after another. Generally, though, Google has taken the lead in innovation. In particular, the following three features are highly valued by Google advertisers:

- ✔ **Minimum payments.** As I describe later, search advertisers bid on the value of the keywords associated with their ads. Those bids determine the ad's position on the results page and the top amount the advertiser pays when searchers click the ad. However, Google uses a complex formula to determine the *lowest* amount the advertiser must pay, per click, to maintain position on the page — and that is the amount Google charges. All this is clarified later. The point here is that Google streamlines expenses by charging the least possible amount for advertisers to compete effectively for position on the page.

- ✔ **Success breeds success.** Unlike other PPC systems, Google factors an ad's success into the cost of keeping that ad in a high position on the page. Position is partly determined by bid amount, but a very successful ad with a low bid on a keyword can place higher than an unsuccessful ad with a higher bid on that keyword. Success is measured by *clickthrough rate,* or *CTR.* Here again, relevancy is the name of the game. Google cares so much about providing its searchers with relevancy on the search results page (in results listings *and* advertisements) that it rewards relevant ads with discount pricing for high placement.

- ✔ **Conversion tracking.** Getting a searcher to click your ad is the first step; making a sale is the next step. The sale can be whatever the advertiser wants from the customer; the desired action could be a simple site registration or signing up for a free newsletter. Whatever you want the customer to do on your site after clicking through your ad, Google helps track your success, or the *conversion rate.*

All this and more is bundled into the Google AdWords keyword advertising program. If you've used Google, you've seen AdWords in action. Figure 6-1 shows a Google search results page with two AdWords ads, matching the keywords *cold climate gardening.*

Broader searches (on the single keyword *gardening,* for example) return pages with eight ads in the right column. In some cases, Google places ten ads on the page: two above the search listings and eight in the right column. Figure 6-2 shows a search on the keyword *baskets,* with AdWords ads above and to the right of the index listings.

Figure 6-1:
AdWords
ads are
displayed in
the right
column of
search
results
pages.

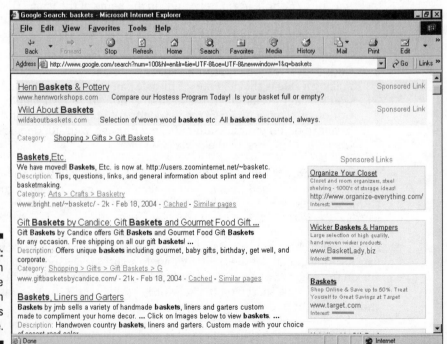

Figure 6-2:
Up to ten
ads are
displayed on
any results
page.

What You Need to Get Started with AdWords

The two factors that have kept advertising in the realm of relatively large companies for years are

- ✔ High cost
- ✔ High commitment

These two factors characterize blanket advertising, in which exposure of arguable value is purchased in large, expensive, irrevocable blocks. In refreshing contrast, Google AdWords features

- ✔ Low cost
- ✔ No commitment

Anybody can advertise in the AdWords program. The traditional barriers to advertising on a global scale are demolished.

It *is* possible to spend a lot of money advertising on Google, but the point is not cheap advertising but cost-effective advertising. The absence of commitment, in terms of a campaign's duration and expense, enables advertisers to cut losses instantly and work to improve their *return on investment (ROI)*.

You need only two things to start an AdWords campaign:

- ✔ Five dollars
- ✔ A landing page

A *landing page* is the clickthrough destination, the URL underlying your ad's link. Most advertisers spend quite a bit more than five dollars, but that nominal amount is all Google requires to activate an account. Likewise, most advertisers own considerably more Web property than a single landing page.

However, as I write this chapter, I'm managing a small AdWords campaign for a non-profit institution promoting a single event publicized with a single Web page. This small-time approach isn't unusual, even for thriving Internet businesses that sell a single product from a single page or affiliate businesses whose ads link customers directly to somebody else's order-taking page. In that latter case, the advertiser might own merely the right to link to another company's landing page.

Democracy and small-business friendliness are important, attractive attributes of search advertising. The smallest of small-time players can join in, battling it out for screen space with major media corporations. Survival and success depend on smart targeting, good research, and tenacious adaptation more than on the brute force of spending. True, deep pockets help when bidding on expensive keywords, but as I discuss in the following chapters, avoiding keyword traps is part of nimble marketing in Google.

Understanding How AdWords Works

Enough theory. Here's how AdWords works. I save detailed instructions in setting up an account and developing a campaign for Chapter 7. As a preview, the following list outlines the basic steps of designing and running ads in Google, in roughly the order in which most people proceed:

✔ **Start an account.** Starting an AdWords account is pain-free and expense-free. You don't even have to be certain that you'll ever run a single ad. Opening the account simply lets you into Google's AdWords staging area, called the Control Center (see Figure 6-3), where you create and deploy campaigns. No ads are displayed, and no billing occurs, until you *activate* the account, at which time you provide your payment information. Opening the account gives you access to the Keyword Suggestion Tool, a necessary campaign-planning device.

Figure 6-3: The Google AdWords Control Center.

✔ **Write ads.** Google provides guidelines for composing the highly compressed copy that goes into an AdWords ad. (Figure 6-4 shows an ad-composing screen.) This copy is called the *creative,* as in, "I'm going to rewrite the creative of my ad." AdWords advertisements are extremely short bursts of text, so it's no surprise that they're difficult to write. (Any writer will tell you that expressing a message concisely is far more difficult than composing long, voluble, drawn-out, wordy sentences that repeat redundancies and ramble on loosely and aimlessly, continuing beyond the point that they're intended to convey, seemingly without end, until the writer mercifully runs out of steam or his editor intervenes, whichever comes first.) Google imposes guidelines that establish a uniform style throughout the AdWords column. Within those rules, experimentation is key. Savvy AdWords marketers determined to maximize effect create multiple ads for each group of keywords, and then watch their reports carefully to see what works.

✔ **Assign keywords.** This crucial task determines the search result pages upon which your ad appears. In truth, you should be assigning keywords continually, even before you open an AdWords account. I make the point throughout this book. Sorry about the repetition, but keywords represent the one Google marketing thread that runs through everything, from designing a site to building your PageRank, from advertising on results pages to publishing Google ads in the AdSense program. At this point in your evolution as a Google advertiser, keyword selection becomes an intensely focused affair, with money riding on sharp, competitive choices. Google offers plenty of help, as shown in Figure 6-5.

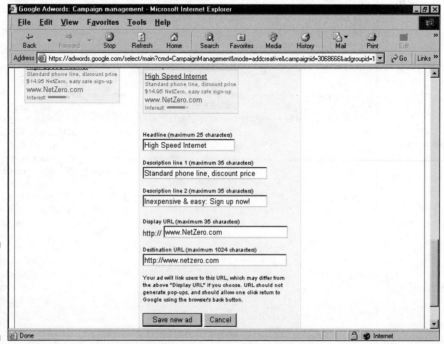

Figure 6-4:
Writing
AdWords
creative (the
ad text).

✔ **Bid on keywords.** At this point, you choose how much you're willing to pay for the keywords associated with your ads. Specifically, you select a maximum *cost-per-click* (*CPC*) that you'll pay per group of keywords. You may adjust the maximum CPC for each keyword. Another group of key-words, applying to one or more ads, can be implemented with a different cost-per-click maximum (for the entire group and individual words). When it comes to running the campaign and paying your bills, Google often charges less than your maximum — in fact, Google always charges the lowest CPC to keep your ad in the position it would attain by paying the maximum. (See the "Getting into position" sidebar.)

✔ **Edit keywords.** This step and the previous two steps happen at once. Adjusting your maximum CPC and your keywords are part of a single process — the most important process of your campaign. Google pro-vides estimates of your ad's performance at various CPC levels, on a keyword-by-keyword basis. Chapters 7 and 8 delve into selecting and bidding on keywords.

✔ **Specify a budget.** You can set a daily maximum for clickthrough expenses. Google can optimize the timing of your ad displays to spread out your ad displays and clickthroughs over a 24-hour period. Ideally, your ads run evenly throughout the day, and you hit your daily budget on the nose. Google sometimes overshoots and exceeds the daily budget by as much as 20 percent, but it never charges advertisers more per month than 30 times the daily budget.

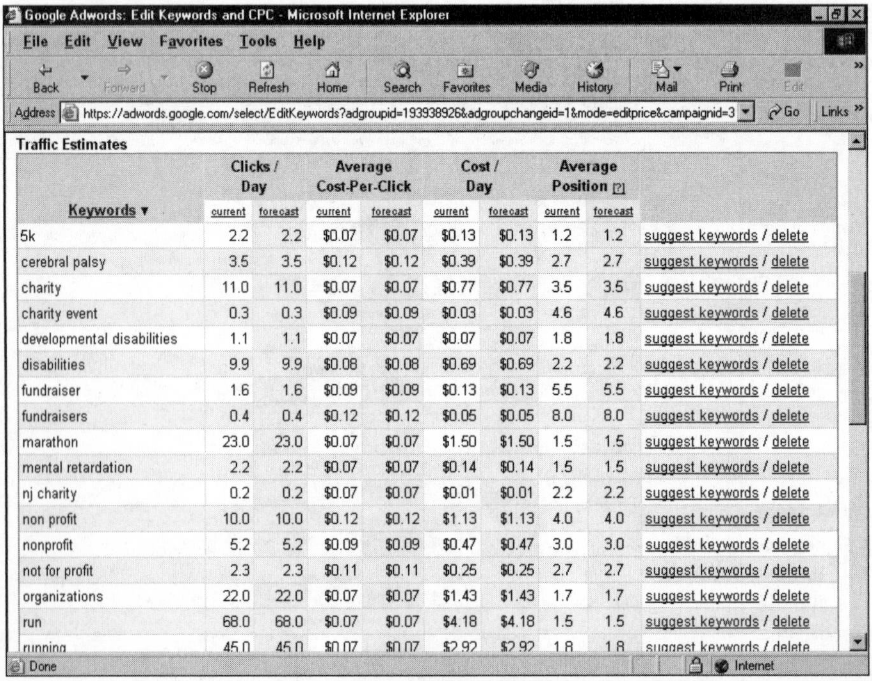

Figure 6-5: Google's Traffic Estimator is one of several tools for selecting and optimizing keywords.

	Clicks / Day		Average Cost-Per-Click		Cost / Day		Average Position [?]		
Keywords ▼	current	forecast	current	forecast	current	forecast	current	forecast	
5k	2.2	2.2	$0.07	$0.07	$0.13	$0.13	1.2	1.2	suggest keywords / delete
cerebral palsy	3.5	3.5	$0.12	$0.12	$0.39	$0.39	2.7	2.7	suggest keywords / delete
charity	11.0	11.0	$0.07	$0.07	$0.77	$0.77	3.5	3.5	suggest keywords / delete
charity event	0.3	0.3	$0.09	$0.09	$0.03	$0.03	4.6	4.6	suggest keywords / delete
developmental disabilities	1.1	1.1	$0.07	$0.07	$0.07	$0.07	1.8	1.8	suggest keywords / delete
disabilities	9.9	9.9	$0.08	$0.08	$0.69	$0.69	2.2	2.2	suggest keywords / delete
fundraiser	1.6	1.6	$0.09	$0.09	$0.13	$0.13	5.5	5.5	suggest keywords / delete
fundraisers	0.4	0.4	$0.12	$0.12	$0.05	$0.05	8.0	8.0	suggest keywords / delete
marathon	23.0	23.0	$0.07	$0.07	$1.50	$1.50	1.5	1.5	suggest keywords / delete
mental retardation	2.2	2.2	$0.07	$0.07	$0.14	$0.14	1.5	1.5	suggest keywords / delete
nj charity	0.2	0.2	$0.07	$0.07	$0.01	$0.01	2.2	2.2	suggest keywords / delete
non profit	10.0	10.0	$0.12	$0.12	$1.13	$1.13	4.0	4.0	suggest keywords / delete
nonprofit	5.2	5.2	$0.09	$0.09	$0.47	$0.47	3.0	3.0	suggest keywords / delete
not for profit	2.3	2.3	$0.11	$0.11	$0.25	$0.25	2.7	2.7	suggest keywords / delete
organizations	22.0	22.0	$0.07	$0.07	$1.43	$1.43	1.7	1.7	suggest keywords / delete
run	68.0	68.0	$0.07	$0.07	$4.18	$4.18	1.5	1.5	suggest keywords / delete
running	45.0	45.0	$0.07	$0.07	$2.92	$2.92	1.8	1.8	suggest keywords / delete

Getting into position

The AdWords system is popularly known as a type of advertising in which you purchase keywords by bidding on their value. But that interpretation reveals a crucial misunderstanding. It is not possible to own a keyword. You bid for a position in the AdWords column of a search results page. The AdWords column is dynamic and positions change frequently, so you might not own a certain position for long if the competition is tough.

One reason Google's system is so attractive and cost-effective is the constant downward pressure Google applies to actual costs. Every advertiser in the AdWords column pays the lowest possible per-click cost to remain in the position earned by that advertiser's bid. Say your bid of 50 cents earns you the top spot on the search results page for the key phrase *collectible coin trading*. Your closest competitor bids 40 cents as a maximum CPC for the same or similar keywords, and lands on the same search results page in position number 2, below your ad. When a searcher clicks your ad, you're billed 41 cents, the minimum cost to maintain your position above number 2.

✔ **Activate the account.** Activation puts your payment information on file and readies your account for live campaigns. Google charges a one-time activation fee of five dollars. (A reactivation fee is also levied when a repeatedly deactivated account is reactivated more than twice. Google deactivates underperforming keywords and campaigns.)

✔ **Start the campaign.** AdWords campaigns are under the advertiser's control (except for Google's automated deactivation system, which discontinues underperforming keywords and accounts). You may pause campaigns and adjust every aspect of them on the fly.

Seeing the Big Picture: The Google Ad Network

So far, I've described how search advertising in general, and AdWords in particular, run circles around blanket advertising in these ways:

✔ **Search advertising is democratic.** Anyone can launch a global ad campaign, in contrast to the high cost and commitment level of traditional media advertising.

✔ **Search advertising is cost effective.** This is especially true in AdWords because Google charges less than your CPC bid when possible.

✔ **Search advertising has built-in relevancy.** Blanket advertising has built-in irrelevancy.

✔ **Google AdWords is a pay-per-click system.** Advertisers pay for only prequalified leads, not for unqualified exposure.

✔ **AdWords offers detailed control of the campaign.** This contrasts with the all-or-nothing blanket approach.

I haven't mentioned another aspect of the value of Google AdWords: the tremendous reach inherent in Google advertising. Google distributes AdWords advertisements in three important venues:

✔ **Google search results pages.** These pages display Google's proprietary search results in the Web, Groups, and Directory sections and also in Froogle.

✔ **Google's search engine partners.** Google provides AdWords ads to the search results pages of other engines, including Excite, Teoma, About.com, AskJeeves, Netscape, Go.com, AOL Search, and iWon.com. (See Figure 6-6.)

Figure 6-6:
Search results at Netscape.com don't look like Google, but they come from Google. So do the ads.

✔ **Google's content network.** This portion of the AdWords distribution network encompasses the thousands of Web pages that run AdSense ads. These destinations, large and small, are called *content sites* or *content pages*. AdSense ads are just AdWords ads running on partner sites that are not search engines. (See Figure 6-7.) Some of these sites are major media outlets, such as Forbes.com. Others are small entrepreneurships operating affiliate businesses or merely providing information. In all cases, Google attempts (and largely succeeds) to target AdWords ads to content pages based on its understanding of the information on the page instead of by generating them directly by keyword search.

Even without the content network, your ads enjoy astonishing distribution power, appearing in eight search engines besides Google. Aggressive advertisers cover all the bases; *all* advertisers use Google.

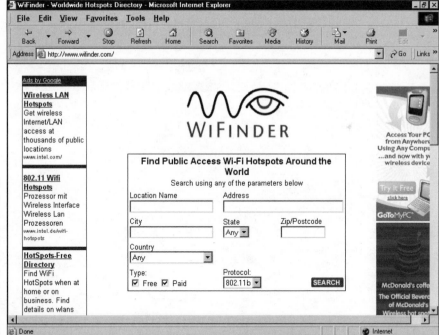

Figure 6-7:
Google's
AdSense
program
generates
AdWords
ads for
content
sites.

Chapter 7

Designing Your AdWords Campaign and Starting an Account

A successful AdWords campaign demands ongoing effort, but in that effort are opportunities for correction, refinement, and improved returns. There is no "throwing the switch" of an AdWords campaign in the same sense as in traditional advertising, where a media purchase is contracted and runs along a predefined course. Instead, successful AdWords advertisers continually experiment with new variables, remove underperforming aspects, and brainstorm new angles. AdWords is addictive.

Remember these two points:

✔ Starting an account does not necessarily start your campaign.

✔ Starting your campaign does not represent the end of your work.

On the second point, it is vitally important to be clear from the start: A successful AdWords campaign requires ongoing testing and experimentation. I don't mean a successful campaign "thrives on" testing, or "would benefit from" testing. I mean that success *requires* testing. Without an initial period of testing and experimentation, you will almost certainly fail. I won't be so fierce later, so hear it now: It is painfully easy to fail at AdWords. Almost all successful CPC advertisers failed before they succeeded.

With careful planning and an understanding of campaign elements, you can minimize the pain and expense of the inevitable period of trial and error. Before putting ads into play, read as much of Part II as your impatience allows. Google's assurance that you need only five dollars and 15 minutes to get started is literally true, but actual experience is far more complicated. You should get involved with Google AdWords *methodically and carefully*.

The purpose of this chapter is to give you a better idea of how you budget, organize, and track an AdSense campaign, write ad copy, and research keywords. When you understand those tasks, you'll be sufficiently well-informed to open and activate an account. Then, with your account activated and at least one ad in distribution, you'll be ready to read the other three chapters in Part II. Chapter 8 details the administrative tools. Chapter 9 explores the maintenance and improvement of the campaign's building blocks — Ad Groups and keywords. Chapter 10 rounds up miscellaneous points and deals with multiple campaigns.

Now, onwards to the nitty-gritty of the AdWords program.

The Big Picture: Campaigns, Ad Groups, and Keywords

The AdWords sign-up process, which I describe later in this chapter, makes it seem as though running an ad campaign were an effortless, 15-minute process. Indeed, it can be — though launching a campaign with so little preparation is like hang-gliding without a breeze. Even if you've planned your budget and have a list of keywords, you should give some thought to the organization of your campaign.

Google provides organizational layers to your campaign that make it possible to test different marketing angles, track their performance, and discontinue ineffective approaches while letting robust ads run. You must use these organizational features to some extent, and I encourage you to become as fluent in their use as possible.

This section helps you conceive your campaigns according to the framework furnished by AdWords, which is shown in Figure 7-1. You can always backpedal from a campaign that you've organized with insufficient attention to detail, and reorganize it more usefully. But you can avoid that headache by planning, from the start, in highly defined marketing modules.

An AdWords account contains three organizational levels:

✔ **Keywords.** Keywords are the terms people use to search, and they trigger your ads. Almost every keyword is assigned an individual cost-per-click value.

✔ **Ad Groups.** Ad Groups contain clusters of keywords, each of which is associated with one or more ads.

✔ **Campaigns.** Campaigns contain Ad Groups.

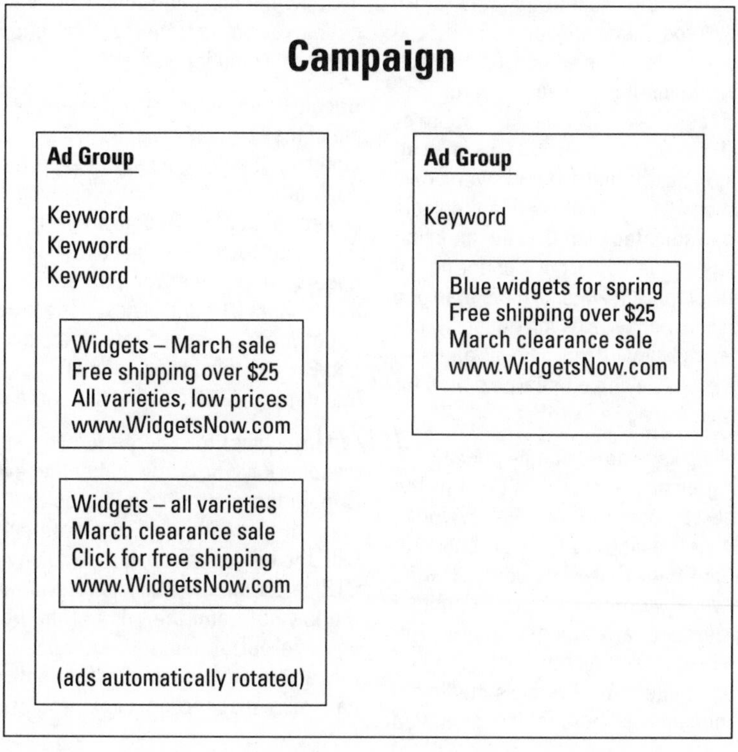

Campaign

Ad Group

Keyword
Keyword
Keyword

Widgets – March sale
Free shipping over $25
All varieties, low prices
www.WidgetsNow.com

Widgets – all varieties
March clearance sale
Click for free shipping
www.WidgetsNow.com

(ads automatically rotated)

Ad Group

Keyword

Blue widgets for spring
Free shipping over $25
March clearance sale
www.WidgetsNow.com

Figure 7-1:
Each Ad
Group in a
Campaign
contains
one or more
keywords
and one or
more ads.

You might be thinking (yes, I can see your thoughts, so please clear all images of Carrot Top from your mind), "How peculiar that ads don't represent an organizational level." Ads are associated with one or many keywords. You may associate one ad with one keyword; one ad with multiple keywords; multiple ads with one keyword; or multiple ads with multiple keywords. Each of these configurations can make up an Ad Group. The defining feature of an Ad Group is the keyword(s) associated with it, not the ad(s). Strange, I know. Let it go for now; I return to Ad Groups later.

Google's strong medicine

Google doesn't tolerate failure among its advertisers, but its standards of success might differ from yours. Google is concerned with just one campaign statistic: the clickthrough rate (CTR). After an AdWords Campaign generates 1000 impressions, Google takes action on the ads associated with underperforming keywords. The standard of acceptable performance is, more or less, one half of one percent (0.5%) CTR. If an ad fails to elicit 5 clickthroughs out of every 1000 impressions, on average, Google might disable the keyword associated with that ad, meaning that the ad is prevented from appearing on search pages for that keyword. (If more than one keyword is associated with the ad, Google tracks the CTR for each keyword individually, and prevents ads from displaying on search pages for those underperforming keywords.)

Before disabling keywords, Google puts an "At risk" warning next to them, as shown in the figure. The next step is to "Slow" the keywords, which really means slowing the distribution of ads associated with those keywords. During this slowdown, keywords not at risk continue performing normally, and ads associated with those healthy keywords appear unhindered on search results pages. But Google's medicinal pill is bitter because *all* instances of a slowed keyword across all Ad Groups are slowed, even if in some of those instances the ads associated with those keywords are performing adequately. You must correct the problem by eliminating keywords from the Ad Groups in which they are executing badly.

Google's focus on clickthrough rate is an example of the company's obsessive concern for the quality of the Google search experience. If ads don't attract clicks when displayed on certain results pages, in Google's eye it means that those ads are not relevant to the page and don't deserve to be on it. You perhaps don't care as much about CTR and almost certainly care more about your conversion rate on the clicks you *do* get. But you must keep your CTR up to Google's standard to avoid slowing the entire campaign.

When it comes to underperforming, slowed, and disabled keywords, remember that even though Google targets the keyword as the faulty element of the campaign, the problem could lie with the ad copy. True, the usual culprit in poor CTR performance is lack of relevance between the keyword and the ad, and the best way to improve performance is to choose keywords that are more relevant. But ineffective ad copy can also discourage clickthroughs, and it's worth trying a correction there before deleting the keyword. However, after Google brands a keyword "Disabled," that's the end: You must pluck the word out of the Ad Group.

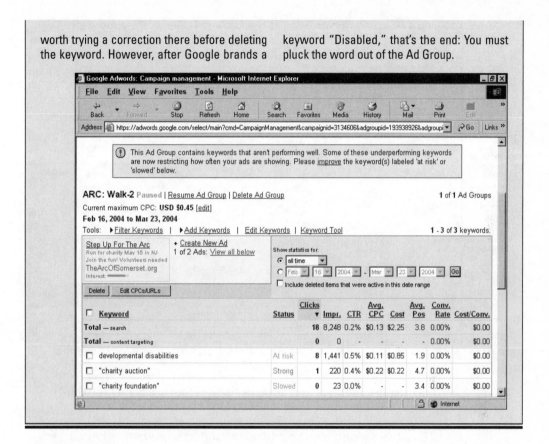

Planning the first level: Campaigns

Throughout this book, I speak so much about "the AdWords campaign" that you might think your AdWords account is necessarily dedicated to a single campaign. Not so. Here, I must distinguish between the generic campaign, which is your overall marketing initiative as it applies to advertising on Google, and the AdWords Campaign, which is a distinct organizational tier.

An AdWords account may contain multiple campaigns (see Figure 7-2). Although I strongly recommend making organizational divisions within a campaign (as I describe in the following section), running multiple campaigns is not essential in many cases.

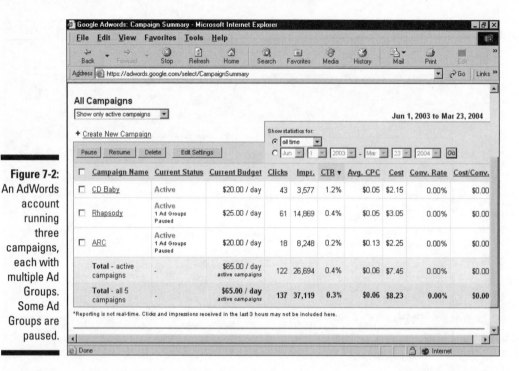

Figure 7-2:
An AdWords account running three campaigns, each with multiple Ad Groups. Some Ad Groups are paused.

Two major considerations lead advertisers to set up a second (and third) campaign:

✔ The advertiser is marketing different products, represented by ads, keyword groups, and landing pages that have nothing to do with each other. Even in this dispersed circumstance, you can accomplish the boundaries you need by working with Ad Groups within your campaign. But establishing a new campaign structure makes the Control Center pages neater and enables simpler naming of Ad Groups. Think of campaigns as marketing books, and Ad Groups as chapters in those books. Whether you want one book or several depends on the diversity of your marketing initiatives.

✔ The advertiser wants to launch ads with campaign settings that differ from an existing campaign. Google provides seven settings that affect all ads in a campaign. Campaign settings can be convenient and inconvenient. On one hand, global settings are cumbersome because you can't exempt specific ads from their effect. On the other hand, the ability to set variables across the entire campaign is a valuable shortcut.

Knowing how to organize your marketing effort into AdWords campaigns requires a clear understanding of the Campaign settings. Google divides the Edit Campaign Setting page (see Figure 7-3) into several sections.

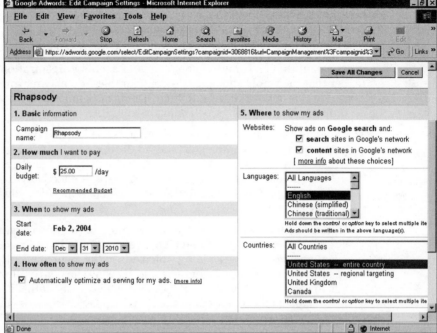

Figure 7-3:
Campaign
settings
apply
globally
to all Ad
Groups
in the
Campaign.

Here are the settings of each campaign that you need to consider when organizing your entire AdWords structure:

✔ **Name.** From an organizational viewpoint, the campaign name is probably the least important setting. Of course, you want to name your campaigns distinctly. If the name is the only difference among your planned campaigns, you might as well lump them together and distinguish them in Ad Groups.

✔ **Daily budget.** This setting is where you choose your spending cap per day. (Later sections of this chapter cover AdWords budgeting in detail.) This important setting, by itself, could determine a dedicated campaign in your AdWords account, even if it advertises a product similar to one in a campaign with a higher or lower daily budget.

Suppose that you sell kayaks and kayak supplies. Normally, you would probably consider your entire business to be under one campaign roof. But if you market a landing page filled with inexpensive accessories (water boots, paddling gloves, roof racks) separately from a landing page dedicated to the relatively expensive boats, you might decide to budget more money per day to a campaign driving traffic to the latter page. Such a decision would be based on a host of considerations such as relative profit margins, clickthrough rates, and your maximum CPC. Tinkering with this setting on a campaign-wide level is possible only if you make intelligent and thoughtful divisions of your marketing strategy in advance.

Adamant though I am that you plan your account organization, remember that the whole shebang is reconfigurable. You may rearrange your campaigns and Ad Groups anytime. Doing so is not exactly a drag-and-drop process, though, so planning is advisable.

- **Campaign schedule.** Here, you determine start and end dates for the campaign. Because all campaigns (and Ad Groups within campaigns) may be paused and resumed at will, this variable usually isn't changed from its default end date, which is December 31, 2010 — effectively an indefinite campaign run. However, setting an end date is useful when you can't monitor the campaign closely.

- **Optimization.** Google optimizes the rotation of the various ads within your campaign — at the Campaign level, not the Ad Group level. Optimization involves determining which ads in the campaign enjoy higher clickthrough rates than other ads and skewing the distribution of your ads toward those that perform better. You may turn off this feature at the Campaign level, but not at the Ad Group level (where it would probably be more productive).

- **Content site distribution.** You may also distribute your ads across the Google content partner network. This network consists of content sites that have agreed to enable AdWords ads to appear on relevant pages. This network does not include search sites that Google licenses to, such as AOL Search and Netscape. Your campaign can be distributed throughout the content network of non-Google sites at your discretion.

- **Languages.** All advertising is language specific, determined by the language in which the ads are written. Google can isolate the language used by individuals based on their Preferences setting. When you set a language choice at the Campaign level, all your ads should be written in that language, and they are all directed at Google users in that language.

- **Countries.** Related to the language setting, this variable allows you to target users by their geographical location. Google locates its users based on their IP address, which works in most (but not all) cases. Currently, you may target your campaign to any combination of dozens of countries or fine-tune your targeting to a U.S. region or a combination of U.S. regions.

Note: Chapter 10 contains more detail about language targeting and geo-targeting.

Those new to AdWords have no way to evaluate the relative importance of campaign settings or to forecast the optimal division of their marketing. So, with the voice of experience, let me recommend that you pay close attention to three campaign features in particular: the daily budget, language targeting, and location targeting. Those three settings are the most important and are the variables most worthy of earning a campaign dedicated to them. Being able to adjust these settings across a suite of Ad Groups is vitally convenient. The targeting they represent is so crucial in some marketing plans that defining campaigns by these settings might be more important than dividing the account by product line. Ideally, though, major organizational criteria coincide, so that product type, budgetary requirements, language targeting, and geo-targeting all suggest the same campaign divisions.

Planning the second level: Ad Groups

Ad Groups are the gears that propel your campaign. They're the most important unit of most organizational plans. Every account contains at least one campaign, and every campaign contains at least one Ad Group. (See Figure 7-4.) For this reason, Ad Groups are unavoidable, yet they are easy to disregard. The 15-minute plan hyped by Google establishes a simple Ad Group in a solitary campaign. Advertisers who let their marketing rest with that simple scheme never get their hands on the real power of AdWords: the power of highly specific targeting and CPC budgeting.

Ad Groups are somewhat misnamed — they're not necessarily groups of ads. Ad Groups are not necessarily groups of keywords, either, but they're *more likely* to contain clusters of keywords than clusters of ads. I touched on this peculiar subject earlier in the chapter. Here, I reiterate the four possible combinations that might make up an Ad Group:

- One ad associated with one keyword
- One ad associated with multiple keywords
- Multiple ads associated with one keyword
- Multiple ads associated with multiple keywords

The last of these is perhaps the most common, but good reasons exist to create Ad Groups with a single keyword, or a single ad, or both. In fact, Google encourages precision and diversity. The more detailed you get, the more maintenance is required, with the reward being greater precision in tracking results in the account.

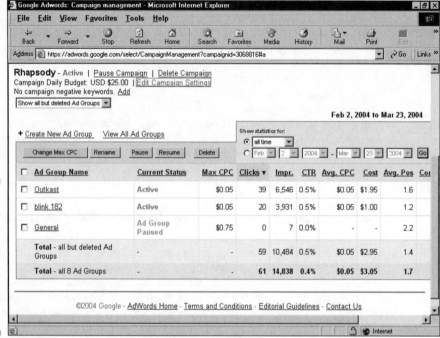

Figure 7-4:
This
AdWords
Campaign
contains
three Ad
Groups, one
of which is
paused.

Ad Groups are defined by keywords more than by ads in two ways. First, as I noted, an Ad Group is more likely to contain a group of keywords than a group of ads. (See Figure 7-5.) Second, and more importantly when conceiving of Ad Groups, the better strategy is to build Ad Groups around targeted keywords than around ad copy.

As with all other aspects of Google marketing (repeated to the point of tedium in this book), Google is all about keywords no matter how you approach it. Ad Groups should be conceptually founded on keywords, not ad text. You might want to think of Ad Groups as keyword groups.

Ad Groups are bundles of marketing energy that connect four essential constituents of your campaign:

✔ Keywords

✔ Ads

✔ CPC bids

✔ The landing page

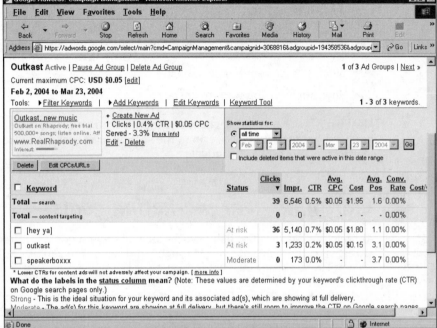

In formulating an Ad Group, you first identify your marketing goal — even
before choosing keywords or writing ads. Then you identify your target customers by the keywords they will most likely search for. These keywords form
the core of your Ad Group. Researching these words and phrases requires
ingenuity, persistence, testing, and familiarity with interactive tools.

After you've determined a preliminary set of keywords, you create one or
more ads. (Google has you create the ad first and then load up the keywords,
as I describe in the next chapter. But Google's procedural order doesn't
match smart conceptual order. Base your Ad Group, and your entire marketing thrust, on keywords.) With your keywords and ads in place, you set a
maximum cost-per-click for the entire Ad Group and individual CPCs for separate keywords if you want. Your landing must be ready by the time you
launch the Ad Group, but besides that obvious requirement, it doesn't
matter when you construct it.

Setting Your Goals

Two considerations rise to the top for every new AdWords advertiser:

- ✔ What do you want to accomplish?
- ✔ How much do you want to spend?

Most likely, your marketing goal corresponds with one of the objectives listed in the following section. Read on to the section after that for a discussion of how to set your AdWords budget.

Clarifying your marketing goals

Although AdWords advertising works on a different model than traditional advertising, the range of goals is roughly the same. You can use AdWords to accomplish six major Internet marketing goals:

- ✔ **Develop leads.** Leads eventually turn into sales, ideally. How that conversion occurs varies widely among industries and business models. A lead might consist of a registered site visitor, a newsletter subscriber, or simply a visitor who bookmarks the site for future visits.

- ✔ **Sell your products.** Major e-commerce sites use the AdWords program to propel direct sales.

- ✔ **Sell someone else's product.** This is the realm of affiliate marketing, which is prominent in AdWords. Affiliate ads are always marked with the word *affiliate* (or the abbreviation *aff*) in the ad copy.

- ✔ **Increase impressions.** For sites that earn advertising revenue, the value of traffic lies in generating the largest number of ad displays.

- ✔ **Capture coordinates.** Capturing the visitor's e-mail address (and perhaps mailing address) allows the business to develop a more direct relationship with that person, leading to direct communication, repeat visits, or eventual sales.

- ✔ **Build a brand.** Brand recognition is enhanced differently in AdWords than in traditional media advertising. AdWords ads do not build brand recognition by means of graphics, like a banner, TV, or magazine ad. However, some advertisers see value in driving traffic to a Web site that does use graphics to increase recognition. Brand-building may also occur when people see AdWords ads for something that they don't associate with a business, such as Wal-Mart ads appearing for the keyword *jewelry*.

Driving traffic is the overwhelming purpose of AdWords advertising, and that single imperative ties together all six marketing goals just listed. The ingredients of a successful AdWords campaign remain the same regardless of the traffic's purpose: relevant keywords, bidding for effective positioning, and ad copy that elicits clickthroughs. The single ingredient that changes most according to your campaign's purpose is the landing page, because that is where you receive and convert traffic.

Understanding the AdWords budget

The budget of an AdWords campaign is much more elastic than the budget for traditional advertising. You control not only how much your AdWords traffic is worth on a per-click basis, but also how much you spend, overall, on the campaign. You may augment or diminish your AdWords operating budget at any time.

The AdWords budget structure contains two major parts, each of which has two components. Here's how it works:

- ✔ **CPC budget.** The cost-per-click budget is set at two levels: keyword and Ad Group. (In Figure 7-6, three keywords are being set for the same maximum CPC.) Using the keyword setting is painstaking work, and many advertisers stick with a CPC bid covering all keywords in the Ad Group.

- ✔ **Total budget.** Total AdWords budgets are derived from a daily limit that you place on your campaign expenses. The daily budget is a Campaign setting, and places a ceiling on the total daily expenditures of all the Ad Groups in that campaign. The second component of your total budget is the overall daily ceiling of all AdWords campaigns, if you operate more than one. Paused campaigns do not contribute to the overall total budget.

A monthly budget lurks in the background but doesn't appear on your account screens. The monthly budget is calculated by multiplying the daily budget by the number of days in the current month. This figure is used to guide Google's overbilling allowance; Google may overrun your daily budget by 20 percent during any day but may not overbill your monthly budget. If an accounting overrun of clickthroughs occurs at the end of any month, Google issues a credit to your account.

Your CPC budget represents a *maximum* amount to pay for clickthroughs. In nearly all cases, you pay less per click. As described in Chapter 6, Google charges the least amount needed to maintain the page position earned by your bid.

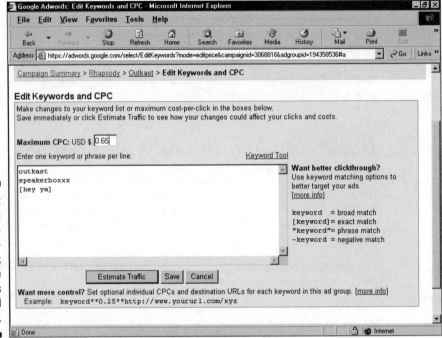

Figure 7-6:
Adjusting
the maxi-
mum cost-
per-click
for all three
keywords
of an Ad
Group.

With your marketing goal clear and the budget parameters understood, you're ready for two major tasks:

✔ Preparing your site to receive AdWords-generated clickthroughs and convert visitors to your goal

✔ Determining your budget in dollars and cents

The next two sections cover these points.

Preparing Your Landing Page

Too many people launch an AdWords campaign without sufficient attention to the important element that exists outside Google: the landing page. The landing page is where visitors who click through your ads meet your sales and conversion presentations. The typical downfall of a landing page is the belief that it needn't contain anything special — that the index page (the site's home page) or another page of a site can do double-duty as a landing page. In some cases, this presumption is true, especially at up-and-running e-commerce sites. The bookstore Alibris.com, for example, uses ads keyed to author names to send clickthroughs to those authors' pages at the site. Because the Alibris e-commerce engine is in full throttle throughout the site, no special landing page is necessary.

The story is different for sites not selling products or sites new to the game of buying traffic. Converting unpaid traffic is not as urgent a proposition as converting paid traffic. When the conversion rate determines the success or failure of an AdWords campaign, you need to pay special attention to the landing page, which receives paid traffic. Here are three tips:

- **Don't use the index page.** Although the index page of a site might seem like the best (and certainly easiest) choice for a landing page, it serves a different function. An index page gives a broad overview of the site and presents a full array of navigational links. These front pages encourage exploring and surfing, which are not productive behaviors from a need-to-convert viewpoint.

- **Keep the landing page tightly focused.** Don't distract your paid visitors. Focus on the single task you want each visitor to perform, and optimize the landing page for that one task. In this context, optimization bears little resemblance to keyword embedding and tagging described in Chapter 4. You're not trying to give the landing page a high PageRank in Google. In fact, your landing page might not be linked to or appear in Google's index at all. Optimize the landing page toward conversion. Make conversion the only subject of that page, and don't offer links to other portions of your site if following those links takes the visitor away from the conversion task.

- **Make the landing page action oriented.** Editorial content for its own sake has no value on a landing page. Of course, the page displays words and sentences, but they should encourage a conversion action. (See Figure 7-7.) Whether the conversion is signing up for a newsletter or buying a product, the visitor should feel that the action is the ticket off the page. Look at Amazon.com's book pages. Visitors to those pages aren't encouraged to admire books, or talk about books, or read about books — they're encouraged to *buy* books. The same is true with eBay, Lands' End, CDBaby, and other online stores that convert powerfully.

Most likely, each AdWords Campaign deserves its own landing page. You might consider creating distinct landing pages for each Ad Group or even each ad. Even if the landing pages are similar, their distinct URLs offer an easy way to track clickthroughs.

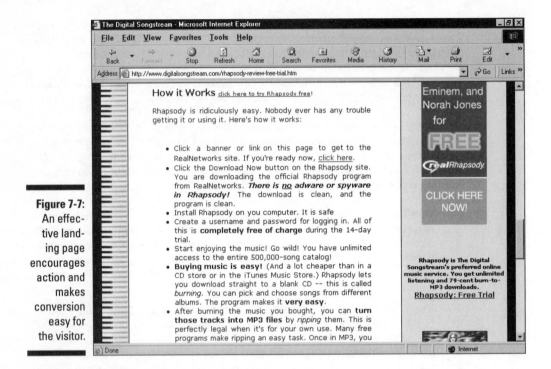

Figure 7-7:
An effec-
tive land-
ing page
encourages
action and
makes
conversion
easy for
the visitor.

Productive Budgeting

The amount you spend to purchase traffic depends, essentially, on what the traffic is worth to your business. This factor is where your marketing goal meets your budget. A positive return on investment (ROI) is easy to quantify when the campaign is geared to selling products directly. In that case, your return is calculated simply by subtracting expenses from sales. As long as the result is a positive number, your budget can be sky-high, because every dollar spent on clickthroughs yields (on average) a profit.

"Spending" is perhaps a misnomer when budgeting in AdWords, which comes close to being a direct sales channel. (A direct sales channel is one in which the consumer can take immediate action that results in a sale.) As with any other advertising venue of this sort, ad spending takes on a new light when it can be directly connected to gain. What limits should be placed on a budget whose every spent dollar returns (on average) more than a dollar in revenue? No limit, obviously. You might not make a living on a very slim profit margin — for exam- ple, if every $1.00 spent returns $1.01 in average revenue. However, even a one-penny profit justifies the ad campaign and encourages the advertiser to increase its daily budget. Naturally, if you're experiencing a slim profit margin in AdWords, you might need to find ways of increasing that margin and selling more profitably through other channels.

With all this in mind, the real question becomes, What is your experimentation budget? Here's another, admittedly harsher way to phrase it: How much can you afford to lose before you figure out how to make a campaign profitable?

As I mentioned earlier in this chapter, a successful AdWords campaign requires initial experimentation to shake out the bugs. During this debugging, keywords are discarded, new keywords are added, daily and per-click budgets are tweaked, and the campaign structure is sometimes torn down and rebuilt. Each test of the budding campaign costs some amount of money, and that amount is variable. (More on the dollars and cents later.) Take comfort in one happy realization: Utter failure is the cheapest option. Not that I wish anyone failure, but the truth is that if your campaign fails to generate clickthroughs, you're not billed. Your only expense while grinding through multiple failures is the five-dollar fee every third time you reactivate your account.

Of course, almost every campaign with substantial ad impressions induces some clickthroughs, even if the CTR is insufficient for both you and Google. You must pay for those clicks. But the streamlined payment model makes the testing phases relatively painless financially.

After you find the sweet spot in which working keywords match ideal bidding levels, and your campaign generates profitable clickthroughs, it's time to open the floodgates and expand your budget dramatically. When clickthroughs yield a positive ROI, you want as many clicks as possible and should be happy to pay for them.

Aggressive budgeting, with important limits, is usually a smart move with AdWords. Consider your AdWords experience as consisting of two phases:

- ✔ Testing
- ✔ The ongoing operation of a mature campaign

The purpose of testing is to determine whether your keywords, bids, clickthrough rate, ad copy, and landing page work together for a gainful ROI. A certain volume of impressions is needed to determine whether the current configuration works. (When testing, your impressions can be thought of as a statistical sample that becomes more meaningful as it becomes larger.) Google regards 1000 impressions as a meaningful sample, and begins slowing the distribution of underperforming keywords after that number has been reached, campaign-wide.

Your priority should be to get the news, good or bad, as quickly as possible. The key to avoiding overspending dangerously during AdWords testing is a combination of vigilance and the daily budget setting. AdWords doesn't allow you to build in a campaign stop based on the number of impressions, like a stop-loss order for a stock. If that setting were possible, you could set the campaign to stop after 1000 impressions and go to the beach for the rest of the day. As it is, the daily budget is your stop-loss order. You can also use the End date setting to stop the campaign after one day. *Then* go to the beach.

Keeping in mind the need for testing, the preference of receiving meaningful feedback quickly, and the desire to avoid overspending, the following is one step-by-step plan for budgeting an AdWords test. Don't worry for now about the mechanics of creating an Ad Group or using the Traffic Estimator; these points are covered later in the chapter, in the "Creating an AdWords Account" section. (Chapter 9 delves into both points in more detail.)

1. **Create an Ad Group.**

   Your Ad Group consists of keywords and at least one ad associated with those keywords, plus a cost-per-click bid that applies to the entire Ad Group.

2. **Using the Traffic Estimator, observe what Google estimates you will spend per day, and decide whether you can afford one full day of testing.**

   The Traffic Estimator (see Figure 7-8) is not infallible, but it does give you a ballpark idea of the campaign's cost.

3. **On the Edit Campaign Settings page, adjust your daily budget.**

   You might want to peg your daily budget to Google's estimate of daily cost, or you might want to set it lower. The campaign will end before the day ends if you spend your daily budget amount first. There's not much point setting the budget higher than Google's suggestion for a one-day test. Remember that Google reserves the right to overrun your daily budget by 20 percent, but never overbills a campaign's monthly budget total.

4. **Still on the Edit Campaign Settings page, set an End date *if* you can't closely monitor the campaign's progress.**

   This setting is valuable if you believe that you'll get enough reporting data on the campaign's first day and might not be available to pause the campaign manually.

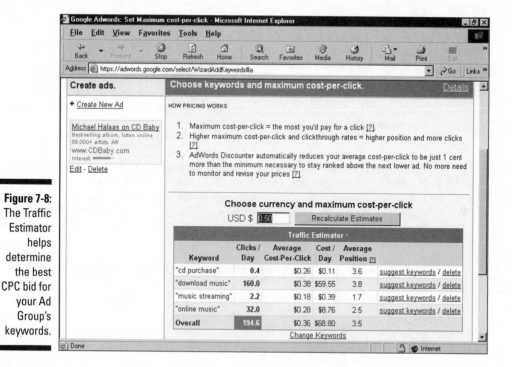

Figure 7-8:
The Traffic Estimator helps determine the best CPC bid for your Ad Group's keywords.

TIP

When setting your Ad Group's maximum cost-per-click (CPC), ignore Google's initial suggestion that appears in the bid-entry box. Nobody knows where those preposterous default suggestions come from; I believe Google pulls them in from *The Twilight Zone.* Play with different CPC amounts and observe what they do to your estimated ad placement and your estimated daily expense. Acquiring the number one position for your keywords might seem too expensive, and knocking your CPC in half could keep you in the second or third spot while getting your daily expenses under control. Fiddle with the CPC amount until you find the estimated sweet spot for your budget and visibility needs.

The lesson here is that arbitrarily setting a low daily budget while testing, purely in the interest of saving money, merely prolongs the test. There's no way to avoid purchasing the clicks necessary to sustain the campaign until it reaches a decent number of impressions. The faster you correct failed tests, the sooner you get to a profitable campaign. The fastest track to positive ROI is a willingness to make the daily expenditures necessary to test quickly.

Writing Effective Ads

AdWords ads usually contain between 10 and 15 words, including the title and not counting the display URL. Specifically, ad titles are limited to 25 characters, and each of the two lines of copy may contain 35 characters. (See Figure 7-9.) That's concise advertising! Hence the ease and challenge of writing copy in the AdWords program.

It might seem strange that AdWords ad copy is called the *creative,* when so few words are involved. But constructing such a small presentation that *works* is definitely a creative project. You don't need to compose a paragraph-long sales message or use flowery language. Heck, you don't even need to write in complete sentences. But most writers will tell you that it's harder to write short than to write long. Fancy languages and complex sentences work against you in AdWords.

Only three principles apply to the creative portion of an AdWords ad:

- ✔ Be relevant
- ✔ Be accurate
- ✔ Compel the click

The biggest downfall in writing an AdWords creative is trying to convert the customer in the ad. Conversion happens at your site, not in the ad. The 10–15 words in an AdWords text box can't possibly deliver a mature sales message. The only purpose of your ad is to get clicked, so craft every word in that tiny space toward luring the click.

To that end — compelling the clickthrough — relevance is crucial. Google shuts down ads that don't attract an adequate proportion of clicks for certain keywords. If the ad doesn't relate to the page on which it's displayed (which really means it doesn't match the mindset of the people searching that page), the problem might be the keyword or the creative. Nip the creative problem in the bud by always writing with tight relevance to the keyword(s) associated with the ad.

The need for relevance is why so many successful advertisers create multiple Ad Groups in a campaign, each of which consists of one ad associated with one keyword. Search Google for an author's name, for example, and look at the ads for Amazon.com, Alibris.com, and other e-tailers. The best copy of those ads contains the name of the author you searched. That means the store created a unique ad for each author (or lots of authors, anyway) in the store, with the author's name as the keyword.

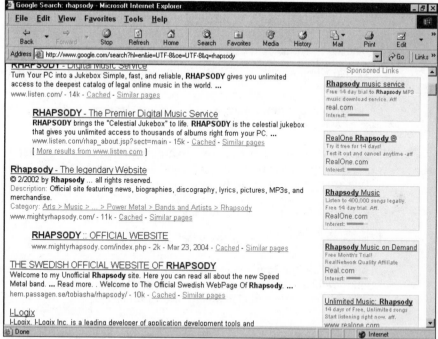

Figure 7-9:
Not exactly haikus, but AdWords ads are studies in concise writing.

Relevant ads that compel the click cover two of the three guiding principles when writing the creative. The third point is accuracy. Accuracy doesn't necessarily contribute to the clickthrough rate of an ad. If the ad promised a million dollars to those who click, it would probably enjoy a stratospheric CTR. But, of course, the conversion rate would remain at zero as disgruntled visitors discovered the lie. Never promise more (or less!) than you deliver on the landing page. Let your audience know what to expect in return for their clicks. A click is an investment, and each visitor wants a return on that investment.

Besides these overriding principles of writing an effective creative, Google enforces certain style points:

- ✔ No exclamation points in the title.

- ✔ No double punctuation (!! or ??) for emphasis. Single exclamation points and question marks are allowed below the title.

- ✔ No capitalization for emphasis. You may capitalize acronyms of common terms or organizations, such as MBA or ASCAP. Emphasis is achieved through direct relevance to the keyword, because Google **bolds** any instance of the keyword in the ad.

✔ No repeating words for effect

✔ No misspellings

✔ No chatspeak, such as "free trial 4 u"

✔ No eliminating spaces between words, tempting though it is to conserve space

✔ No bad grammar, such as "Click of free trial," even though you barely have room for a complete sentence

These style rules are enforced both automatically and by humans. No rule-breaking ad slips through for long, and ads that don't adhere to the house style are pulled out of circulation until corrected.

Google spells out its style guidelines here:

```
adwords.google.com/select/guidelines.html
```

I also advise that you spend a half hour reading AdWords ads. If you're an online retailer, do your research in Froogle. Otherwise, search for your competitors in Google and also ads in other industries.

The controversial call to action

Traditional advertising routinely includes a call-to-action message: "Act now!" "Call today!" "Have your credit card ready and order by phone!" Such loud declamations are disallowed by the AdWords program on stylistic grounds. More subdued calls to action are allowed, although there's disagreement among AdWords advertisers, and even inconsistency from Google, about their value. When the AdWords program started, Google was categorically against calls to action. Now, with more experience under its belt, Google acknowledges the value of such calls, and many advertisers swear by them. In the selection of AdWords ads in the figure, three ads contain gentle calls to action and the bottom ad is aggressive.

If you use a call to action in your ad copy, you must conform to specialized and subtle style rules. Most importantly, your call to action can't be generic, along the lines of "click here," "click now," or "visit this site." Specific calls to action that refer to the product, the service, or the result of the product or service are encouraged. For example, phrases such as "click to start a free trial," "buy discount music today," and "visit now to view today's rates" are acceptable and probably effective. Even so, you may not use specific calls to action that use the display URL as part of the sentence, as in this example:

View today's rates by visiting:

www.Low-Rates-Today.com

Calls to action might or might not be the most effective style for your campaign. If in doubt, create two ads for each Ad Group, one with a call to action and one without, and then track their effectiveness using third-party tracking software. A simpler way to track the ads would be to create separate Ad Groups for ads with and without calls to action. Perhaps even simpler, go back to the two ads in the same Ad Group, but create two different landing pages. In that scenario, you can track the traffic of both landing pages in your site logs.

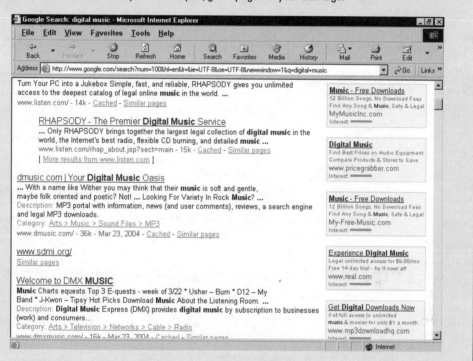

Creating an AdWords Account

If you've read this chapter to here, you have a good grip on how an AdWords account is structured and how an AdWords campaign proceeds. If you've read up to this point but skipped Chapter 6, and feel a little shaky in your understanding, I urge you to absorb Chapter 6 before proceeding with this section.

Here, I walk you through opening an AdWords account. The steps aren't difficult, and Google offers brief instructions on each screen. But in opening an account, you prepare your first AdWords campaign (or, to be more accurate, the first draft of your first campaign), so you should have the basics under your belt first.

All right, then. Time to ease into the AdWords marketing lifestyle. Follow along:

1. **Go to the AdWords page at**

   ```
   adwords.google.com
   ```

2. **Click the button labeled Click to begin.**

3. **Select your target language and country, and then click the Save & Continue button (see Figure 7-10).**

   You might be thinking, "Whoa! I'm just trying to set up the account, not build the campaign!" If so, relax. This is just Google doing its own marketing by roping you into the first steps of campaign design. (Google figures you're more likely to finish the process if you're forced to start it.) Google walks you through basic geo-targeting (this step), setting up an Ad Group, and writing an ad.

   Your selections aren't important at this stage, but if you've thought ahead to your target languages and countries, go for it. If not, leave the default selections or click English (under Languages) and United States — entire country (under Countries). Chapter 10 explores issues of geo-targeting in detail. You may change these initial selections at any time.

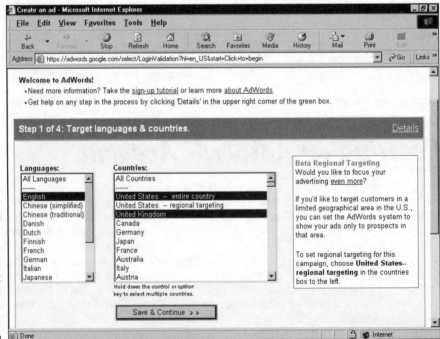

Figure 7-10: Select one or more target languages and countries.

4. Create an Ad Group.

Simply type a name for your first Ad Group. Remember, you can change or delete the name at any time. Simply call it *test group* if you want to get past these steps quickly.

5. Scroll down the page and write an ad (see Figure 7-11), and then click the Create Ad & Continue button.

Writing ads is a concise art that I discuss previously in this chapter. Spend time on this step if you like, or throw something together quickly and move on. Fill in every box. Remember, the display URL should be short because it's visible in the ad. The destination URL is the Web location of the landing page.

6. Choose keywords (see Figure 7-12), and then click the Save Keywords button.

Keyword selection is a complex and important issue that dominates a big chunk of Chapter 9. If you haven't absorbed that information and engaged in painstaking keyword research, the keywords you enter at this step are nearly meaningless. Google provides a few hints, scratching the surface. Throw some keywords into the box and move on.

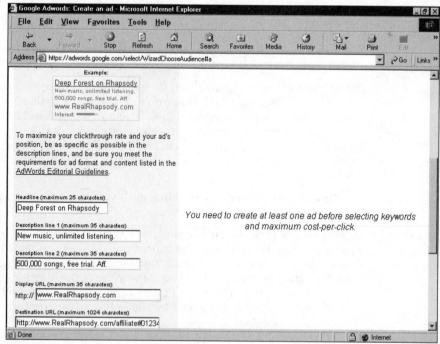

Figure 7-11:
Write your first ad, but don't labor too hard. You'll undoubtedly change it later.

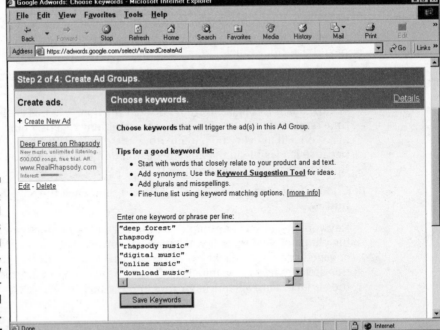

Figure 7-12:
Keyword
selection is
an ongoing
process.
You'll likely
change your
initial
choices.

7. **Select a maximum cost per click for your keywords, and then click the Calculate Estimates button.**

   Chapter 9 discusses setting CPC for individual keywords in an Ad Group. Never mind that now. And while you're in the mood to disregard things, never mind Google's suggested CPC. Delete that figure and type some value that seems fair to you. It doesn't matter what it is — you'll adjust the CPC in the next step. After clicking the Calculate Estimates button, the screen reloads with the Traffic Estimator's information columns filled in.

8. **Adjust the maximum cost per click until you're satisfied, and then click the Save & Continue button.**

   Here, you're shooting for a reasonable daily budget and a respectable page position for your ads. The information columns estimate the volume of clickthroughs per day for each keyword, the average cost (per click and per day) for each keyword, and the average position for each keyword. (Look back to Figure 7-8.) Every campaign is in constant flux, its costs and positions determined by competing advertisers and search patterns in Google.

9. **On the next page, click the Continue to Step 3 button.**

   This page offers you a chance to create a second Ad Group. You certainly may, but for our purpose (which is just getting the darn account open), plow onward.

10. **Type a daily budget, and then click the Save & Continue button.**

    This is where you determine the maximum you want to spend, per day, to operate this Ad Group.

11. **Enter your personal information, read the terms and conditions, and then click the I agree — Create my AdWords account button.**

12. **When you receive Google's verification e-mail, click the link in the e-mail to establish your new account.**

When you follow the preceding steps to establish your AdWords account, you don't *activate* the account or put your newly created ad in distribution. Your new Ad Group awaits you in the AdWords Control Center, inside the account.

A separate procedure activates the account and begins your campaign. That process is mercifully shorter than opening the account. Just do this:

1. **Go to the AdWords home page here:**

   `adwords.google.com`

2. **Log in to your account using the e-mail address and password you established in Step 11 in the preceding list.**

3. **In the Control Center (which is discussed with gusto in Chapter 8), click the My Account tab.**

4. **In the My Account section, click Billing Preference.**

5. **On the Billing Preferences page, fill in your contact and payment information.**

6. **Click the Save Changes button.**

Entering and saving your billing information activates the account and initiates the distribution of the ad in the Ad Group you created to open the account. If your selected keywords are popular search terms, and your daily budget is high, you could begin generating thousands of impressions and (possibly) a truckload of clickthroughs with frightening speed — within minutes. This is not the time to shut off your computer and go to the Neverland Ranch. There might not ever be a good time to go to the Neverland Ranch. Never mind that. If you want to put on the brakes, click the Campaign Management tab and use the Pause button to temporarily stop your campaign.

Finding Your Ads at Work

When you do release your campaign upon the Google realm, it's natural to want to see your ads at work. Easy enough — just search on one of the keywords in your Ad Group. Theoretically, ads begin displaying instantly upon activating a campaign. Indeed, I have seen instantaneous deployment of my ads. I've also waited more than an hour before ads started to appear. Keep a couple of points in mind if you don't see your ads immediately:

✔ Google is fast, but some delay is natural. Wait at least an hour before sending an e-mail to customer service.

✔ If your daily budget is on the low side relative to your CPC maximum, full deployment of your ads on matching search pages would burn up your daily cost limit quickly. For this reason, Google calculates (in the background) how many clickthroughs it takes to reach your daily budget, and estimates how many impressions are necessary to amass those clickthroughs. Then Google spreads out the distribution of your ad so that it appears steadily through all parts of the day. When this scenario is in effect, it might require 3, 5, 10, or 100 searches on your keyword to generate one display of your ad.

Chapter 8

Understanding AdWords Statistics and Reports

***

In This Chapter

▶ Viewing account statistics

▶ Peering into campaigns and Ad Groups

▶ Creating AdWords reports

***

*T*he preceding chapter introduced the parts of the AdWords Control Center you use to create the initial Ad Group required to open an account. That chapter offered a glimpse of screens for writing ad copy, assigning keywords and estimating their traffic, determining Campaign settings, establishing cost-per-click (CPC) bids, and setting a daily budget.

There's more to the Control Center than the few screens you see when opening an account. It's not an exaggeration to say that devoted AdWords advertisers and agents spend the bulk of their work day in the Control Center, especially if they don't use third-party tracking and reporting tools to measure click-throughs and conversions. Google's Control Center is not perfect (and I pick apart some imperfections in the next chapter), but it is a complex, sophisticated suite of research, creative, and reporting tools.

You can see in Figure 8-1 that the Control Center presents three organizational tabs. Rather than divide its functionality according to those tabs, however, it's more useful to consider what the Control Center does for you in the course of your day-to-day AdWords-obsessed life.

Four basic functions come into play:

> ✔ **View your campaigns in progress.** The Control Center provides a lay-ered view of your entire account: your individual Campaigns, each Ad Group in a campaign, and the performance of every ad and every key-word associated with your ads. All this information flows onto your

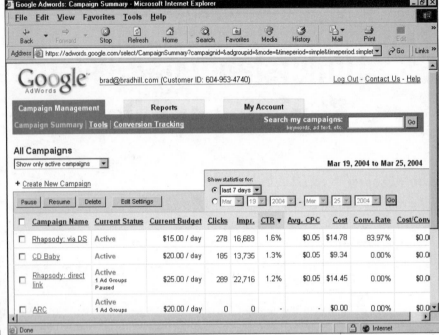

Figure 8-1:
The
AdWords
Control
Center,
where
advertis-
ers view
campaigns
in progress.

Control Center screens rapidly, but not exactly in real time. I've seen early statistics of an added marketing element show up within minutes. At the most, allow a three-hour delay for impressions and clickthroughs to come into view and jive with each other. When campaigns are running continuously, without intermittent pausing and resuming (see Chapter 10), you must cut three hours of slack when you look at them. The only way to get a complete, static snapshot of marketing statistics is to pause one or more elements of your account and then allow three hours for the dust to settle.

✔ **Report your marketing statistics.** The Control Center's information screens are flexible and robust in their capacity to offer views of your advertising at work. AdWords reports take your marketing metrics to the next level by offering more detailed, customized views and automatic e-mail delivery of the reports.

✔ **Research keywords.** This book describes non-Google keyword research tools, but the AdWords Control Center provides everything needed in many cases. The Keyword Suggestion Tool and Traffic Estimator give any marketer plenty of ideas for experimentation and refinement.

✔ **Adjust basic account properties.** The Control Center keeps track of your billing and payment information, display language, and log-in password.

This chapter is primarily concerned with statistics and reports. Chapter 9 is more involved with the creative side of the Control Center — producing new Ad Groups and selecting keywords.

Viewing Account Statistics

The Control Center presents three essential views of your AdWords marketing. These views are like boxes within boxes. The account holds your Campaigns; your Campaigns hold your Ad Groups; your Ad Groups hold your ads and keywords. The Reports section chops up the information into innumerable configurations, like a Japanese chef working on a grill with one of those big knives at one of those cook-at-the-table restaurants. (I obviously don't know what I'm talking about, but the image came to mind.)

For each of the three main account views, you can see a table that lists your costs, impressions, clickthroughs, clickthrough rate (CTR), conversion rate, and the average position of your ad(s) on the page. In each view, you may determine the timeframe (to the day) for which the numbers are calculated. All this takes place in the Campaign Management tab.

The account overview

Clicking the Campaign Management tab leads you directly to an overview of the entire account, as shown in Figure 8-1. The search box to the right is for advertisers running multiple campaigns, Ad Groups, and ads. Use that box to search for campaigns, Ad Groups, keywords, and ad text.

The Campaign Summary page (refer to Figure 8-1) contains several columns of information. Together, they convey an essential overview of your campaigns:

- ✔ **Campaign Name.** Simple enough; this is the name of your campaign.

- ✔ **Current Status.** Campaigns may be active, paused, or deleted. Deleted Campaigns are not really deleted, oddly. They're in limbo and may be out of sight, but they're still available for examination. Even odder, deleted campaigns contribute to total statistics, in a unique row separate from the total statistics of active campaigns (see Figure 8-2). This extra totaling occurs even when the deleted campaign is hidden from view. Whenever you want to see your deleted campaigns, use the All Campaigns drop-down menu to select Show all campaigns. (That setting also brings paused Campaigns into view.)

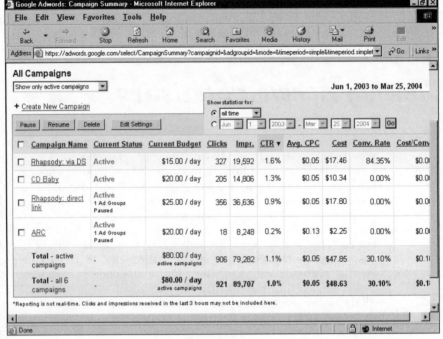

Figure 8-2:
Deleted
Campaigns
contribute
their
obsolete
statistics
to the
bottom line.

✔ **Current Budget.** This column displays the daily budget for each campaign and totals them at the bottom.

✔ **Clicks, Impr.,** and **CTR.** These columns detail your campaign-wide ad distribution, breaking it down into clicks (clickthroughs of the Campaign's ads), impressions (ad displays), and CTR (clickthrough rate, calculated by dividing clicks by impressions). The CTR column is vitally important, because Google requires certain CTR levels for campaigns and keywords. If the campaign's CTR sinks below 0.5 percent, Google might step in to remedy the situation. Even if the campaign's CTR remains stoutly above that threshold, individual keywords inside the campaign might get into trouble.

✔ **Avg. CPC.** This view does not divulge your cost-per-click bid for any Ad Group in the campaign, but it does reveal the average cost you're paying for all clicks, campaign-wide.

✔ **Cost.** This column totals up the cost-to-date for the campaign, by multiplying clicks by costs-per-clicks.

✔ **Conv. Rate** and **Cost/Conv.** These columns fill with numbers when the campaign uses Google's Conversion Tracking, which I describe in Chapter 9.

Use the drop-down menus above the table to define a date period. Click the upper radio button to select from the pull-down menu of time frames. Click the lower radio button next to use the month-day-year menus.

Note the check box to the left of each campaign. Click one or more to select campaigns to pause, resume, or delete. You may also adjust Campaign settings for multiple campaigns on a single screen. I describe the Campaign Settings page in Chapter 7, but I want to revisit that screen here. Figure 8-3 shows the Campaign Settings screen when more than one campaign is selected with check boxes. As you can see, small arrows (they're yellow) appear next to settings that you may apply to all checked campaigns. (The Campaign name is the only setting that must remain unique.) As you adjust settings for the first campaign, click the yellow arrow whenever you want that new setting to take hold in the others. You may scroll down and enter new values, overriding the arrow, at any time.

Seeing inside the campaign

To drill into any campaign and see its Ad Groups, click any campaign link in the Campaign Name column (back in Figure 8-2). Figure 8-4 details the inside of a campaign, showing several Ad Groups. Many of the features on this page are the same as those in Figure 8-2, so I won't repeat them here. Note that deleted Ad Groups work just like deleted campaigns in that they remain accessible and their statistics contribute to the bottom line.

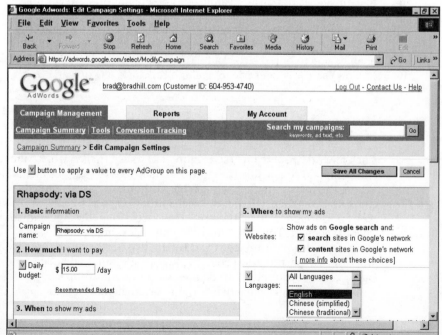

Figure 8-3: Adjust Campaign settings across multiple campaigns.

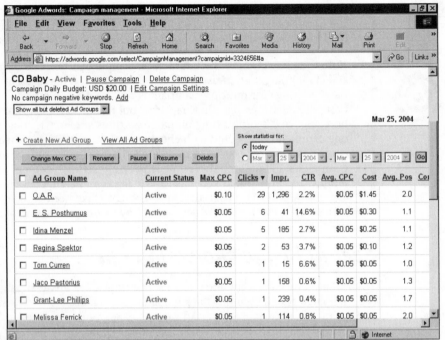

Figure 8-4:
Viewing the
Ad Groups
statistics of
a campaign.

You use the check boxes next to the Ad Groups (just as you use the ones next to campaigns) to pause, resume, and delete multiple Ad Groups simultaneously or affect just a single item. You may also select multiple Ad Groups and click the Change Max CPC button. As with the Campaign settings across multiple campaigns (see the preceding section), the Change Max CPC feature enables you to enforce the same CPC bid across selected Ad Groups. The (yellow) arrow is your friend again in this task, as you can see in Figure 8-5.

Seeing inside the Ad Group

Click any Ad Group name (see Figure 8-4) to see the keywords and ads in that Ad Group. Getting inside the Ad Group is where the rubber meets the road. Where the pedal hits the metal. Where other half-baked analogies that I can't think up take place. On these screens lurk Google's evaluations of your keyword performance, in all their mystery, occasional threats, and sometimes encouragement. This page is where your click, impression, and CTR statistics are broken down by keyword and by the two parts of Google's extended network: search partners and content sites. In addition to detailed reporting, this page contains your ad(s) associated with this Ad Group's keywords, with the chance to edit those ads, delete them, or create new ones.

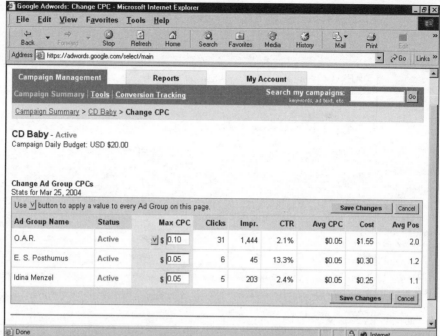

Figure 8-5:
Set the
maximum
CPC bid
across
multiple Ad
Groups.

The table that you see within an Ad Group (see Figure 8-6) present statistical totals above the reporting details. A curious arrangement, and there's nothing to do about it. Notice, also, the two Total rows — one for "search" and one for "content targeting." These cryptic labels need some explaining.

If you read Chapter 7, you might remember that you have a choice, in Campaign Settings, to run your ads across the Google network of sites. (If you're next to the computer, try going to Campaign Settings to see that choice.) Specifically, you can opt to distribute all the ads of any campaign in one of four distribution patterns:

- ✔ **Just on Google's search pages.** These pages include search results pages in Web search, Google Groups, Google Directory, and Froogle. Your ads must run on these sites, regardless of how you adjust the other two settings.

- ✔ **On Google's search pages, plus Google's search partners.** These other search sites include Web-search portals to which Google provides AdWords advertising. As of this writing, these sites include Excite, About.com, Teoma, AskJeeves, Netscape, AOL Search, and Go.com. You may opt in or out of this extended network of search sites. If you opt in, your keyword statistics corresponding to Google pages plus other search pages are totaled in the Total — search row.

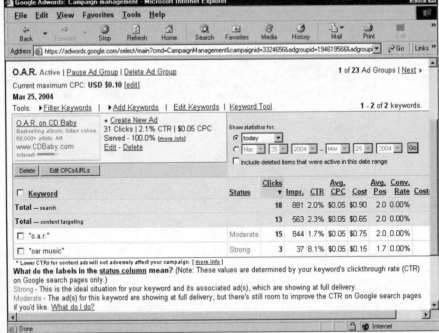

Figure 8-6:
Looking
inside an
Ad Group
at statistics
for each
keyword
and, in this
case, the
only ad.

✔ **On Google's search pages, plus content sites in Google's network.**
Content sites are AdSense publishers that run AdWords ads (see
Chapters 11, 12, and 13). On these sites, ads are chosen according to relevance to the content of the pages on which they appear, whereas on
search pages, ads are matched by relevance to keywords used at those
search engines. You may opt in or out of the content network. If you opt
in, your keyword statistics corresponding to the content network are
totaled in the Total — content targeting row.

✔ **Distribute everywhere.** By opting into both the extended search network
and the content network, your ads appear throughout both those systems
and on Google's pages. Keyword statistics for the entire arrangement are
totaled on the row containing the keyword (see Figure 8-6), below the
Total rows. These totals combine the broken-out totals (search and content targeting).

In reading about how the totals work, you perhaps noticed that you don't get
keyword statistics corresponding to *only* Google pages. You get Google pages
plus extended search pages bundled into one line of totals, but no statistics
describing how your ads are performing on Google exclusive of the extended
networks.

In my opinion, this lack is an outright deficiency, but you're not totally clueless about how your ads are faring in Google. The Control Center issues one of five status levels for each keyword, displayed in the Status column. These status levels are

- ✔ **Strong** and **Moderate.** (Both in green.) Strong and Moderate keywords are cooking along fine. No action is necessary.

- ✔ **At risk** and **Slowed.** (Both in yellow.) At risk keywords are in imminent danger of being disabled by Google. Slowed keywords cause the ad(s) associated with those keywords to suffer infrequent displays until you correct the situation.

- ✔ **Disabled.** (In red.) Disabled keywords take their associated ads out of circulation on search pages and content pages matching those keywords. You may resuscitate your disabled keywords, but keeping them alive becomes harder after they have been disabled.

Note: Chapter 9 explains in detail how to correct keywords that are at risk, slowed, or disabled.

Figure 8-7 illustrates a keyword statistics screen in an Ad Group, on which three different status levels are exhibited. The warning atop the page (whose red background is quite alarming in color) appears when any keyword on the page has been slowed. Figure 8-8 illustrates another page with the Disabled status in full display.

Look at Figures 8-7 and 8-8, particularly at the keywords labeled At risk (*developmental disabilities*), Strong (*charity auction*), and Disabled (*maroon 5*). Look at the CTR column for all three keywords. Notice anything peculiar? The Disabled keyword (*maroon 5*) owns a robust clickthrough rate of 1.7 percent — well above Google's danger threshold of 0.5 percent. The *charity auction* keyword, labeled with the Strong status, owns a weak CTR of 0.4 percent. The keyword immediately above it (*developmental disabilities*), labeled At risk, has performed better than the Strong keyword!

None of this seems to make any sense, but there's a simple explanation. Google computes a separate clickthrough rate based on the performance of ads on Google's search pages, exclusive of the extended search and content networks. Google uses that CTR to evaluate the performance of keywords and their ads. Performance on the extended networks doesn't matter in determining whether a keyword is slowed or disabled. However, Google doesn't provide the result of this Google-only CTR calculation, preferring instead to furnish the status warning system instead. Because that crucial CTR number is not broken out from the total CTR figures that *do* include the extended networks, the status warning (and status praise) sometimes seems out of touch with reality as expressed in the CTR numbers. This strange reality warp occurs when an ad performs much better or much worse in the extended networks than it does on Google's pages. (The disparity isn't too uncommon.) File this odd fact away for now; I come back to it with a vengeance in Chapter 10.

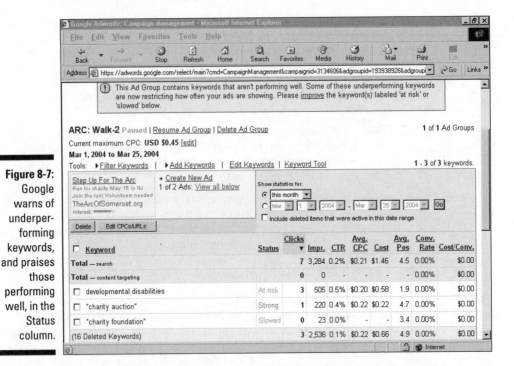

Figure 8-7: Google warns of underperforming keywords, and praises those performing well, in the Status column.

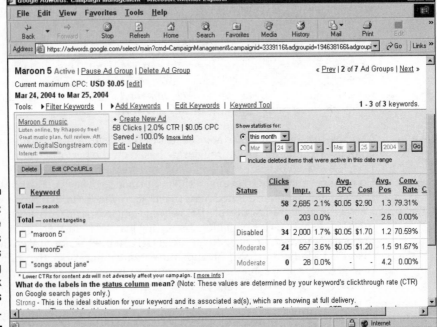

Figure 8-8: Google disables keywords after placing them at risk in the Status column.

One final note about this page: You can see how your ads are positioned on Google pages by looking at the Avg. Pos column, which shows you the ad's average position in the AdWords column. No more than ten AdWords ads appear on any Google search page. You can achieve a higher position through a combination of a higher cost-per-click and a better clickthrough rate.

Creating AdWords Reports

The Control Center's most potent statistical features are located in the Reports tab. Click that tab to see something resembling Figure 8-9. This screen shot illustrates the Reports main page after several reports have been run. The right-hand column offers quick links to recent and saved reports. You may also have created reports updated periodically and sent to you automatically through e-mail.

The six preset report modules in the Report Center spit out usefully assembled information, without any adjusting of their settings. However, you *may* adjust the presets. Figure 8-10 shows the Keyword Report form ready to deliver a report of one campaign (adjusted from the default, which is all campaigns), showing information about all disabled keywords (adjusted from the default, which is Any status).

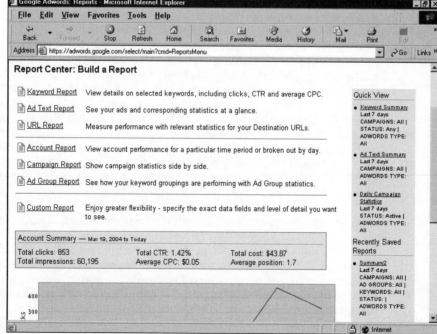

Figure 8-9: Click the Reports tab to see a selection of report modules, links to recently created reports, and saved reports.

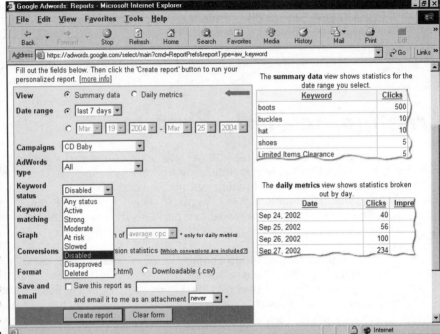

Figure 8-10:
The
Keyword
Report form,
ready to run
a search for
disabled
keywords
in one
campaign.

This Keyword Report in Figure 8-10 is one I use all the time — a few times each day, believe it or not. If you have a dozen or more Ad Groups, it becomes too difficult to repeatedly look into each one to see whether Google has put at risk, slowed, or disabled any keywords. Running a quick report reveals the presence of badly performing keywords and their performance statistics. (Although, as mentioned, you don't get the statistics that really count — those describing the keyword's performance on Google pages exclusively.) I typically run that report for all campaigns simultaneously; when I'm checking for disabled keywords the result looks like Figure 8-11. (Note that in this example, the CTRs of the five disabled keywords are above the 0.5-percent threshold, and four of those keywords are much higher. This weirdness illustrates why it's a good idea to run this report; the overall CTR, as reported on the Campaign Management screens, gives no cause for worry. In that situation, disabled keywords can go unnoticed for a long time.)

Make sure you become familiar with the Custom Report. Figures 8-12 and 8-13 illustrate just a few of the detailed controls at your disposal. The Custom Report blends the features of all the preset report modules and adds more power, such as the ability to enter specific keywords (Figure 8-12) and specify many settings with check boxes (Figure 8-13). One of the beauties of the Custom Report is that you can build columns based on individual lines of ad copy.

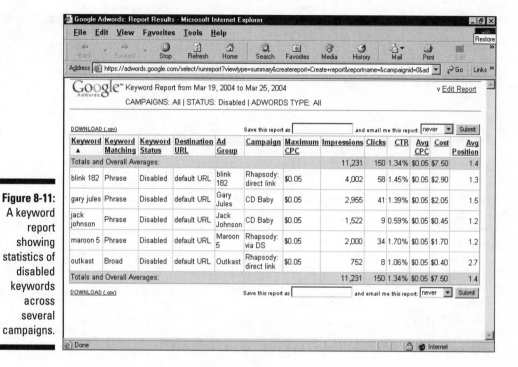

Figure 8-11: A keyword report showing statistics of disabled keywords across several campaigns.

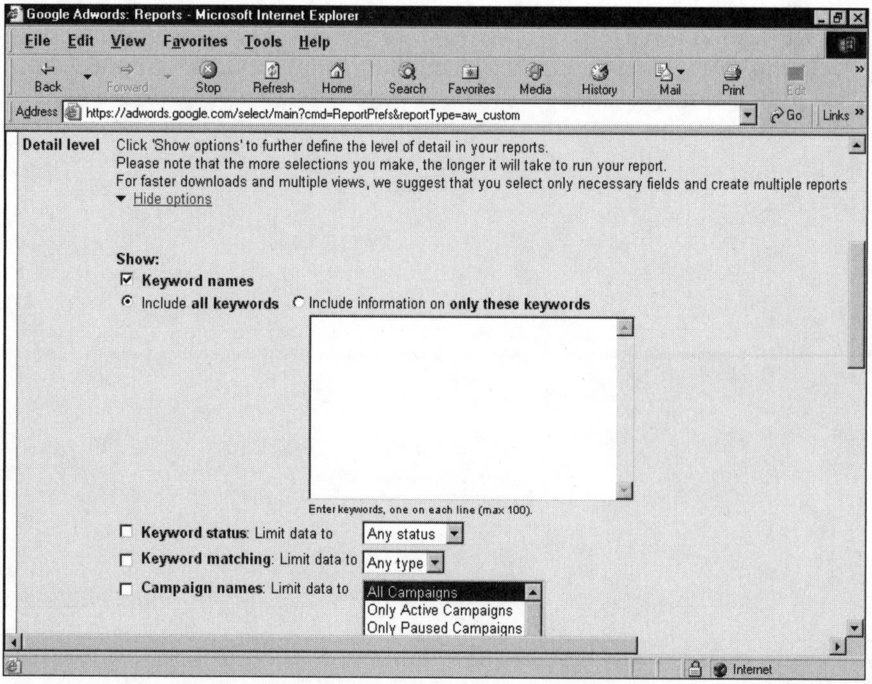

Figure 8-12: Part of the Custom Report form, where you may specify keywords.

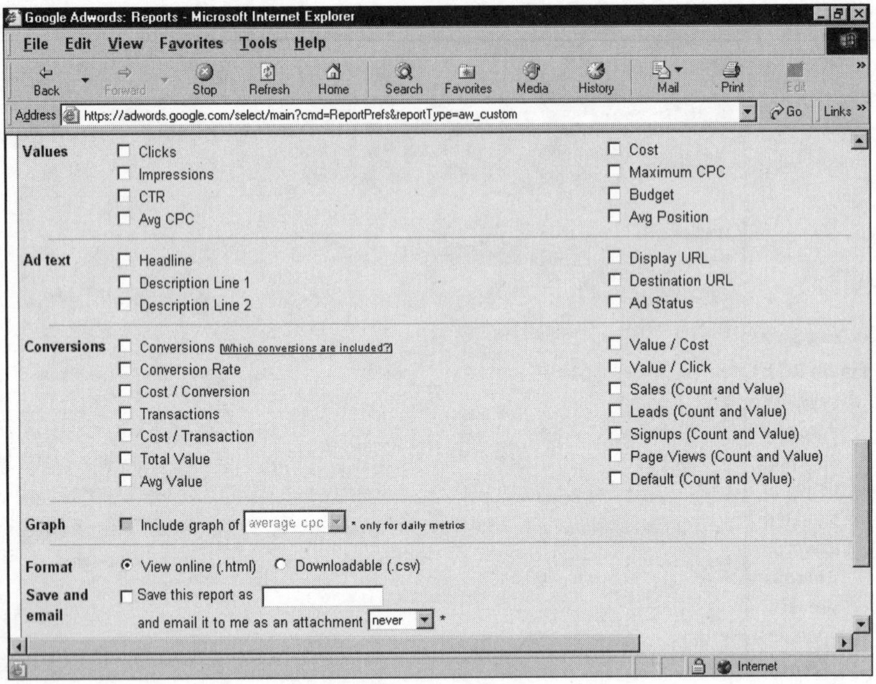

Figure 8-13:
Another
portion
of the
extensive
Custom
Report form.

In addition to arranging for reports to be e-mailed on a preset schedule (bottom of Figure 8-13), you may save the report as a CSV database file. A CSV (comma-separated value) file can be imported to spreadsheet programs and then displayed in various ways for statistical analysis.

Chapter 9

Creating Effective Ad Groups

• •

In This Chapter

▶ Creating Ad Groups

▶ Editing keywords, ads, and bids in Ad Groups

▶ Using the Keyword Suggestion Tool

▶ Brainstorming imaginative and productive keywords

▶ Utilizing keyword-matching options

• •

A d Groups are the fundamental marketing units that propel your AdWords campaign. If keywords are the sparks of AdWords success, Ad Groups are the flames. And, one hopes, your campaign is a roaring bonfire. But forget the heated analogy. The point is that success in AdWords depends largely on the effective creation and manipulation of Ad Groups.

Why is the Ad Group the most powerful element of your campaign? Because it contains the four motors of your advertising and conversion strategy: ads, keywords, bid prices, and destination pages. As such, the Ad Group defines what your advertising campaign looks like, who it is shown to, how much it costs, and the location where your business meets your customers.

Although it might seem excessive to devote an entire chapter to Ad Groups, the truth is that I could probably write an entire book about them. (Such a book would also include pictures of my editor's dog and my personal ruminations on Leno versus Letterman.) So be happy that I'm limiting this examination of Ad Groups to one chapter.

Here you find strategies and mechanics that are not covered elsewhere. The mechanical aspects include creating Ad Groups in the Control Center and editing their parameters (keywords, ads, and bid prices). The strategic issues include the competitive struggle for placement on the page (effective bidding) and putting your ads on productive search pages (researching and selecting keywords). The important crafts of writing good ads and composing dynamic landing pages are covered in Chapter 8.

Creating New Ad Groups

You create Ad Groups in AdWords Campaigns. You can't open an account without creating an Ad Group, even if you never deploy that initial effort. Assuming that you own an AdWords account, then, you have some experience with the mechanics of creating an Ad Group. Busy advertisers open new Ad Groups frequently. Here's how it happens:

1. **In the Control Center, click the Campaign Management tab.**

2. **In the Campaign Name column, click any campaign.**

   Naturally, you should click the target campaign of the new Ad Group. If you don't want the new Ad Group to be influenced by that campaign's global Campaign settings, click the Create New Campaign link instead of an existing campaign. Do not hesitate to begin new campaigns, and lots of them. When you do open a new campaign, Google walks you through the Campaign settings, and then returns you to this point and marches you through the creation of a new Ad Group.

3. **Click the <u>Create New Ad Group</u> link.**

4. **Enter the name of the Ad Group.**

   I used to include the campaign name in my Ad Group titles, but I lost that habit after experiencing screen clutter when running AdWords reports. There's no need to duplicate the campaign name in the Ad Group title, because the campaign name is always visible somewhere on the screen when you drill into its Ad Groups.

5. **Scroll down and compose your ad, and then click the Create Ad & Continue button.**

   If this Ad Group is not the first Ad Group of the campaign, Google supplies the most recently created ad of the campaign to work with. So you're not necessarily creating the ad from scratch. Even if the ad copy differs substantially from the previous ad, chances are good that you won't change the display URL and the destination URL. This convenience saves time when mass-producing Ad Groups with ads that are nearly identical.

6. **Enter your keyword(s), and then click the Save Keywords button.**

7. **Enter your bid in the Traffic Estimator, and then click the Calculate Estimates button.**

8. **Adjust your bid and recalculate the traffic and placement estimates until you reach a good balance of cost versus position.**

Later in this chapter, I discuss bidding strategies and the importance of knowing your return on investment (ROI) needs. For now, try for an average position of four or higher (which means 4.0 or *lower* in the Average Position column), without committing to paying more than you think a clickthrough is worth. See Figure 9-1.

9. Click the Save & Continue button.

Your Ad Group is created, and begins running immediately. That immediacy always takes me a bit by surprise. For some reason I expect a confirmation and review of my selections, like you see in an online shopping cart, before the Ad Group is launched to the public. The Save & Continue button sounds like a mid-process button, not the final launch button that it is.

If you want to stop the process, immediately click the <u>Pause Ad Group</u> link after Step 9. Even in those few seconds of activity, you could generate hundreds of impressions and some clickthroughs if your keywords are popular. So get in the habit of deliberating on your Ad Group choices before clicking that final Save & Continue button.

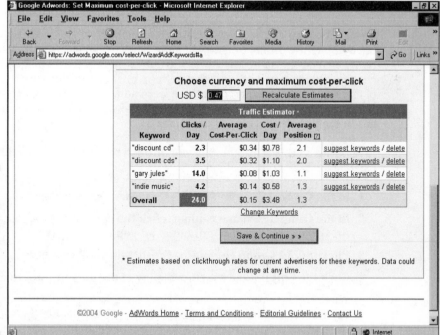

Figure 9-1:
Balance
page
position
with
what you
think the
keywords
are worth,
per click.

Editing Elements of an Ad Group

After you set up your Ad Group, the work begins. Rarely does an Ad Group run for long without issuing a call for maintenance. That call might derive from your examination of your Ad Group's performance. You might be pressed into action by Google's clamping down on an underperforming keyword. You might discover that a lower-than-expected conversion rate at your site is resulting in a negative ROI for your campaign, and you need to revise your bids in several Ad Groups.

Whatever the reason for tweaking, you will eventually find yourself needing to know (quickly, sometimes) how to edit your ads, keywords, and maximum bids.

Editing ads

You use the same screen to edit, delete, and create ads in an existing Ad Group. Editing and creating ads are essentially the same process. In this section, I concentrate on editing as a way of modifying an ongoing Ad Group.

If you choose to create a new ad, which can also be an effective way to try out a different wording or a new landing page, Google runs both ads concurrently against the same keywords and shows you each ad's distribution percentage. Running two ads in one Ad Group might seem like a less precise type of marketing, and it would be if there were no way to determine individual statistics for each ad. But you can easily break apart the data of concurrent ads in the Reports section (see Chapter 8).

At any rate, in this section I walk you through the mechanics of editing an existing ad. Follow these steps:

1. **In the Control Center, click the Campaign Management tab.**

2. **In the Campaign Name column, click the campaign that contains the Ad Group running the individual ad you want to edit.**

3. **Click the Ad Group containing the ad you want to edit.**

4. **Click the <u>Edit</u> link next to the display of the ad you want to edit.**

   When the Ad Group has only one ad, the <u>Edit</u> link is positioned above the statistics table, next to the display of your ad. If multiple ads exist, the <u>Edit</u> links appear with the display of your multiple ads, below the statistics table, as shown in Figure 9-2.

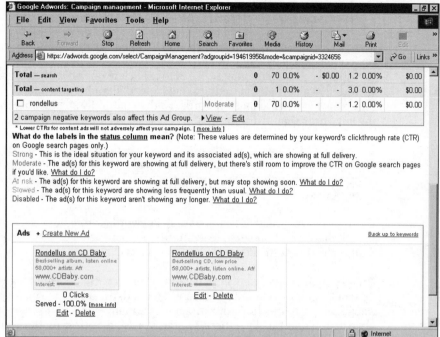

Figure 9-2:
When an
Ad Group
contains
more than
one ad,
scroll
below the
statistics
table for the
Edit links.

5. **On the edit screen, make changes to your ad.**

   As you no doubt recognize, this screen is the same as the ad-creation screen. Type your edits, and watch the display lines change when you click out of the edit box.

6. **Click the Save changes button.**

   Your ad begins appearing in its new version immediately.

Of course, you may delete ads instead of editing them. Doing so is a one-click process, and that click should be directed at the <u>Delete</u> link below any displayed ad on your Ad Group page. Deleting the only ad of an Ad Group does not make the Ad Group implode and vanish. (You must select an Ad Group and click the Delete button to obliterate that Ad Group.) If you delete the sole ad of your Ad Group, you are no longer marketing to keywords of that Ad Group. But the Ad Group structure remains in your campaign, waiting for you to create a new ad for it.

Adding and editing keywords

Most advertisers adjust keywords more frequently than they adjust ads. This phenomenon is partly due to most advertisers using more keywords than ads. (In other words, common practice is to associate one ad with many keywords.) Advertisers and their marketing agents spend alarming amounts of time brainstorming and researching keywords, so they naturally spend more time tweaking keywords than tweaking ads.

Then there's the fact that when Google slows or disables keywords, ads are slowed or disabled on search pages for those faltering keywords. The natural impulse, rightly or wrongly, is to correct the keyword. (It's the right impulse most of the time.)

Finally, the overwhelming emphasis on keywords throughout the SEM (search engine marketing) universe leads to the popular belief that successful keyword selection is the key to AdWords success.

True enough, creating successful keywords is crucial. Without a keyword, an ad can't run. And without a relevant keyword, the ad won't run for long. Campaigns of any respectable duration endure many ups and downs with their keywords. I don't believe there's an AdWords advertiser on the planet who hasn't had a keyword disabled or a campaign slowed. And even if Google doesn't lower the boom, ROI considerations force resourceful advertisers to continually refine their keyword selections.

Almost certainly, you will need to modify your keywords at some point (and probably often). The following steps walk you through the mechanical part of editing and adding keywords. I get into strategic considerations later.

1. **In the Control Center, click the Campaign Management tab.**

2. **In the Campaign Name column, click the campaign containing the keywords you want to edit.**

   You can't edit shared keywords across campaigns.

3. **Click the Ad Group containing the keywords you want to edit.**

   You can't edit shared keywords across Ad Groups in a campaign. However, you can make one specific campaign-wide keyword edit: adding negative keywords that apply to every Ad Group in the campaign. Negative keywords represent one of four keyword-matching options that I describe later in the chapter. For now, assume that adding negative matching is not the kind of keyword edit you're after.

4. **Click the <u>Edit Keywords</u> link.**

   Note the <u>Add Keywords</u> link right next to it. The two resulting screens — one for editing keywords, the other for adding keywords — are nearly identical.

   The Edit Keywords page (see Figure 9-3) includes a box showing your CPC bid, giving you the chance to adjust it as you edit your keywords. Furthermore, on that screen, nothing stops you from adding keywords while you're editing existing keywords. So there's never any reason to use the <u>Add Keywords</u> link.

5. **Edit your keywords, add new keywords, and adjust your CPC bid, as necessary.**

6. **Click the Estimate Traffic button for further adjustments of your bid, or click the Save button to finish.**

   See Chapter 7 for a guide to using the Traffic Estimator.

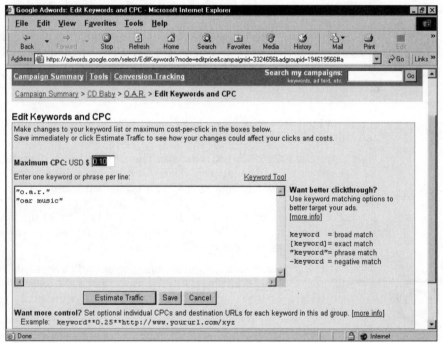

Figure 9-3: You can adjust keywords and bids on one screen.

Editing your bid

The Control Center provides three ways to edit the crucial CPC (cost-per-click) bid. This is the bid that helps determine your ad's position on search pages. Normally, the bid applies to all keywords in an Ad Group, but you may also specify unique bids for individual keywords. Following are the three methods of tweaking your CPC bid:

✓ **Using the <u>Edit Keywords</u> link.** I describe this method in the preceding section, in the discussion about editing keywords. The same screen allows keyword editing and CPC editing.

✓ **Using the <u>Edit Keywords</u> link, but this time with a different method for determining keyword-specific CPC bids.** As you type new or edited keywords, separate your bid amount from the keyword by two asterisks (**), putting the bid amount on the same line as the keyword. Here's an example:

```
ancient coins**0.45
```

Do not use a dollar sign. In addition to specifying a unique CPC bid for each keyword, you may include a unique destination page. Just extend the line with another two asterisks, and then type the complete URL of your landing page for that keyword. For example:

```
ancient coins**0.45**http://www.the-coin-trader.com/
new-signups.htm
```

Don't put spaces between any characters. Do type the complete URL, including the *http://* prefix.

✓ **Using the Edit CPCs/URLs button.** This button, located on the Ad Group page, leads to a friendlier interface for entering unique bids and landing pages, as shown in Figure 9-4. Click the check box next to the keywords you want to select, and then click the Edit CPCs/URLs button. (On this screen you don't have to bother with asterisks.) Notice the small arrows in the screen shot (they're yellow on the screen); use the arrows to enforce the same value for all selected keywords.

Use the arrows even if a minority of keywords will eventually receive different CPC or URL values. After setting those values and clicking the arrows, travel down the page and change the keywords that need to be changed.

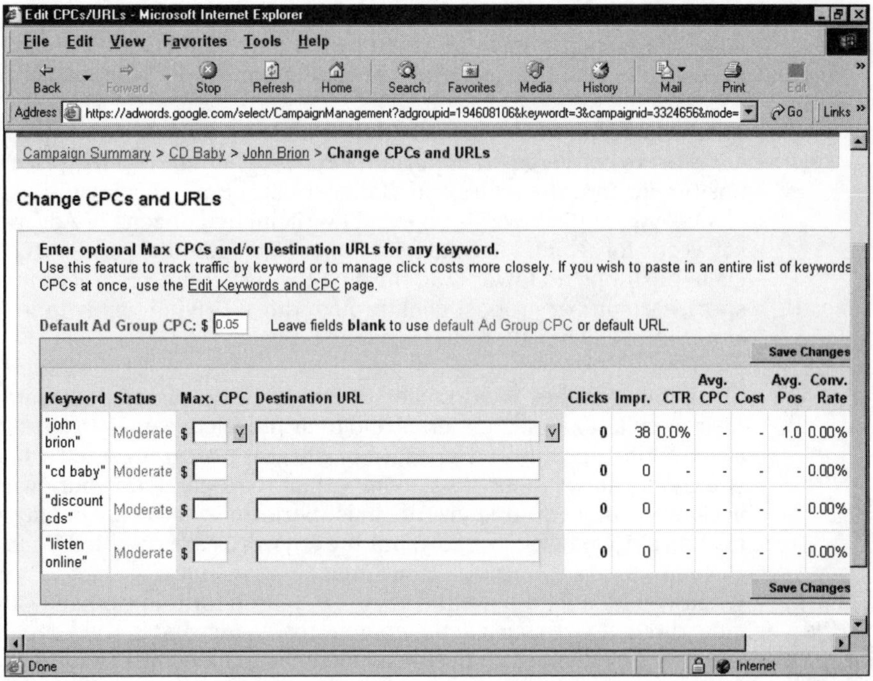

Figure 9-4:
Here's a
friendly
interface for
creating
unique
keyword
values.

Researching and Refining Keywords

Enough mechanics. The remainder of this chapter is mostly about strategic issues. I discuss formulating keyword concepts using the Keyword Suggestion Tool, the widespread reliance on keyword generators, finding keywords by thinking like your customer, and the four keyword-matching options at your disposal. You find out about tactical positioning of ads on search pages, planning for distribution in Google's extended networks, and trademark controversies. I continue the discussion of Google's insistence on relevance at all costs. Let's get started.

Hunting for the ideal keyword

Imagine the gold ring of search advertising: the mythical keyword that's in high demand by searchers but has no competition from other advertisers. That sweet spot in Google where, even if only for a short time, you can reach millions of hungry searchers for the absolute minimum cost per click. In that Eden-like scenario, your ad would be the only paid link on the page, floating majestically in alluring solitude, receiving hordes of dirt-cheap clickthroughs.

That's the ideal. Reality usually differs considerably. Sharp, opportunistic advertisers converge on important keywords, driving up the price of good positioning into the realm of dollars per click. But, amazingly, ideal and near-ideal keyword discoveries do exist. I've launched dozens of Ad Groups with keywords for which I bid the minimum of $.05 per click, and watched the ads claim positions no lower than third on the page (and several times the top spot), earning very robust clickthrough rates. Driving highly targeted clicks at a cost of $50 per thousand is a true bargain.

Chapter 4 describes Wordtracker, which strives to evaluate keywords based on their popularity as search terms and their prevalence on Web sites, to arrive at a competitive profile of a keyword or phrase. Wordtracker is certainly a tool you should know about. It's also important to research on your own, especially in Google, where your keywords must perform well to stay in play. (Actually, the ads perform well or badly, but the keywords are disabled if the ads fail.)

When you identify a potential keyword, search for it in Google — that's the most direct way to survey the competitive landscape in the venue that really counts. Click the Search button a few times to catch ads that are in slowed or spread-out distribution patterns. Notice also how many search results Google finds. These two pieces of information — the number of search results and the number of ads on the page — give you a good idea of the demand (from searchers and advertisers) for that keyword. When demand from searchers (represented indirectly by the number of search results) seems to exceed demand from advertisers (represented directly by the number of ads), you know you have a potentially productive keyword.

Remember that an attractive keyword need not result in millions of page results in Google; hundreds of thousands of links represents a healthy market-place in which to present your ads. With this perspective, look at Figures 9-5 and 9-6. The first screen is Google's results page for the keyword phrase *discount cds*. The second screen shows the results for *budget cds*. The first page shows strong demand everywhere: roughly 2.5 million search results and an AdWords column full of ads. The second page shows strong consumer demand (753,000 results) and faltering advertiser demand.

Is there room in that AdWords column for a third ad? Most certainly, especially because one of the displayed ads is owned by a local shop. Whether a third ad would be successful depends on many factors. But for the moment, it appears that the third spot could be purchased for a low CPC bid. This situation is ripe for testing, and it took me about 30 seconds to find it. Search Google with your prospective keywords and with productive variations!

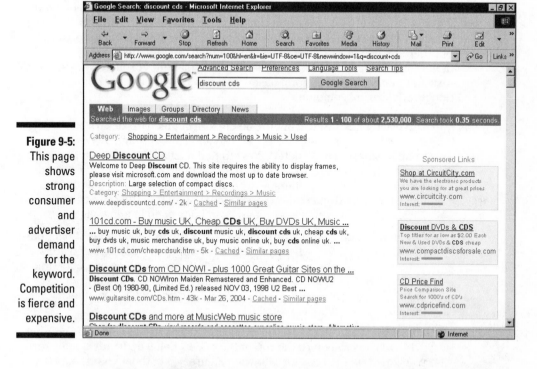

Figure 9-5:
This page shows strong consumer and advertiser demand for the keyword. Competition is fierce and expensive.

Figure 9-6:
This page shows reasonably strong consumer demand and weak advertiser demand. Inexpensive space is available.

One possibility to remember as you strive for the perfect keyword is counter-intuitive. Namely, being lower on the page can deliver better results than top placement. The point of bidding up a keyword is to attain a higher position. But there's some question as to whether a high position necessarily means better visibility, and there's even more question about correlated advertising results. Consider these factors, based on anecdotal experience shared by the Google advertising community:

✔ **Top-placed ads suffer from drone clickthroughs.** Tire-kickers, it's widely supposed, veer straight for the top ad and click through it with no intent to do business. Those determined to find useful information and products are just as likely to click further down the AdWords column of ads. Also, determined searchers — who are often the best leads and most likely future customers — comparison-shop in the AdWords column, clicking several in succession and examining each landing page.

✔ **Competitive ad-bashing normally targets the top-placed ad.** It isn't particularly ethical, but when competitors want to drive top-placed ads out of their lofty position, they click through the ads, driving up costs (and driving down ROI) for the advertiser. Such hostility is usually not directed at lower-placed ads. (Google is alert to such ad-bashing and penalizes those who are caught.)

✔ **Top-of-page ads might not be as visible as ads in the AdWords column.** AdWords ads roll up to the top of the page when 9 or 10 ads qualify for placement on the page, as shown in Figure 9-7. In those cases, only 8 ads are placed in the AdWords column. While reaching the top of the page (where Google used to sell cost-per-impression sponsored links) is an accomplishment and an honor, there's some doubt about the effectiveness of that perch. Google users are accustomed to glancing over to the right when checking out the ad portion of search results. And "ad blindness," in which the viewer disregards top-of-page, horizontal ads, is also common. (For more on ad blindness, see Chapter 13.)

Here's an example of a lower placement beating a higher placement. The report in Figure 9-8 shows the Ad Groups of a campaign. Notice the performance of the Josh Turner Ad Group. Although its average page position is the second-lowest of the group, its CTR is the highest, by far.

Notwithstanding everything I say about low positions having certain advantages over high positions, one aspect of high placement gives it undeniable value. Google's extended advertising networks present ads differently from Google, in ways that dramatically reward the top spot. On AOL Search, for example, often only a single ad is presented on the results page (see Figure 9-9), and I have experienced outstanding clickthrough rates on ads claiming that spot.

Figure 9-7: AdWords ads roll up to the top of the page when every spot is taken.

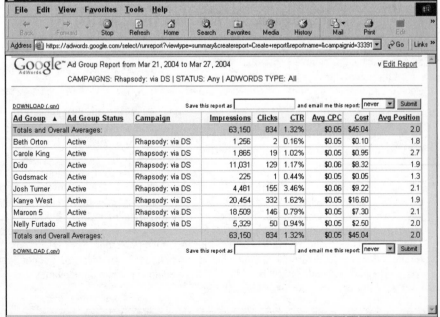

Figure 9-8: A low position can lead to high clickthrough rates, as shown by the Josh Turner Ad Group.

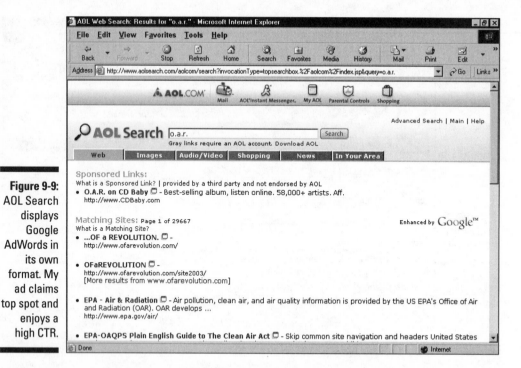

Figure 9-9:
AOL Search
displays
Google
AdWords in
its own
format. My
ad claims
top spot and
enjoys a
high CTR.

Placement: It's not just bidding

One crucial feature of the Google system that all advertisers must remember is the two-part formula that determines the placement of ads on Google pages. Bidding price gets most of the attention in this department, as competing advertisers slug it out with clickthrough dollars for premium placement atop the AdWords column. But clickthrough rate (CTR) is as important as the bid price.

The specific formula multiplies the two. If one advertiser bids 50 cents for a keyword and develops a CTR of 1.4 for that keyword, his or her ad would place second to an advertiser who bids 40 cents (10 cents less) and develops a CTR of 1.9. A third advertiser bidding only 35 cents would rise above both competitors if his or her CTR were 2.2. Here's how the ads would be ordered:

$$35 \text{ cents} \times 2.2 \text{ CTR} = 0.77 \text{ (1st place)}$$

$$40 \text{ cents} \times 1.9 \text{ CTR} = 0.76 \text{ (2d place)}$$

$$50 \text{ cents} \times 1.4 \text{ CTR} = 0.70 \text{ (3d place)}$$

This formula creates turbulence in the AdWords column: you never know for sure where your ads will land. The competitive situation is always changing. Don't attempt to game the formula. Google cares overwhelmingly about the clickthrough rate because it reflects relevance, and the company rewards advertisers with successful ads by placing them higher — sometimes much higher — than they might have earned by their bid rate alone. Success breeds success in AdWords. Smart advertisers concentrate less on bidding wars than on relevancy wars.

The content network (AdSense sites) presents its own twist on placement value. Many AdSense publishers choose horizontal banner-like displays of AdWords ads, in which four ads are positioned side-by-side. A good argument can be made that none of those positions is more valuable than another, and that argument speaks to the cost-saving value of dropping out of the top spot. (AdSense also provides publishers with a vertical display, in which the top spot is arguably more visible and productive than lower positions.)

When considering your performance in the content network, you drop off the radar when your ad is ranked below the fifth position, because none of the ad displays in the AdSense program contains more than five ads. Most of them contain four, and some of them contain two or one. (See Figure 9-10.)

These ramifications are interesting, but I must issue a closing reminder of this crucial fact: Google evaluates your ad performance strictly on Google's pages. Although you get clickthroughs on the extended networks, pay for them, and see them reported in the Control Center, they don't count toward the official CTR that Google uses to reward or punish your ads. Keywords are slowed and disabled according to how their associated ads perform on Google's pages, and nowhere else.

Figure 9-10: AdWords ads on an AdSense publisher's site. If your bids did not earn fourth place or higher, your ad would not appear here.

Using the Keyword Suggestion Tool

The most dangerous keyword strategy is one that's too broad. Broad keywords are usually thoughtless keywords, and Google advertising punishes lazy marketing. The danger is not even so much that you lose money deploying overly general keywords; worse, you lose time. You probably can't get the clicks you need with wide, fuzzy targeting, yet you'll accrue an enormous number of impressions before you can make a cup of coffee. Then Google will shut you down before your statistics have even arrived in your Control Center.

Targeted relevance is the key. The more precise your targeting — which is to say, the more precisely your ad's keyword matches both your ad copy and the searcher's keyword — the more magnetic your ad. One way to find out what your potential customers are searching for is to ask Google. The Keyword Suggestion Tool is Google's way of answering your question.

The Keyword Suggestion Tool is no more than three clicks away from anywhere in the Control Center:

1. **Click the Campaign Management tab.**
2. **Click Tools.**
3. **Click Keyword Suggestion Tool.**

The Keyword Suggestion tool is designed to spit out search terms related (in varying degrees) to one or more keywords you entered. The best results come from not mixing and matching unconnected keywords, though Google allows any combination.

Google delivers three lists of keyword suggestions, though the organization is a little confusing:

✔ On the left side of the page, under More Specific Keywords, is a list of words and phrases matching your entry — most are phrases. These are broad matches that might trigger any ads associated with the keyword you entered, if that keyword is set on broad matching. (I cover keyword matching later in this chapter.) In the example of Figure 9-11, the list of phrases would probably trigger any ad associated with the *mp3* keyword. That popular keyword is too broad for most advertisers, but the more specific key phrases might not be. Of course, you need to choose relevant items from the list.

✔ On the right side of the page, under Similar Keywords, are two lists. The top list consists of expanded broad matches to the keyword you entered. Any keyword in this list would trigger your ads if your keyword were set on broad matching. The Similar Keywords list is not as related to your keywords as the More Specific Keywords list.

✔ Also on the right side of the page but further down are more suggested keywords, but these don't trigger ads associated with the keyword you entered. I often find that these words are the most useful. This list is where Google's contextual intelligence shines in the Keyword Suggestion Tool. The best new, yet related, ideas are in this list. Most of the keywords and phrases here do not include the keyword you entered but are related *in concept.* This type of relationship is extremely valuable and sometimes difficult to invent without assistance. And, because Google gets its ideas from its immense database of search terms that people have entered, you know these are viable search queries.

Thinking like a customer

The sad truth is that business people often don't think the way their customers think. As consumers, we see this frustrating reality every day in the products we complain about. When advertising on Google, and in particular when selecting keywords, the big challenge is understanding the mind of potential customers as they enter the search engine. Even if you know what they're looking for, do you know the search terms they'll use to find it? That is the question that counts.

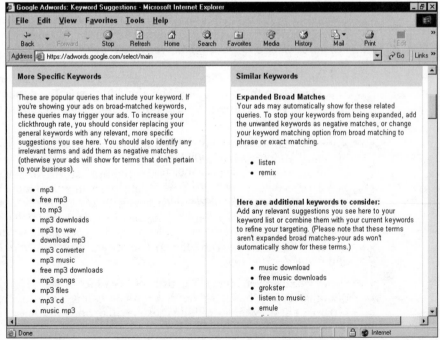

Figure 9-11:
The list of additional keywords contains great concept-related ideas.

Breaking the addiction to keyword generators

Much fuss is made in the CPC-advertising world about keyword generators and suggestion tools. In this book I promote not only Google's Keyword Suggestion Tool, but also standard workhorse tools from Overture and Wordtracker. Each one is a fine research aid.

But my experience has led me to believe that these interactive assistants are best used to fill in the gaps of brain-powered research. It's impossible to think of every permutation of a word or a concept. And it's certainly beyond human capacity to consolidate, in a flash, millions of search results and rank their keywords by relevance and frequency. But the human mind excels in imagination, and that's where great keyword ideas come from. After you have great ideas, use the keyword generators to flesh them out with related words, commonly searched phrases, and important misspellings.

You must find your own specific terms that match your product or service, of course. But to get on the same page (literally) as your potential customers, who are trying their best to find you, consider exercising your mind with these thought inversions:

- ✔ **Solution versus problem.** As an expert in your field, you think in terms of solutions. But a customer's mind is filled with the problem. Searchers commonly express their queries as questions, not answers; problems, not solutions. So although your impulse might be to advertise on the keyword *landscape grade repair,* your customers are probably running to Google with queries like *how do I stop my basement from flooding.* There's not a search engine in the world that expects its users to enter solutions and answers in the search box. You shouldn't expect it, either. Build keyword lists not just around your products, but also around the questions that will lead to your products as answers.

- ✔ **Knowledgeable versus naive.** Assume that your potential customers are naive about the terms that define your industry. We all tend to think everyone knows what we know. When you brainstorm for keywords, dedicate some keyword lists to avoiding buzzwords and industry "in" phrases. You might fill some Ad Groups with keywords such as *home improvement contractor, landscaping materials,* and *retaining walls.* But don't neglect other keyword opportunities to reach potential naive customers who might be searching for *healthy grass, golf green in back yard,* and *fixing dog damage.*

- ✔ **Using versus discovering.** You use your product or service, and you no doubt get repeat business. But a certain percentage of your customers are brand new. When attracting these people, don't assume that they search with the mindset of someone who is familiar with what you offer. Imagine that you know nothing about your industry. What words lead to a first discovery of your business?

All these inversions are similar, in that they all require you to erase your self-knowledge, approaching your own product with a fresh mind. One trick is to ask your friends, acquaintances, family, and even strangers what search terms they would use to find what your offer. The beauty of AdWords is that you can perform keyword experiments. If the keywords get disabled for poor performance, you probably don't want them anyway.

People type all sorts of things into Google, including mistakes. Even misspellings return results — and sometimes ads. How does an ad get roped onto a search page for a misspelled keyword? The advertiser anticipated that misspelling and put it in the ad's keyword list, that's how, and that advertiser is in the excellent position of being perhaps the only relevant link for the searcher who hit a typo. Thinking up every plausible way to misspell your keywords is a grueling chore, but every serious advertiser does it.

I recently experienced the benefit of productive misspellings. I ran a series of ads keyed around the names of musicians and bands. I wanted an ad for the group Blink-182, and it occurred to me that many searchers probably wouldn't know about the hyphen (or, trusting Google, simply wouldn't bother typing it in) and would also omit the space between *blink* and *182*. So I included two keywords: *blink-182* and *blink182*. Indeed, the proper spelling ended up getting disabled by Google for poor CTR, while the misspelling delivered outstanding results.

Complying with Google's need for relevance

Throughout this book, I talk about Google's obsessive enforcement of relevance on its pages. The AdWords program doesn't hold to lower standards. You might not realize it because of the smooth automation with which the Control Center operates, but every ad in the system is cleared by a human. These gatekeepers check stylistic considerations, but simple relevance is equally important. Don't attempt to blanket Google with irrelevant ads. Google will probably stop you — and their prevention would save you time, because nobody would click on irrelevant ads.

The quality of ads on a search results page is as important to Google as the quality of its editorial search results. It is all content to Google, content that is judged and responded to by people searching the index. Google doesn't want anything on the page that fails to meet its standard of relevance.

The gray area of trademark infringement

The standard of relevance for which Google is renowned is tested painfully by some companies for allowing competing companies to place ads on their search pages. By "their" search pages, I mean pages answering search queries about that company. The complaining companies claim that their trademarks are violated, a claim implying that the company thinks it owns the search results page.

Perhaps the most celebrated trademark case involved an environmental organization that ran AdWords ads critical of a cruise company, and associated those ads with keywords related to the cruise company. On the surface, this tactic might seem no less sporting than attack-and-response ad campaigns, common in political advertising. Political opponents might hate each other, but they don't claim trademark infringement when the ads get dirty.

The problem on Google arises in the very concept of relevance. Everyone wants Google's search pages, including the ads, to express a high level of relevance. When an advertiser reaches across competitive lines to appropriate a keyword normally associated with a rival, the rival can charge that the relevancy of "its" results page has been compromised, and the users of that page (the searchers) have been betrayed. Google is responsive to such arguments, or at least cautious enough in the early days of this new type of dispute, to generally accede to requests for editorial control of the situation. In the example just mentioned, the environmental organization's ads were taken down within a day.

The lesson for advertisers is simple: Don't make obvious crossovers into competitive territory to plug your products. That goes for affiliate advertisers, selling other companies' stuff. You can see this caution played out on Google's search pages. Search for a well-known company, and you rarely see its competitors' ads. If you do, you *never* see those ads mentioning the competing company by name.

Using keyword-matching options

Google provides four ways to treat your keywords so that it interprets them exactly the way you want. These treatments, called matching options, are similar to the search operators used on the front end of Google. (You might want to refer to *Google For Dummies* for a complete discussion of search operators.) One of those search operators — the quote operator — is the same as one of the keyword-matching operators discussed here.

The four keyword-matching options at your disposal are

- ✔ Broad matching
- ✔ Negative keywords
- ✔ Phrase matching
- ✔ Exact matching

Keyword matching is powerful stuff and sometimes ignored by advertisers. In the rush to launch a campaign, it's tempting to throw in untreated keywords (which default to the broad matching option) and let them ride. Slowed accounts and disabled keywords are often the result of such carelessness. Read on to find out about these four important options.

Broad matching

Do nothing, and your keyword is broadly matched to a potentially huge array of related keywords. Your ad might be displayed on search results pages for variations of your keyword, misspellings of your keyword, or conceptual similarities to your keyword. Broad matching is convenient, because you let Google do the work of researching keywords. With a single word, you cover a lot of search queries.

On the other hand, broad matches might not work for your ad, and Google is the sole determinant of broad matching if you don't balance a broad match with a negative keyword (see the next section).

Broad matching is risky, and most experienced advertisers use it cautiously. If a broadly matched keyword is disabled by Google (a common occurrence), you may put it back in play with a different matching option. Narrowing the effect with phrase or exact matching often makes a sputtering keyword suddenly potent.

Negative keywords

Placing a minus sign (hyphen) immediately before a keyword excludes that keyword from matching your keyword and triggering an ad impression. Negative matching looks like this:

```
-keyword
```

Google recently introduced a valuable feature that assigns negative matches to the entire campaign — every Ad Group. The Campaign page contains an Add link for creating a campaign-wide list of negative keywords. That link becomes a View/edit link after you add at least one negative keyword.

Figure 9-12 illustrates the screen on which you create the negative word list for the entire campaign. Note the Clean Sweep feature on the right, which lets you extract negative keywords individually embedded in Ad Groups and reassign them to the entire campaign.

Phrase matching

Phrase matching uses quotation marks around a key phrase, like this:

```
"coin trading"
```

The quotes force Google to match your keyword to queries in which the quote-enclosed words appear exactly as spelled and as ordered. Google still broad-matches the phrase to related words and concepts but keeps the quoted phrase intact. Don't use phrase matching on a single word.

Exact matching

Putting brackets around a key phrase is the most restrictive treatment. Exact matching looks like this:

```
[coin trading]
```

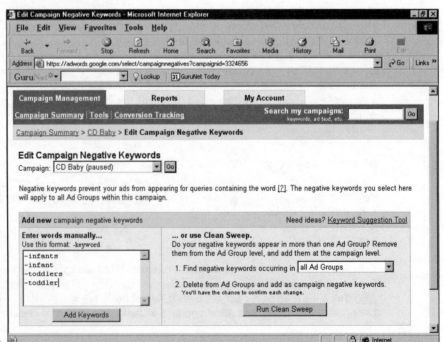

Figure 9-12:
Use this screen to add negative keywords that affect your entire campaign.

This match forces Google to place the ad only on pages responding to the exact query, with no other related matching. If any other words appear in the query, your ad will not be called onto the results page. Don't use exact matching with single words.

A useful keyword-matching tool lurks under <u>Tools</u> in the Campaign Management tab. Go there and click <u>Change Keyword Matching Options</u>. This interactive timesaver lets you change all of one type of match to another type of match, throughout an AdWords Campaign, as shown in Figure 9-13.

Rather a blunt tool for advertisers with carefully tailored keyword lists containing different matching options, this tool is good for running experiments on campaigns built entirely on broad matching. If you are running all broad matches, and if the campaign is struggling, changing all broad matches to phrase matches might prove a worthy experiment. Note that the first drop-down menu (see Figure 9-12) invites you to take all broad-, phrase-, and exact-matched words and change them into one type of matching.

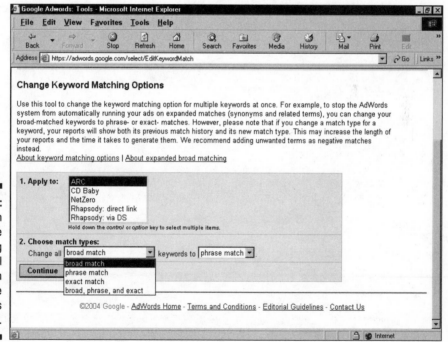

Figure 9-13:
You can change the matching option of all keywords in an entire AdWords Campaign.

Chapter 10

Managing Ongoing Campaigns

• •

In This Chapter

▶ Pausing and resuming campaigns and Ad Groups

▶ Reactivating a slowed account

▶ Reviving disabled keywords

▶ Understanding geo-targeting

▶ Setting up conversion tracking

• •

This chapter is about the daily operation of AdWords campaigns. I emphasize five important topics in this chapter:

✔ Pausing and resuming campaigns and Ad Groups

✔ Understanding why accounts are slowed, and knowing how to reactivate a slowed account

✔ Coping with slowed and disabled keywords, situations that can be baffling to the uninitiated

✔ Understanding and choosing geo-targeting

✔ Implementing Google's conversion tracking feature

Pausing and Resuming Portions of Your Campaigns

One advantage of AdWords advertising is the control you have over stopping and restarting portions of your marketing. Following are some reasons why you might want to interrupt your advertising:

✔ **Budgetary.** Your return on investment is suffering and your business is leaking marketing dollars.

✔ **Assessment.** You want data from different portions of your overall enterprise to settle without ongoing activity distorting your ROI calculations.

This factor is especially pertinent to affiliate marketing, in which the marketer must balance site statistics, AdWords statistics, and reporting statistics at the affiliate agency.

✔ **More assessment.** You need time to catch your breath in AdWords, survey the account, and analyze your ROI.

✔ **Breakdown.** Not your breakdown, I hope, but the breakdown of some portion of your AdWords effort. You may stop and restart elements of your campaign down to the Ad Group level. You may also delete keywords, but you can't pause and resume keywords short of plucking them out entirely and then building them back in.

The pause-and-resume system in AdWords allows you to stop activity without losing settings. The system responds quickly, if not quite instantaneously. However, it can take up to three hours for reporting statistics in the Control Center to catch up with paused reality. When a campaign is running, of course, statistics never catch up to reality — there's always a lag of no more than three hours.

Little instruction is required for pausing campaigns and Ad Groups. In the case of campaigns, you can do the job from the top page of the Campaign Management tab, like this:

1. **Click the Campaign Management tab.**

2. **Use the check boxes to select one or more campaigns you want to pause.**

3. **Click the Pause button.**

You pause and resume Ad Groups in the same manner, but from the Ad Group page. Specifically:

1. **Click the Campaign Management tab.**

2. **In the Campaign Name column, click any campaign.**

3. **Use the check boxes to select one or more Ad Groups.**

4. **Click the Pause or Resume button.**

Paused campaigns and Ad Groups continue to display their statistics (see Figure 10-1) and to contribute those numbers to your account or campaign totals. However, the display of those statistics is date-sensitive. So if you use the date menus to specify a day in which some Ad Groups were paused for the entire day, those Ad Groups show no data.

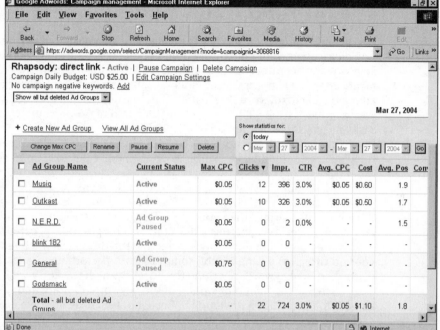

Figure 10-1:
Paused Ad
Groups
continue
showing
statistics
and
contributing
them to the
bottom line.

Repairing Broken Campaigns

Sometimes things can go wrong. Specifically, Google puts its nose in your account, inhibiting the distribution of your ads. This grim fact is frustrating at first to nearly every advertiser, but it's all in the cause of relevance, which in the end is the key to everyone's success.

Things can go wrong with your marketing effort that have nothing to do with Google's intrusions and corrections. You might not convert leads to sales on your site. You might spend too much for clickthroughs, generating high click-through rates (CTRs) but dragging down your return on investment (ROI). These issues seek a variety of solutions ranging from product pricing to site design to advertising strategy. The purpose of this section is to show you how to deal with the problems that arise and are solved in the AdWords Control Center, namely, recovering from slowed and disabled account elements.

Reactivating a slowed account

Google puts the brakes on your campaigns for one basic reason: low CTR. Google assesses your clickthrough rate on two extreme levels: keyword by keyword and account-wide. For the most part, Google begins these measurements after 1000 impressions. Under certain circumstances (for example, after a disabled keyword is reinstated), fewer impressions are counted. If your account's total CTR is below the threshold of 0.5 percent, which necessarily means some of your keywords are below that level, Google might (probably will) slow the account. If the overall account CTR is acceptable, Google slows individual keywords when they don't perform up to spec.

When the account is slowed, the Control Center displays a notice. You may *reactivate* the account whenever you like with a single click of the button in the notice. Every third time you do so, Google charges your account five dollars. Nearly everyone accrues a few of those charges, but be careful about reactivating the account without correcting the problem, which resides in your Ad Group(s). Fixing troublesome keyword performance is a matter of discarding the keyword, rewriting the ad with which the keyword is associated, changing the matching option of the keyword, or adjusting the bid amount to encourage a higher clickthrough rate. These creative issues are discussed in Chapters 8 and 9.

Recovering disabled keywords

Google never stops the activity of an advertiser's entire account, though it does slow the distribution of all ads when the account isn't performing well. At the keyword level, Google does stop ad distribution completely when an ad is failing on its keywords' search pages. Three factors must correspond to motivate Google to disable a keyword:

- ✔ The associated ad must accrue at least 1000 impressions, unless it's a formerly disabled keyword in use again.

- ✔ The CTR must fall below 0.5 percent for ads in the top page position or below slightly lower thresholds for lower positions.

- ✔ The performance meltdown must happen on Google.com, regardless of the ad's performance on the extended distribution networks.

Google first issues the At risk warning in the Status column of the Ad Group page, as described and illustrated in Chapter 9. Google might also slow the ads associated with the failing keyword. Then, if you make no corrections, Google lowers the boom and disables the keyword, meaning that ads associated with that keyword no longer appear on any pages in Google and throughout the extended networks.

When bad things happen to good keywords

Not uncommonly, Google slows or disables keywords that appear to be thriving. This phenomenon is a source of mystery to new advertisers, who watch in horror as Google takes their best keywords out of play. The advertiser's best keywords are not necessarily Google's best keywords. The reason for this contradictory scenario is that Google computes the deciding CTR on advertising performance on Google's search pages only. It does not factor in ad performance on its search or content partner sites.

If an advertiser chooses to distribute ads to the search network and content network (in Campaign settings), the Control Center's statistics for the campaign total all metrics generated throughout the networks. Ironically, Google doesn't break out the important numbers regarding performance in Google. Instead, Google implements the "At risk" warning system — a surprisingly blunt tool in an otherwise laser-sharp reporting environment.

Frustration can run high when good, productive, profitable keywords are disabled. I've seen keywords with an overall CTR above 3.0 fall under the knife because their hidden performance numbers on Google were below the 0.5 threshold. The question naturally arises, Why do some ads perform so well outside Google and so poorly on Google search pages? Several reasons contribute to this puzzle. Important sites in the extended networks display ads differently from Google, and those display differences can work favorably for certain ads. Perhaps consumers are more accustomed to the presence of advertising in Google than on other sites. Whatever the reasons, expect to run into the situation.

The AdWords community has buzzed with complaint about this issue, wondering why advertisers are not offered a choice of getting off Google's pages entirely. If advertisers are allowed to opt in and out of the Google Network, why not the home site? After all, when robust keywords are disabled because of Google-only performance, everybody loses — the advertiser, the search network owners, the content publishers, and Google.

Following are two facts to know when a keyword is disabled:

- ✔ Keywords in good standing continue operating at full throttle, triggering the appearance of your ads.

- ✔ Keyword phrases that include a keyword that is failing elsewhere in the account are slowed along with the failing keyword, even if those phrases are performing well in their Ad Groups. So, if the keyword *mp3* is disabled, the phrase *portable mp3 player* is disabled also, no matter where it is used in your account.

You may resuscitate a disabled keyword, but the process is not as easy as the one click that reactivates a slowed account. Google *really* doesn't want underperforming ads appearing on its pages, and it regards a low CTR as a mark of poor relevance. Therefore, advertisers may not simply turn the keyword back on in the same Ad Group. Here are your options:

- ✔ **Ignore the disabled keyword.** Let it stay disabled and forget about it.

- ✔ **Delete the disabled keyword.** Doing so gets rid of the problem but doesn't reactivate an account when it has been slowed by a slowed or disabled keyword.

- ✔ **Change the matching option of the keyword, leaving it in the same Ad Group.**

- ✔ **Delete the keyword from its Ad Group and put it in another Ad Group.** This option, while allowed, brings an extraordinary level of scrutiny to that keyword's performance. Google no longer allows 1000 impressions to accrue to resuscitated keywords, and boots them into disability at the first sign of low-CTR trouble. You may continue reviving the keyword in this fashion, but the exercise is futile and frustrating and doesn't address the underlying problem, which is the poor relevance of the keyword to the ad, and the ad to the searcher's keyword.

Pros and Cons of Geo-Targeting

Geo-targeting is one of the newest and most valuable of the Campaign settings. I describe how to select target countries and U.S. regions in Chapter 7. There's really no mystery to it:

1. **Click the Campaign Management tab.**

2. **Select any campaign by clicking its check box.**

3. **Click the Edit Settings button.**

4. **In the scrolling list, select one or more countries.**

   If you want to geo-target U.S. regions, select United States — regional targeting. Then select one or more regions from the new list that appears.

Geo-targeted ads appear on the search pages of people residing in the selected countries or regions. Google is reasonably accurate in determining the location of users.

One quirk of this program that advertisers should be aware of concerns the display of geo-targeted ads. As you can see in Figure 10-2, these geographically astute ads promote their own region with an extra line in the ad copy. The problem is, that line isn't always accurate, because of the way the country is divided in the system. For example, in Figure 10-2, the ad for a CD store in New Jersey displays a *Philadelphia, PA* geo-target line. Confusion ensues. I operated a brief AdWords campaign for a non-profit corporation, and their geo-targeted fundraising ads were likewise mislabeled. The organization feared the resulting confusion, pulled back into full U.S. distribution, and watched the CTR plummet. We found other ways in AdWords to market their program, but advertisers should watch how geo-targeted ads appear, and make sure the regional locator doesn't hurt more than help.

That wrinkle notwithstanding, geo-targeting is a fine way to make every ad impression count, and many advertisers hone their geo-placements, building up CTR by withholding their ads from locations where they would be ineffective. Again, it's all about relevance, and geographical relevance is a strong determinant of advertising success in service-oriented businesses.

Figure 10-2:
Geo-targeted ads display the targeted location, not always accurately.

Setting Up Conversion Tracking

Conversion Tracking is Google's answer to third-party software packages that trace traffic through a site. Specialized programs provide a more detailed picture than Google does of where traffic comes from, how it proceeds through the site, and the manner in which it exits. Google's tool is geared to tracking how many clickthrough visitors get through a simple conversion process at the landing site.

In most situations, a customer who clicks through an AdWords ad is asked to perform some sort of behavior on the landing page. If the advertising site merely wants traffic, no conversion is necessarily called for. But most landing pages are geared towards collecting a registration or sign-up or selling a product. Affiliate marketers aim clickthroughs at other companies' sites, so conversion tracking doesn't work for affiliate marketers.

Implementing conversion tracking in your account is simple, but it does require a knowledge of HTML code, at least to the extent of being able to cut and paste preset code into a Web page's source document. After you alter the document, you must upload it to the site's server. Google provides the code.

Without getting technical, here's a description of conversion tracking in action:

1. The advertiser pastes Google's code (which is javascript) into the page to be tracked. In most cases, this page is not the initial landing page, but the page a customer lands on *after* performing a conversion. So, the code might be placed in a "Thank You" page after a newsletter sign-up, for example.

2. Google tracks consumers as they click through ads and land on the advertiser's site.

3. If the customer performs the conversion action and lands on the post-conversion page, Google's javascript tabulates the activity.

4. Google reports conversion tracking statistics in the Control Center.

Google offers two versions of conversion tracking: basic and customized. The customization mostly consists of the ability to put in a price value on a product sold at the target site, so Google can perform ROI statistics on the Control Center pages.

Most advertisers who are unaccustomed to conversion tracking start with the basic version, which does a fine job of tracking how many clickthroughs end up on the post-conversion page. This basic statistic is crucial in calculating the advertiser's ROI and the effectiveness of AdWords marketing.

To set up your account for basic conversion tracking, follow these steps:

1. **Click the Campaign Management tab.**

2. **Click Conversion Tracking.**

3. **Under Basic Conversion Tracking, click the <u>Learn more</u> link.**

4. **Click the Start tracking button.**

   Select a language and your site's security level. If you operate a secure commerce site, your security level on the post-conversion page is most likely *https://*. If not, your page's prefix is the regular *http://*.

5. **Copy the javascript code shown in Figure 10-3.**

6. **Paste the code into your post-conversion page.**

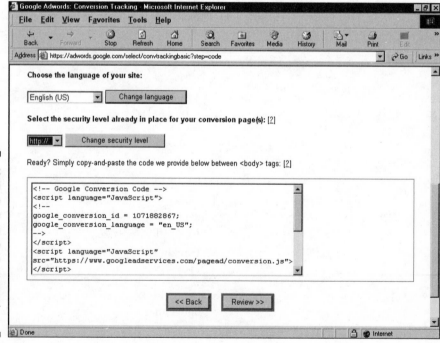

Figure 10-3:
Copy and paste conversion tracking code into your post-conversion page, such as a "Thank You" page.

Part III

Creating Site Revenue with AdSense

The 5th Wave   By Rich Tennant

SCHOOL OF ENTOMOLOGY

PEARSON BUG EXTERMINATOR

"You'd better come out here — I've got someone who wants to run a banner ad on our Web site."

In this part . . .

Up to now, the book has been devoted to optimizing your site, attracting visitors, and converting them to customers. The value of the optimization and advertising process kicks in for Webmasters and companies that carry products or editorial content of value. The purpose of visiting those sites is to buy something or sign up for something.

The Google AdSense service, the subject of Part III, is a program for creating revenue from the site itself, not from products promoted by the site. AdSense is a groundbreaking ad-syndicating program available to nearly anyone with a decent site. A fast-growing segment of Google's business services, AdSense is gaining much publicity and grassroots participation.

As with Google's other services on the consumer and business sides, the democratic nature of AdSense appeals to all types of participants. Small sites with no previous experience running ads can join the game with astonishing ease. Major media empires also use AdSense for its simplicity, contextual relevance, great reporting tools, streamlined ad displays, and outstanding ROI.

This section covers the AdSense program from soup to nuts. Chapter 11 sketches an overview of advertising publishing, ad syndication, and the linchpins of Google's program. Chapter 12 gets you started with an AdSense account, enabling you to run ads. You also discover how to customize the appearance of ads. Chapter 13 covers advanced topics and style considerations.

Chapter 11

Introducing the Google AdSense Program

A dSense is Google's "other half" of the advertising business. After making search advertising famous with AdWords, by enabling anyone to be a global online advertiser, Google introduced a program that enables anyone to get into the other side of the advertising business by publishing ads. I say "anyone" reservedly, because Google limits AdSense in certain ways, whereas AdWords is open to anyone with five dollars and a landing page. (See Chapter 6.)

This chapter surveys the AdSense program in an introductory fashion, from the theory of ad syndication to the particular way Google lets Webmasters publish ads. Chapters 12 and 13 provide more detailed tutorials in applying for the program and publishing ads on your site. The glossary, at the end of the book, includes every important AdSense term you need to know.

The Business of Serving Ads

If you follow tech stocks, and especially if you followed them during the 1990s, you know about the importance of ad revenue to online media sites. Since its inception as a public company, Yahoo!'s quarterly earnings have been largely about the company's advertising revenue. Heck, you don't need to follow Wall Street to understand the connection between on-screen ads and Internet revenue — just go to nearly any newspaper site and watch the pop-ups.

Serving ads is big business across all media. In fact, the magazine industry isn't really an editorial industry at all; it's an advertising industry. We readers think of pages of content interspersed with ads, which get in the way of articles and stories. But publishers view it quite differently. To the publisher, ads *are* the content. Articles and stories are merely the vehicle which drives advertising content into the hands of readers. TV? An ad industry. Programs are excuses for ads. Television is a medium for delivering scheduled advertisements into the home, and that's the *only* purpose of its Emmy-Award-winning dramas and comedies. (An exception is a few cable channels that earn revenue through subscription fees to cable companies.)

The Internet is more complicated because an online business can actually transact a product sale, earn a service commission, or take a content subscription directly from a Web page. Nevertheless, advertising started out as the main business model of the commercial Internet, and it remains one of the three fundamental revenue plans in the Internet space. Old-media though it be, advertising drives business online.

Chapter 6 describes how search advertising drives a new-media twist into the heart of old-school blanket advertising used in television and magazines. Instead of built-in irrelevancy, search advertising builds in targeted relevancy. Instead of pushing ads to passive, often sullen recipients, keyword advertising matches business with consumers who are actively looking for something, pulling keyword-related content to their screens. And whereas blanket advertising forces clients to pay for large amounts of irrelevant impressions, search advertising charges only for clickthroughs to the advertiser.

The advantages are good for everyone — the advertiser, the consumer, and the search engine serving the ads. The enhanced control and streamlined costs of keyword-based advertising have rocked the business world and are poised to change the face of ad-based commerce on the Internet. Google is really onto something. And with AdSense, you can ride on Google's coattails. AdSense enables Webmasters to share Google's clickthrough revenue derived from the AdWords program. The little effort that's required is covered in the three chapters of this part. AdSense is like a big, unexpected gift to Webmasters who, until now, have lacked a nearly effortless way to cut their sliver of the global media pie.

The AdSense Overview

Google AdSense is an extension of Google AdWords. Specifically, the AdSense program allows non-Google Web sites to display Google advertising (AdWords ads), and then share the revenue Google charges advertisers when site visitors click through the displayed ads. Clear as mud? Well, look at it this way: Google ads appear not just on Google but on thousands of sites all over the Web. These sites serve as syndicators of Google ads. (See Figure 11-1.)

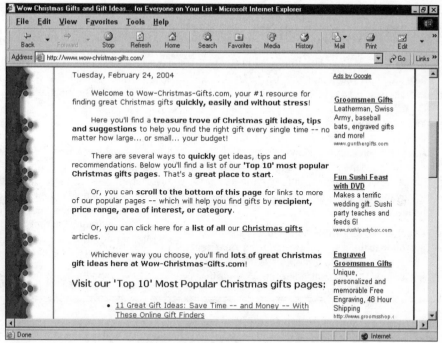

Figure 11-1:
Google
AdSense
in action.
This holiday
gift site
publishes
AdWords
for other,
not directly
competitive,
gift sites.

So, what does this seemingly slapdash distribution of Google ads do to the vaunted relevancy of AdWords and search advertising? On Google, AdWords ads are associated with keywords and are displayed when somebody searches on those keywords. When the advertiser does a good job choosing keywords related to the advertised site or product, relevancy is automatic and chances are good that the ad is of interest to the Google user. What kind of relevancy ensues when AdWords ads are displayed on a non-Google site — a site that is, in most cases, not even a search engine?

Google builds relevancy between ads and their host sites by analyzing the sites and determining keywords appropriate to them. This task might seem presumptuous, but remember how much experience and success Google has in crawling, absorbing, understanding, and indexing Web pages. After all, Google is in the keyword-matching business and is arguably better at making those matches than any other company in the world. So if you trust Google to find Web pages matched to keywords, there's no problem trusting Google to display relevant ads on AdSense sites. It's all about keywords.

The optimization piece of the AdSense puzzle

Relevance is the name of the game at Google, no matter how you approach it. On the front end, searchers seek sites relevant to their keywords. On the back end, advertisers seek relevant matches between their ads and consumers using the search engine. When it comes to AdSense, relevance is likewise crucial to the content publisher. The Webmaster needs ad displays relevant to site content. If the ads are irrelevant, visitors ignore them at best and are annoyed with them at worst.

Google does its part by applying its relevancy algorithm to the content site, deducing what it's about and serving up targeted ads. My experience is that Google does a fine job . . . *when* the site is well optimized. Here, I'm harking back to Chapter 4, and pulling the Google business process full circle. The major elements of building your business with Google — optimizing the site, building PageRank, advertising in AdWords, and syndicating with AdSense — are tied together by keywords. In this case, publishers in the AdSense program get the relevancy that they — or, more accurately, their sites — deserve. Finely optimized pages, with clear keyword associations built into their tags, headers, and editorial content, get the most finely relevant AdWords ads. Relevancy brings higher clickthrough rates and more revenue.

Evaluating Your Site's Eligibility for AdSense

The AdWords program is available to anyone willing to pay for qualified clickthroughs. Google prevents the display of ads that are not sufficiently relevant to gain a minimum clickthrough rate, sparing consumers irrelevancy on their search results pages. Above all, Google protects the consumer search experience on the Google site. Next on the food chain is the AdWords advertiser, whom Google strives to protect from poor-quality exposure. For that reason, Google limits AdSense host sites in certain ways.

To keep the value chain sparkling throughout the AdSense network, Google establishes the following basic guidelines and terms-of-service rules:

- ✔ **Vanity sites aren't allowed.** This limitation is perhaps confusing because some sites start out as personal expressions but add informational, editorial, and service value over time. Google is the only arbiter of these situations. A 15-year-old who puts up a Web page showing pictures of her dog probably wouldn't be allowed to run AdSense ads. An amateur historian who describes Civil War reenactments and collects articles probably would be allowed to run AdSense ads. AdSense sites don't have to be commercial, but they must contain content of some substance. Google leans toward professional sites, whether they're operated by individuals or companies.

✔ **Content sites are scrutinized for appropriateness.** Like many terms-of-service rules applying to hosted content, Google's guidelines prohibit running AdSense ads on sites that promote illegal behavior, pornography, or gambling. In a similar vein, excessive profanity can get an AdSense site excluded from the program, as can content promoting hate or violence. Copyright infringement of any sort (music, books, video) is also out of the question.

✔ **The site must be functional.** This is basic optimization. Make sure your links work and that the site is available to visitors without undue delay or difficulty. Remember, Google crawls the entire site and can easily discover dysfunctional navigation.

✔ **You may not reference the displayed ads in your content.** Just let the ads appear. Don't talk about them, and — most importantly — don't advise your visitors to click them. Don't click the ads yourself. (See a special warning about this point in the last paragraph in this section.) Don't offer incentives for clicking the ads or plead with visitors to support your site by clicking *any* advertising on any page running AdSense ads. You should probably avoid mentioning any of your advertising throughout the site. Google is serious about protecting the clickthrough quality on behalf of its advertisers. Clickthroughs are supposed to represent qualified leads to the advertiser. If you dilute the quality of your site's clickthroughs, Google will cut you off like a stern bartender at closing time.

✔ **Use only supported languages.** Google currently supports sites whose main language is English, French, German, Italian, Dutch, Portuguese, Japanese, or Spanish. AdWords advertisers have access to greater language support, including Danish, Finnish, and Chinese. But the issue is not just displaying ads in the language of your site but also crawling and identifying your site effectively.

✔ **Competing ads are not allowed.** Before you advertising veterans get alarmed, Google means "competing" in a strict sense. You can't run other ads derived from search engines, or text ads that look substantially similar to AdWords ads. You're certainly permitted to run banner ads (see Figure 11-2) and, in most cases, simple sponsored links. Affiliate links are definitely allowed.

To be accepted into the AdSense program, Google must check out your site's suitability. Interested parties simply apply online (a short contact form, which includes your URL for their review). Once accepted, participating sites begin by simply placing AdSense HTML code on their Web pages. (I describe this in more detail in the Chapter 12.) AdSense ads start appearing almost immediately. When that happens, Google is alerted to the presence of a new AdSense site in the network and reviews the site for eligibility. Sites that fail to qualify are discontinued soon after they begin hosting ads.

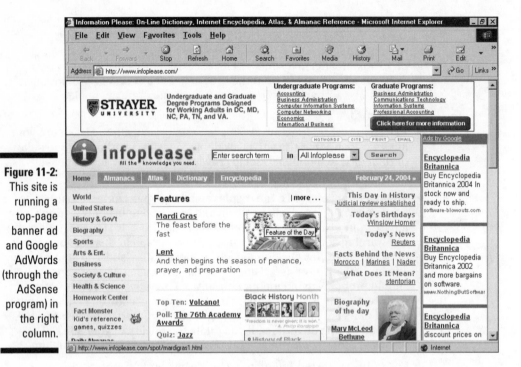

Figure 11-2:
This site is
running a
top-page
banner ad
and Google
AdWords
(through the
AdSense
program) in
the right
column.

The exact order of events is as follows:

1. **Apply for and open an AdSense account.**

   As with other Google accounts, starting an account is free. The AdSense
   program has no activation fee nor do you have to provide payment information. However, you do need to provide a Social Security number or
   tax ID number as well as an address so that Google can pay you. The
   necessary tax-form submission is accomplished online — no need to
   print and mail any forms.

2. **Select an ad style for the AdWords ads that will appear on your pages.**

   Google provides interactive pages so that you can choose a display
   configuration and the colors of the ad text and borders, as shown in
   Figure 11-3.

3. **Clip the code.**

   As you select display properties, Google creates HTML for pasting into
   your page(s), as shown in Figure 11-4. The code uses javascript to call
   the ads and pull them from Google to your site.

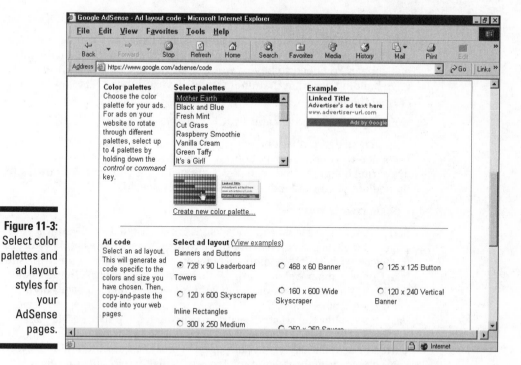

Figure 11-3:
Select color
palettes and
ad layout
styles for
your
AdSense
pages.

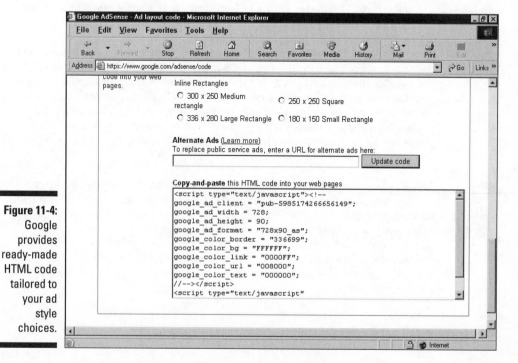

Figure 11-4:
Google
provides
ready-made
HTML code
tailored to
your ad
style
choices.

4. **Incorporate the code.**

Here, you put Google's code into your page documents. You decide which pages will run AdWords displays, and where on the page the ads will appear. You need to have a working knowledge of HTML, or use a page-building program that understands javascript and lets you drag it around the page.

5. **Upload your new pages and wait.**

Your new pages, embedded with Google's code addition, must be uploaded to your server, of course. In most cases, Google ads start appearing instantly when the pages are visited. If you visit your own site immediately after uploading, you'll probably see ads.

6. **Google crawls your site.**

Soon after your AdSense-enhanced site is first visited, Google crawls your pages. Google is extremely responsive to new AdSense sites and performs a relevancy crawl within minutes, in many cases. Whether or not your site is in Google's main Web index, it is still crawled for AdSense. In the (usually brief) time between uploading your AdSense-enhanced pages and Google's AdSense crawl, the ads served to your site might not seem relevant. Google fills the ad space with broadly targeted public service ads, in most cases. Keep watching your pages — click your browser's Reload button or sequentially visit your pages. In most cases, within minutes you see a change from broad, untargeted ads to highly relevant, sharply targeted ads. The better your site is optimized, the more relevant its ads will be.

Note: Chapter 12 probes the details of each of these steps. Google's AdSense pages also walk you through the steps in simple fashion. If you're certain your site is eligible, and you want to dive in without reading Chapter 12, feel free. Experienced Webmasters can't damage their sites with AdSense. You can always bail out, temporarily or permanently, by simply removing the AdSense code from one or more pages. (Each AdSense page operates independently.) And you can always make changes when you want to alter the display properties of the ads.

AdSense is not a path into Google's main Web index. In reading this chapter and in understanding that Google crawls every AdSense site, you might think that clipping AdSense code and planting it on your pages is the quickest way to get your site crawled. This tactic is neither a quick nor a slow way of getting into the Web index and starting a PageRank. Google's AdSense index is separate from the Web index. Being in one does not put you in the other and doesn't hasten the other to crawl your site.

Bringing a page up to spec for AdSense

The AdSense program can motivate you to make a personal site more professional and to make a bit of money from operating that site. Both design and content considerations apply, as described in Chapter 4. The key is to offer some kind of user experience that isn't just about you. Not that you aren't a fascinating person. But think about your target audience. If your site is aimed at friends and family, it's probably inappropriate as an AdSense host. Furthermore, if your audience is very small and your traffic is low, the AdSense program won't make you much money anyway.

Broaden your audience and increase your traffic by deepening your content and optimizing your site. If you describe a hobby at your site, add articles and links and optimize your tags. Build your pages around keywords and aim for a higher placement on Google's search results pages for those keywords. Building your site's PageRank leads to greater AdWords success.

Being accepted in the first place is mostly a matter of the site's attitude. Imagine a larger audience seeking serious information, even before you actually have that audience. Google's paramount interests are that users have a good experience by seeing the most relevant ads and that advertisers, in turn, get good exposure to interested users.

Weblogs (blogs) may be considered for the AdSense program, but they're not guaranteed entry simply because they're content sites. Developing a smart, interesting blog on a focused topic (not just random personal observations) can yield AdSense revenue. As with other sites, Google will determine your blog's viability for the program.

If you'd like to be in the AdSense program but are in doubt about whether your pages are eligible, there's one answer: Try.

Perhaps the quickest way to be booted out of the AdSense program is to click your own ads. I strongly warn you against this practice because it is so tempting. What could be easier than earning a little money by clicking the mouse? Don't do it. Don't tell your friends to do it. Google is very good at identifying unusual click patterns and locating their source. Google knows the IP address of every computer that touches the Google system, so your fraudulent clicks would be identified instantly. Ganging your friends into your site to click ads would likewise be uncovered quickly. Google usually issues warnings about content indiscretions, but clicking your own ads is considered a heinous abuse of the system, unworthy of lenience or second chances. Out you would go.

Content-Sensitive Ads . . . or Not

Success in the AdSense program depends on relevancy. That basic fact is true for Webmasters of AdSense sites, for AdWords advertisers who allow their ads to be distributed in the AdSense network, and for Google itself. Two factors can inhibit the relevancy of ads on your site:

✔ Weak optimization

✔ Quickly changing content

You have control over the first problem. Optimize your pages according to the principles and techniques described in Chapter 4. Mainly, that means constructing pages around core keywords, and embedding those words in your text content, headers, and HTML tags in proper proportions.

The second problem arises on pages that change focus frequently. A topically restless site normally implies poor optimization, but in many cases actually reflects quick growth (new pages) or dynamic changes that are part of the site's purpose (such as a news site). Whatever the case might be, quick content changes can leave your AdSense ads somewhat behind.

Google is aware of this situation and recrawls all participating AdSense sites with some degree of frequency. "Some degree of frequency" . . . why am I so vague? Because Google is a secretive company, and this issue is yet another point at which Google shuts its trap. I have gone to the ropes with Google on this point, and here is what I can tell you for certain:

✔ The AdSense crawling schedule is automated.

✔ The crawling schedule varies from site to site.

✔ Participants in the premium AdSense program (see Chapter 15) are crawled more frequently and reliably.

✔ If your content shows a history of daily change, chances are good (but not guaranteed) that your site will be crawled every day.

✔ Remember that the AdSense index is distinct from Google's main Web index, and the crawl schedule of one index has nothing to do with the other.

The upshot: If you change the focus of your content infrequently, Google might take a while to catch up and deliver relevant ads again. If you regularly change editorial focus, Google probably keeps up with your site pretty well, serving ads nimbly.

Running AdSense on Existing and New Sites

Most AdSense publishers incorporate the program into existing Web sites to generate extra revenue. As long as the site qualifies according to Google's standards of professionalism, implementing AdSense takes no more than a few minutes.

AdSense is such a good deal that a question naturally arises: How about creating sites specifically as additions to the AdSense network? In other words, does Google allow Web pages that were created exclusively to display AdSense ads? The answer is twofold:

- ✔ Officially, no
- ✔ Practically, yes

I'm not advising any attempts to fool Google. The best answer to this question is complex. Google forbids pages whose only or main purpose is to display AdSense ads. Those lame business attempts are cut out of the system with alacrity. However, the motivation for creating a Web site isn't really the point. Google doesn't interview Webmasters and doesn't try to discern *why* a page was created. Google cares about results, and the results it most cares about are relevancy, user experience, and value for its advertisers. When examining sites for eligibility in the AdSense program (and such examinations are human processes, not automated ones), Google looks for solid content enhanced by ads — not ads enhanced by scraps of content.

Whether you start a site with the intent of monetizing it with AdSense, or start it with other business plans and incorporate AdSense as a supplement to your main strategy, you should construct the resulting Web site according to the same principles. Optimization, PageRank, relevancy, and usability are the foundation stones of Google-related success no matter which part of Google you angle into first. Build a site dedicated to AdSense revenue if you like, but it won't work to slap up a few bare-bones pages and throw AdSense ads onto them. You'll probably be kicked out, and even if you aren't, you won't make any money. Build your content, build your PageRank, start drawing traffic, and then start your AdSense account and you'll be fine.

Show Me the Money

I vowed to never use a movie tagline as a section header. How depressing. Okay, I'm over it.

When contemplating AdSense revenue, two questions naturally come to mind:

- ✔ How much can a Webmaster make?
- ✔ What percentage of clickthrough revenue does Google pass on to AdSense Webmasters?

The answer to the first question is all over the map. Revenue levels depend on site traffic, ad relevancy, clickthrough rates, and the value of the keywords associated with the ads displayed on your site. Read the AdWords chapters for a detailed tutorial — for now, just know that AdWords advertisers bid for placement on Google pages by offering to pay certain maximum amounts on each keyword they assign to their ads. Some keywords are far more valuable than others.

Because AdSense buttons and banners (which I explain in Chapter 12) display one, two, four, or five ads, whereas a Google page displays up to ten ads, you're hosting ads from the top bidders of the keywords associated with your site and its ads. You're sharing revenue from the biggest players and highest rollers. Still, some ads yield spectacular clickthrough revenue (dollars per click) and others yield miniscule clickthrough charges (pennies per click).

The second question is unknown. Google doesn't publicize the revenue split. Nobody outside the company knows what percentage of a clickthrough goes to the AdSense Webmaster. Google operates what is probably the only affiliate program in the industry that refuses to divulge the terms of payment. The frequency is not a secret: Google pays monthly. But the split is shrouded in mystery.

Don't think there isn't a great deal of grumbling throughout the AdSense community about this peculiar state of affairs. A tribute to Google's clout, the company's secrecy hasn't stopped thousands of Webmasters from signing up. My experience and the consensus of the community lead to the conclusion that Google is sharing generously at this point. At any rate, right now AdSense provides worthwhile money to well-trafficked and finely optimized sites.

Working Both Sides of the Fence: AdSense and AdWords

Here's another question that ambitious Webmasters and publishers are asking: Can we run AdSense and AdWords accounts at the same time? Can we run an AdWords ad to drive traffic to an AdSense site? Or, to phrase this in yet another fashion, can an AdSense page be the landing page of an AdWords site?

No matter how the question is phrased, the answer is yes. Google allows you to work AdWords and AdSense in sync. Whether such a tactic is advisable is another question. On the surface, paying for clickthroughs (in AdWords) to get clickthroughs (in AdSense) seems futile. But consider the following two circumstances:

✔ Pay less for your AdWords ads than you receive for AdSense clickthroughs. Your AdSense ads represent the highest-bidding advertisers for certain keywords because lower-bidding advertisers tend not to appear on content sites. If you run AdWords ads for those same key-words, and bid low for them using the Traffic Estimator in AdWords, chances are good that your ad will be positioned lower on the page, and run more cheaply, than others. This gambit requires some experiment-ing, and the last thing you want is for your own AdWords ad to appear on your site as an AdSense ad — leading dizzily right back to your site.

✔ Bid on less valuable keywords leading to the same page. Suppose that you've optimized your page for the keywords *coins* and *coin trading*. You then build an AdWords campaign around more specific and less costly keyword phrases, such as *ancient roman coins*. Your ads might not gener-ate overwhelming traffic, but the traffic won't be expensive, either. With your Web page optimally running AdSense ads keyed to more expensive key concepts (*coins* and *coin trading*), your traffic could result in net gain.

In both these scenarios, remember that not every person who clicks through your AdWords ad to your site will click your AdSense ads. Your AdSense clickthrough rate might be less than 5 percent. So the differential between what you're paying for AdWords and what you're receiving for AdSense must be greater than 1-to-20. For example, if you pay only $0.05 per AdWords click-through, you must average $1.00 per AdSense clickthrough to break even. That's a tough nut to crack.

Playing AdWords against AdSense is a risky strategy. Because the AdWords program gives you the flexibility to try out strategies, you might want to experiment with concurrent AdWords and AdSense usage. But generally, the purpose of AdWords is to drive traffic that returns the investment in clearer and more predictable ways. If you want to add AdSense to the revenue mix, nothing is stopping you. Just remember that an AdSense click takes visitors *away* from your site, a result that is at cross-purposes with most conversion strategies. The best bet might be to place AdSense ads on your post-conver-sion page, where you thank visitors for accepting a newsletter, buying a prod-uct, or registering at the site — whatever the target conversion of your AdWords campaign is.

Chapter 12

Starting an AdSense Account and Publishing Ads

A dSense is a beautiful thing, especially for clearly focused sites that enjoy a reasonable amount of traffic. Once started, AdSense provides easy revenue — sometimes the primary revenue — for information sites. And getting started is simple if you have a basic familiarity with HTML, updating Web pages, and uploading changes to the site server. AdSense is a bit more technical than AdWords, but once launched on your pages, it steams along on its own for the most part, generating passive income. (*You* are passive while the income, which can be remarkably active, rolls in.)

This chapter extends the overview of Chapter 11 into a tutorial in opening an AdSense account, creating the necessary HTML code, customizing the ads you publish, and viewing your account's performance reports. Chapter 13 is more advanced, delving into finer customization, page-design issues, performance strategies, ad filtering, and optimization.

Joining AdSense

The first step in becoming an AdSense publisher is applying for and starting an AdSense account. As with AdWords, opening the account doesn't obligate you in any way and doesn't cost a dime. Nothing about AdSense ever costs you anything.

The AdSense account never requires your credit card information but you must at some point supply tax information so that Google can pay you. That information consists essentially of your tax ID number or Social Security number. (The latter is the appropriate identifier for sole proprietors and small-business operators with no employees.) You use the W-9 form to convey this information to Google. You may fill out and submit that form online or mail a paper version of the form through an anachronistic institution known as the "post office."

AdSense offers three significant features:

✔ **Performance reports.** Use your account to check the number of AdSense ad displays at your pages, the number of clickthroughs, the clickthrough rate (CTR), and your earnings. This information can be delineated by date range.

✔ **Payment reports.** Use this section to check your history of payments received. Google pays monthly, whenever $100 or more is due.

✔ **HTML code for ad layouts.** This section provides HTML code for all available ad layouts and color palettes.

If Google doesn't know you through the AdWords program, you must apply for an AdSense account. The application process takes only a few minutes, but the acceptance process and opening the account can take up to three days. If you're an AdWords advertiser and use the same password for the AdWords and AdSense accounts, your AdSense account starts immediately.

To get going, follow these steps:

1. **Go to the AdSense home page here:**

   ```
   www.google.com/adsense
   ```

2. **Click the Click Here to Apply button.**

3. **Fill in the Email address and Password fields, and then click the Continue button.**

   If you have an AdWords account, you may use its e-mail address and password for your AdSense account. If you don't have an AdWords account, you must enter your e-mail address and create a password, though it can be the same password you use for any other Google account, such as a Google Answers account. For this series of steps, I assume that you don't have an AdWords account.

4. **Fill in all the information required on this page and click the Submit button.**

   Included here is an opt-out check box for periodic newsletters from Google. Don't worry about spam; Google is the least spammy company I know. Frankly, I wish it would send *more* e-mail.

5. **Open the e-mail verification from Google and click the supplied link.**

   This standard e-mail verification procedure lets Google know that you're for real.

6. **Wait for Google's acceptance e-mail.**

   After you receive that, you can log in to AdSense with the password you chose in Step 3.

If you open your AdSense account as an AdWords user, with the same e-mail and password combination, Google skips the formal application procedure through e-mail just described. Instead, Google assumes you're legit and takes you directly to your new AdSense account. Along the way, Google lets you fill out the necessary tax information. Starting your account this way, as an AdWords user, gets you off to a quicker start. If you have an AdWords account, I can think of no reason to open an AdSense account as a new user instead.

Even if you own more than one site, and intend to publish AdSense ads on all your domains, open just one account. If you start a new account for each site, and if Google connects the dots between them, your accounts might all be closed. Some AdSense users *do* have multiple accounts that they procured by writing Google for special permission. If you want to try acquiring your own permission after opening one account, use the <u>Contact Us</u> link on your account pages. The purpose of running multiple accounts is to separate the reporting of different sites, because AdSense currently lumps everything into one set of reports. The account doesn't distinguish Web sites owned by the account holder, even though the account holder is perfectly free to create and paste AdSense code into any site he or she owns. Help is on the way. Google recognizes the demand for site-specific accounting and is working to provide it.

Creating Your AdSense Code

AdSense is a simple, automated program. You need only place a snippet of code into your page's HTML, and then let the ads appear. When your page is visited and loads into the visitor's browser, the code reaches into Google and pulls the appropriate ads onto your page. As with other ad servers, your page content comes from two locations: The editorial content originates from your server, and the ads come from Google's server. This mechanism is invisible to the visitor, and Google ads load extremely fast, thanks to the absence of graphics.

After joining AdSense, Google provides you with a bit of HTML code. You choose which pages you want ads to run on, and paste the code on those pages. For this task you don't need to know much about HTML, but it helps to know a little more when you want to manually alter the code (in Google-approved ways).

REMEMBER

As I walk you through the creation of AdSense code and describe how to paste that code into your page, you might get the impression that you may use only one code sample. Far from it! You may use variously altered versions of the basic code throughout your site — a different layout and different colors on each page, if you like.

Choosing an ad layout and color palette

You start creating your ads in the Settings portion of the AdSense account, as shown in Figure 12-1. Two sections of the Settings tab help create ads that conform to your site's design scheme: the Ad Layout Code section and the Ad Colors section. Actually, both sections deal with ad colors. The Ad Layout Code section offers preset color palettes; the Ad Colors section lets you modify those presets and save them. Here, I look at the Ad Layout Code section, but you can head straight for the Ad Colors page if you want to play with more advanced color controls.

To get to the Ad Layout Code page, simply log on to your AdSense account and click the Settings tab. The screen shown in Figure 12-1 appears. Scroll down to see the page's interactive controls, shown in Figure 12-2.

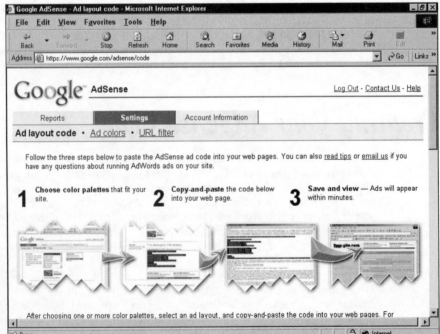

Figure 12-1:
Select an ad configu-ration and choose a preset color palette.

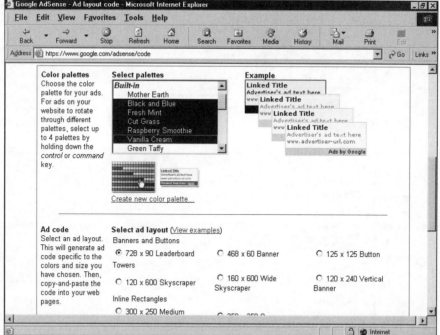

Figure 12-2:
The
interactive
color and
layout
controls.

Then follow these steps:

1. **In the Select Palettes list, choose a color palette.**

   Use the scroll bar to see the full selection of palettes. Click once on a selection to see an ad example on the right. Compare up to four palettes, as shown in Figure 12-2, by making multiple selections. To make contiguous selections, hold down the Shift key and click any two selections. To make noncontiguous selections from the list, click while pressing the Ctrl key.

2. **Choose an ad layout by clicking a radio button next to a banner, button, tower, or inline rectangle.**

   Click the View examples link to see what these ad layouts look like. (See Figure 12-3.) Chapter 13 discusses style and effectiveness considerations when choosing an ad layout.

3. **Scroll down to the Copy-and-Paste box, and select the code.**

   With the mouse cursor inside the box, press Ctrl+A to select the entire code snippet. It's important to clip the whole thing; if you drag with the mouse, you can accidentally leave out a top or bottom line.

4. **Press Ctrl+C to copy the code.**

5. **Paste the code into your Web page document.**

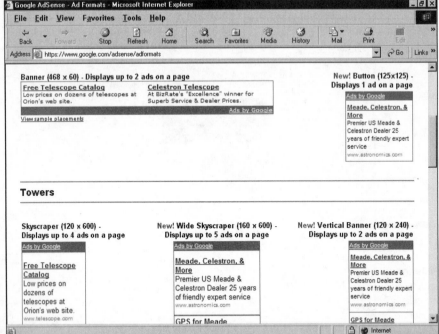

Figure 12-3:
Google
offers
examples of
all ad
layouts.

You may place the AdSense ad unit wherever you want on the page. Those accustomed to working with raw HTML should have no problem positioning the ad unit. Most WYSIWYG (what you see is what you get) page-building programs recognize Google's code as javascript. Therefore, these programs represent the Google code on the graphical layout page like any other javascript element, allowing you to move it around the page until it's displayed correctly. Depending on the program, you might need to upload the page and view it in a browser to see how the ads appear in a live display. Some programs make live calls to specified servers in their WYSIWYG display mode, allowing you to display AdSense ads while rearranging their placement, before uploading the page to the server.

When pasting code in my HTML documents, I find it useful to separate the code, making future color alterations easier. (Chapter 13 discusses such on-the-fly alterations.) Such a separation doesn't affect the page's performance. Figure 12-4 shows a page's source document with Google's code set apart from the surrounding code.

AdSense ad units are not HTML tables, though they resemble tables. But as far as placement on the page is concerned, you can embed ad units into HTML table cells as if they were child tables. Simply place the AdSense code in the appropriate `<tr>` or `<td>` tags. Figure 12-5 illustrates a site that plainly embeds the ad unit in a table cell.

```
www.bradhill[1] - Notepad
File  Edit  Search  Help
<title>BRAD HILL</title>
<meta name="generator" content="Namo WebEditor v5.0">
</head>

<body bgcolor="#25314C" text="black" link="#FFFFCC" vlink="#FFFFCC" alink="white">
<table border="0" width="731" cellpadding="3" cellspacing="2">
    <tr>
        <td width="127" height="59" bordercolorlight="silver">
            <p> </p>
        </td>
        <td width="586" height="59" bordercolorlight="silver">
            <p align="center">


<script type="text/javascript"><!--
google_ad_client = "pub-5985174266656149";
google_ad_width = 468;
google_ad_height = 60;
google_ad_format = "468x60_as";
google_color_border = "25314C";
google_color_bg = "25314C";
google_color_link = "FFFFCC";
google_color_url = "008000";
google_color_text = "999999";
//--></script>


<script type="text/javascript"
    src="http://pagead2.googlesyndication.com/pagead/show_ads.js" target="_blank">
</script>          </td>
    </tr>
    <tr>
        <td width="127" height="59" bordercolorlight="silver">
            <p> </p>
        </td>
```

Figure 12-4:
Make your AdSense code easy to locate by separating it from the surrounding code.

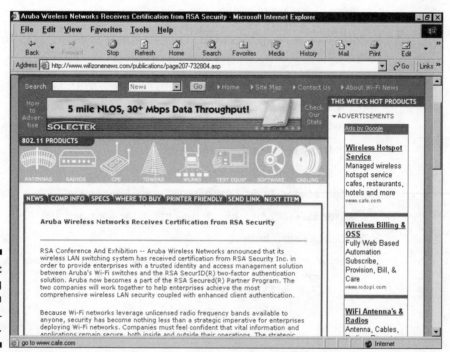

Figure 12-5:
Embedding an ad unit in an HTML table cell.

Making a custom color palette

Google appreciates that the limited set of preset color palettes (described in the preceding section) might not float your boat. Each ad unit consists of five elements whose colors can be changed:

- **Border.** The thin bar at the bottom of each ad, which continues around the entire ad unit.
- **Background.** The shaded area behind the ad's text.
- **Title.** The first line of text; the ad's headline.
- **Text.** The one or two lines of ad copy in the middle of each ad.
- **URL.** The visible URL below the ad text, which might and might not be the destination URL.

The Ad Colors page makes it easy to assign a distinct color value to each of these five elements, thereby creating your own preset color palette. You can name and save your custom palettes, after which they appear on both the Ad Colors page (in a drop-down list of Custom and Built-in palettes) and the Ad Layout Code page (in the scrolling list of palettes).

The interactive palette tool on the Ad Colors page doesn't offer all possible colors, by a long stretch. Specifically, the page provides 222 colors. See Chapter 13 for ways to expand this palette.

For now, follow these steps to use Google's colors in making custom palettes for your ad units:

1. **Go to the Ad Colors page of the Settings tab, shown in Figure 12-6.**

2. **Use the drop-down menu to select a starting color palette.**

3. **Click the radio button next to any of the five ad unit elements.**

4. **Click any color in the color chart.**

   Note that the example ad changes interactively.

5. **Repeat Steps 3 and 4 for each ad unit element.**

6. **In the Palette name box, type a name for your new palette.**

7. **Click the Save button.**

   Your palette's name appears in the Custom Palettes box and in the drop-down list higher on the page. It appears also in the Select Palettes list on the Ad Layout Code page.

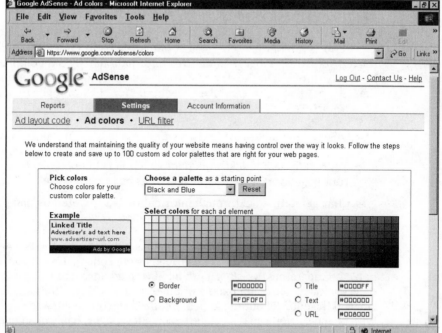

Figure 12-6:
Use this
page to
create new
color
palettes for
your ad
units.

TIP

To get rid of a saved custom palette, click the Delete button below the Custom Palettes box. The deleted palette disappears from that box, from the Choose a Palette drop-down menu higher on the page, and from the Select Palettes list on the Ad Layout Code page.

Inserting your custom palettes into your AdSense code is simple. Here's how:

1. **After saving one or more custom palettes, go to the Ad Layout Code page on the Settings tab.**

2. **In the Select Palettes box, choose one of your custom palettes.**

3. **Using a radio button, select an ad layout.**

4. **Scroll down to the Copy-and-Paste window, and select the entire code sample.**

5. **Copy the code sample and paste it into your HTML page.**

Note: The Alternate Ads box and the URL Filter page make their appearance in Chapter 13. There, I explain how to (in the first case) substitute non-Google ads for AdSense ads, and (in the second case) block certain AdWords ads from appearing in your ad units.

Viewing AdSense Reports

The Reports tab of the AdSense account is where you track earnings and related statistics. Google summarizes information daily but compiles it continuously throughout the day. Statistics are reported quickly but not in real time. As in AdWords, it can take a few hours for clickthroughs to appear in your report.

The AdSense account provides two ways of viewing your clickthrough data:

- **Aggregate data.** Clickthrough information is lumped together from all your pages and sites and presented as an integrated set.

- **Channel data.** Clickthrough information is separated by pages, sites, and even specific ad units, as determined by you.

Before Google introduced AdSense channels in March, 2004, AdSense publishers couldn't see where their clickthroughs were coming from. If you were a publisher operating two sites, both filled with ad units and making good revenue overall, you wouldn't know whether most clickthroughs came from one site and the effort of putting AdSense code in the other site was largely wasted. With channels, you can determine which sites, pages, types of ad unit, or specific ad units are earning for you.

Viewing aggregate data

The AdSense account defaults to the aggregate view. Even if you leave the account in channel view, it reverts to aggregate view when you next log in. Figure 12-7 shows the report screen. Google's terms of service for AdSense prohibit disclosing report statistics, so Figure 12-7 extends down just to the top of the reporting columns, and not to the numbers in those columns.

Google furnishes five columns of information:

- **Date.** Reporting data is summarized daily.

- **Page impressions.** The total number of times your ad units have been displayed to visitors of your site. Each displayed ad unit on any page counts as a single impression, so *do not* divide page impressions by the number of ads in your ad units. (Trying to count impressions of individual ads would not be feasible because you might be using multiple ad layouts, each of which contains a different number of ads.) Google doesn't separate impressions by site, so the Page impressions column reports total displays across all your sites and all their pages.

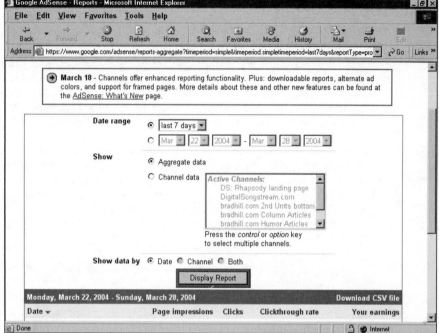

Figure 12-7:
Five
information
columns
summarize
daily
impressions,
clicks, and
earnings.

✔ **Clicks.** The daily number of clickthroughs across all your Web sites and pages running AdSense ads.

✔ **Clickthrough rate.** Calculated by dividing daily clicks by daily page impressions.

✔ **Your earnings.** A daily accounting of money credited to your account, paid monthly when it totals more than $100.

The performance chart can give you some idea of the cost-per-click (CPC) you're earning from your ads. Divide the daily earnings summary by the number of clicks to get an average CPC for that day.

Remember that you're sharing revenue with Google, but the revenue split is not disclosed by Google. I've never heard anyone complain about the phantom split amount — which is to say, people grumble that the percentage is undisclosed but seem satisfied with the amount of money coming in per click. There can be wide disparity in what clicks are worth to you, especially if you operate diverse sites or pages that pull diverse ads. For example, a non-profit site keyed to developmental disabilities is likely to pull ads with lower clickthrough value than a site about digital music.

Totals for impressions, clicks, clickthrough rate (CTR), and earnings are tabulated at the bottom of the performance chart. New accounts can extrapolate annual earnings by counting the number of days summarized, dividing that number into 365, and then multiplying the result by total earnings so far. Using the date-constraining feature described next, you can also wait for a calendar month to pass, and then multiply that month's total earnings by 12. No matter how you extrapolate, remember that CTR often goes down over time if your ad placement is left unattended. Chapter 13 describes strategies for keeping your ad performance fresh over many months of AdSense publishing.

Immediately above the performance table are a series of drop-down menus that invite you to capture reported statistics by time period. The upper menu contains six preset date constraints: today, yesterday, last 7 days, this month, last month, and all time. The default setting, which appears every time you log into the account, no matter which setting was selected when you logged out, is "today." Simply click any item in that menu, and then click the Display Report button.

To fine-tune a date range, click the lower Date Range radio button and use its set of drop-down menus to select a reporting period. Then click the Display Report button. Here, too, Google forgets your setting when you log out. The next time you view your account, the performance report displays statistics for the current day.

Viewing channel data

The second way to view the clickthrough data in your AdSense account is as channel data. AdSense channels are optional; I explain how to set them up in the next section.

You view channel data on the same account screen as aggregate data, but not at the same time. You need to make four clicks to switch from aggregate data to channel data:

1. **Click the Channel data radio button (see Figure 12-8).**

2. **In the list, select which channels to view.**

   To select multiple channels, hold the Ctrl key while clicking channels.

3. **Click the Date, Channel, or Both radio button to select how the display is sorted.**

4. **Click the Display Report button.**

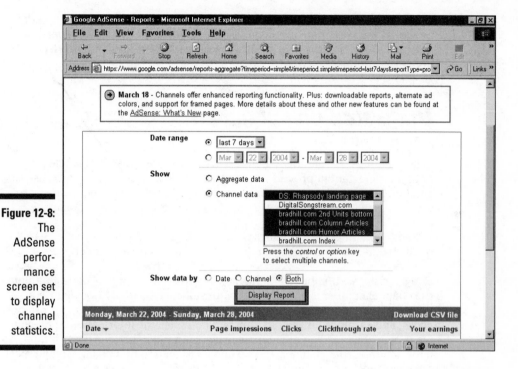

Figure 12-8:
The
AdSense
perfor-
mance
screen set
to display
channel
statistics.

The statistical column headings are the same in channel view as in aggregate view. The Show Data By group of radio buttons makes the following adjustments to the data display:

✔ If you select the Date radio button, Google aggregates the information just as in the aggregate view, but only for the channels you selected in Step 2.

✔ The Channel radio button divides the data by channel and displays it without a breakdown of individual days.

✔ The Both radio button combines these two features, displaying data for each channel and for every day of the time period you selected with the Date Range menus.

Setting Up AdSense Channels

Using channels is a great way (well, the only way) to discover which portions of your AdSense effort are making money. Before Google introduced channels, AdSense publishers were collecting revenue with no idea of where, exactly, it came from. The pre-channel version of AdSense wasn't a bad deal, by any means, but there was a growing clamor for more precise reporting. AdSense channels bring the program to an important level of maturity, and I urge every publisher to use them.

Understanding channels

Google could have simply instituted per-domain reporting, which would have helped publishers running AdSense on two or more sites. That would have been an important improvement, but the channels system takes AdSense to a higher level by being user-configurable. You decide how the channels are assigned and how your AdSense data is broken down on the report page.

AdSense channels are groupings of pages, sites, or ad units. You may use up to 20 channels at once, and you decide what goes into a channel.

Google assigns a number to each channel you create. A line of code containing the channel number is inserted into your AdSense code (by Google or you) and placed in your HTML (by you). That extra line of code tracks impressions, clicks, and earnings for that ad unit, and compiles the information as belonging to that channel. You might have many ad units or just one contributing information to that channel. The ad units assigned to that channel might exist on many sites or just one. The configuration of the channels is up to you.

Following are some common channel uses:

- ✔ **Per-site reporting.** Assign every ad unit on each domain to a separate channel.

- ✔ **Per-page reporting.** If you display one ad unit per page, make each one report to a different channel. If you run two or more ad units on a page, make each page's units report to the same channel. This strategy works only if you operate 20 or fewer pages on your site. (Of course, if you have more than 20 pages, you could select just 20 of them.)

- ✔ **Per-page-cluster reporting.** Assign groups of pages to the same channel. This tactic is useful when multiple pages perform the same function in your site and are similarly trafficked.

- ✔ **Per-format reporting.** If you use multiple AdSense formats and wonder whether one style is more effective than another style, put all skyscrapers in one channel and all horizontal units in another channel. This idea works best when the varied formats are placed on pages that function similarly in your site and are fairly equally trafficked.

Although you can't receive reporting of more than 20 channels, you may create more channels. You select which to activate and deactivate (I get to this in just a bit). Deactivated channels continue to hold their accumulated data; when you activate them, they pick up where they left off.

You can get around the limitation of only 20 active channels. To do so, create additional channels and rotate their activation. This way, you can get fully precise recording of your AdSense performance — just not all at once. Because high-volume sites don't require much time to accumulate meaningful data, a week or so rotation through channel activation could provide a complete picture of AdSense clickthroughs.

Creating channels

You create AdSense channels in a special section of the AdSense account. Follow these steps:

1. **Click the Settings tab.**

2. **Click the <u>Channels</u> link.**

3. **Click the Create new channel radio button, and type the name of your channel.**

   See Figure 12-9. Name the channel descriptively, so you can recognize it on the report page.

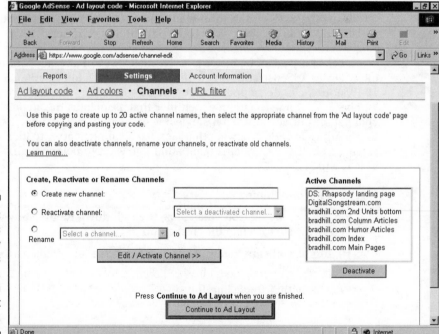

Figure 12-9: Create as many channels as you want. Up to 20 can be active at any time.

4. Click the Edit/Activate Channel button.

Your channel moves to the Active Channels list. Newly created channels are active by default but can be immediately deactivated.

5. After creating as many channels as you want for now, click the Continue to Ad Layout button.

You may return to this page at any time to create channels, deactivate active channels, and activate inactive channels.

6. On the Ad Layout Code page, make the same format and color selections you used when setting up your first version of AdSense code.

This can be tricky. In this step and the next, you're modifying your previous AdSense code by inserting a line that defines which channel the ad unit belongs to. You don't want to change anything else about the display of your ad unit, so you must make the same selections now as you did when first creating the code (see the "Creating Your AdSense Code" section, earlier in this chapter). I describe another way of inserting the channel information after these steps, and that method is easier for anyone comfortable with manually changing simple code.

7. Pull down the Channel menu and select one of your channels.

See Figure 12-10. The AdSense code is instantly updated to include the `google_ad_channel` line.

8. Copy the entire code snippet and paste it into the page(s) containing the ad units that you want to be part of this channel.

If you run many ad units, I have a much easier way of altering your many instances of AdSense code and inserting the channel information. In Figure 12-10, note the code snippet, which is the `google_ad_channel` line. The number in that line is a unique identifier that associates the ad unit with a channel in your account. That single line is the only modification necessary to the AdSense code. Knowing that fact, it's a simple matter to insert that single line in the code of all ad units that you want to belong to that channel. This is what I do:

1. Create your channels.

2. On the Ad Layout Code page, use the pull-down menu (shown in Figure 12-10) to select the first channel in the list.

3. Highlight and copy (using Ctrl+C) the `google_ad_channel` line in the AdSense code.

Copy only that single line.

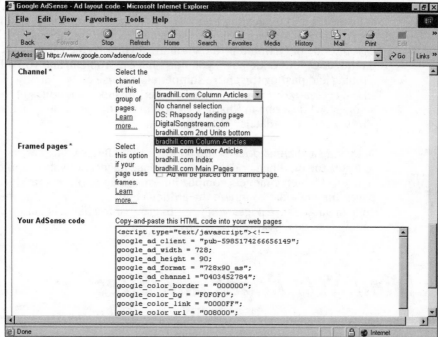

Figure 12-10:
When you
select a
channel on
the Ad
Layout Code
page, the
AdSense
code
instantly
updates.

4. **Paste the line into a text file using WordPad, Notepad, or any text processor.**

   Type the channel name above or below the line of code. You may jot down the channel name and line of code on a piece of paper if you prefer. You're going to repeat this process with each of your channels, so making a text file is probably the best way to establish this record.

5. **Repeat Steps 3 and 4 for each of your channels.**

   You end up with a list of channel names and their lines of code.

6. **Insert the appropriate line of code into each of your AdSense code snippets.**

   Place the line in the same location that Google places it on the Ad Layout Code page: between the `google_ad_format` line and the `google_ad_border` line. That portion of the AdSense code should end up looking something like this:

   ```
   google_ad_format = "728x90_as";
   google_ad_channel ="4855956454";
   google_color_border = "B4D0DC";
   ```

Following this method saves you the trouble of remembering your AdSense code values and replicating them on the Ad Layout Code page. Many publishers run several formats and color schemes; recreating them all on the Ad Layout Code page would be a nightmare. If you saved custom color palettes on the Ad Layout Code page, you don't have a problem, and you might prefer clipping and pasting the entire snippet of AdSense code. But any publisher who has created custom palettes by inserting hex color codes in the AdSense snippet, as I describe in Chapter 13, will prefer the preceding method when altering code for AdSense channels.

Activating a channel doesn't flip a switch that affects your reports. You need to insert the modified code in your AdSense pages. Activation and deactivation affect which channels compile information and place it on the report page. But you must complete the arduous chore of inserting the modified code in *all* AdSense pages you want to group into channels before your activations and deactivations have any meaning.

Adding New Pages and Sites

AdSense is limitlessly expandable because you can add AdSense to new pages and sites anytime. Simply paste your preferred code into any new pages developed for your site. If you use a consistent template across your site, simply putting the AdSense code in the template assures that ads will appear on new live pages. Leave the rest to Google — in time, according to your site's crawl schedule, relevant ads will appear on the new pages. If there's a gap between the time you launch a page and Google crawling it for content, the AdSense program places public service ads on the page.

You may submit new pages to Google's Web index if you like, though it's probably unnecessary (see Chapter 2). If your site is in the Web index, Google usually finds new pages during its deep crawl, which occurs approximately monthly. The best reason for *not* submitting new pages is that the AdSense index is different from the Web index. In both cases, the best bet is to post the page and wait.

Somewhat surprisingly, considering its stringent approval requirements, Google allows AdSense publishers to paste code into entirely new sites located at new domains. No application is necessary. After you're in, you're in, and you have unlimited use of the AdSense code. Keep in mind, however, that Google *does* send a human to every new site that makes a call for AdSense ads to examine it for appropriateness. At that time, or very near that time, Google crawls the new AdSense site for content.

Removing Ads and Stopping Your Ad Publishing

Just as adding new pages and sites is hassle-free, Google puts up no barriers to exiting the AdSense program or reducing your involvement with it. AdSense is entirely configurable on this point; you may publish ads on one page of a large site, all pages, some pages, or across as many domains as you deem productive.

Simply remove the AdSense code from any page you want to be ad-free. Removing a page from the program doesn't penalize other pages or change the quality of ads delivered to your pages. To stop your involvement with AdSense altogether, dump all the code. There's no way to close your AdSense account, nor is there any need to. It remains there, in case you decide to publish ads again in the future.

When you remove AdSense code, remember to adjust your page code to fill the hole you've just ripped in it. If you created a table cell to hold your ad unit, for example, eliminate the cell or put something else in it.

Chapter 13

Enhancing Your AdSense Revenue

- -

In This Chapter

▶ Optimizing your site for AdSense

▶ Optimizing to pull high-value ads from Google

▶ Improving clickthrough rates

▶ Battling "ad blindness"

▶ Keeping your competitor's ads off your site

▶ Using an alternate ad

- -

AdSense is a new program, and a simple one. Starting up is easy (see Chapter 12), and there's no risk. You can't lose money publishing AdWords ads. The worst that can happen with AdSense is that you make no money. I've never heard of anyone making absolutely no money — not a single clickthrough; not a penny earned. Even one low-revenue click through an ad on your page is an encouraging sign that the program works. This chapter is about getting more clickthroughs.

Improving your AdSense performance involves mostly optimization and design issues. It's vital to remember that providing incentives to click your AdSense ads, or merely pleading for clicks, violates the AdSense terms of service and can easily get you kicked out of the program. Relevancy drives clicks. Google's job is to provide relevant ads, and your job is to focus your page's topic clearly so Google can do its job.

This chapter is also about eliminating competition from your pages (or making a business decision to *not* eliminate it) and setting up alternate ads — the two account features not covered in Chapter 12.

Optimizing Your Site for AdSense Success

Success in the AdSense program depends on several factors, most of which are under your control. To get clickthroughs, you need

✔ Traffic

✔ Relevant ads

If nobody is visiting your site, you obviously won't get clicks. If you have traffic but your ads aren't relevant, your visitors won't feel motivated to click them. You might think that it's Google's responsibility to send you relevant ads (especially since I stated exactly that in the introduction to this chapter), but successful AdSense publishers take responsibility for relevancy by giving Google a clearly optimized site to work with. Optimization works both ends of the equation, helping you attract more traffic while helping Google provide relevant ads.

Briefly put, site optimization for search engines (usually called search engine optimization, or SEO) is a bundle of writing, designing, and HTML-coding techniques with two goals:

✔ Creating a more coherent experience for visitors

✔ Improving the site's visibility in search engines

The two goals are tied together by Google's primary mission to provide good content to its users. Google strives to reward visitor-friendly sites with high placement on its search results pages — taking into consideration other factors as well. If you haven't read Chapter 4, this is a good time to soak up its elaborate tutorial in site optimization. That chapter is geared to improving your site's stature in Google, building PageRank, and climbing up the search results page — all to the purpose of attracting traffic.

Promoting your site on other related sites is a tangential aspect of optimization but a pertinent part of traffic building. Building a network of incoming links is the most potent way to improve your PageRank in Google (see Chapter 3 for much more about this). Building links is important also to your success with AdSense. AdSense revenue benefits from all the normal ways that enterprising Webmasters promote their online businesses.

Now, on to relevancy. Relevancy converts visitors to clickthroughs. Ironically, a successful conversion sends the visitor away from your site, which might seem counterproductive. Never mind that for now; if your site provides good information value, your visitors will come back. Later in this chapter I describe how to keep them anchored on your page even when they click an ad.

It's no surprise that the AdSense program is much beloved by Webmasters running information sites, as opposed to service, subscription, or transaction sites that generate nonadvertising revenue. Information sites are often labors of love, having been constructed from the ground up out of passion for the subject. When AdSense burst on the scene, these hard-working, under-rewarded folks began experiencing Internet-derived revenue for the first time. In those cases, AdSense is the only source of site income. More established media sites that build AdSense into the revenue mix are sometimes surprised to find it contributing a larger-than-expected portion of income. No matter what your site's focus or scope, cleanly optimized content delivers more pertinent ads and higher clickthrough rates.

The following is an AdSense-specific checklist of optimization points:

- **Have only one subject per page.** Get your site fiercely organized, and eliminate extraneous content from any page. Don't be afraid to add pages to accommodate short subjects that don't fit on other pages. Let there be no question as to what a page is about.

- **Determine key concepts, words, and phrases.** For each page, that is. Then, make sure those words and phrases are represented on the page. Pay particular attention to getting those words into headlines. Your concentration of keywords should be skewed toward the top of the page. Don't go overboard; your text must read naturally or your visitors (and Google) will know that you're spamming them.

- **Put keywords in your tags.** Take those keywords and phrases from the preceding item and put them into your `meta` tags (the `keyword`, `description`, and `title` tags). See Chapter 4 for details. Don't use any word more than three times in any single tag.

- **Use text instead of images.** Google doesn't understand words that are embedded in images, such as what you often seen in navigation buttons. (Navigation buttons and other images are important in defining the subject of the page and the site.) Replace the buttons with text navigation links.

Try to fulfill these points *before* opening an AdSense account. Ideally, your site is in its optimized state when Google first crawls it. You don't know how often your site will be crawled in the future, so getting properly indexed the first time is key.

These optimization points apply more to home-grown information sites than to database-driven media sites, such as online editions of newspapers, where content deployment is determined by offsite editorial determinants. An online newspaper follows the news, not the other way around, so the topicality of a page might be torn apart by diverse stories. But even sites that drop in their content from offline sources (such as reporters in the field) can optimize their subject categories by organizing site structure along topical lines whenever possible. Keeping to shorter pages of focused content encourages AdSense success.

So far, I've discussed optimization as it applies to sites already built and operating. Such optimization is largely about defining your subject by keywords, and putting those keywords into the page's content and tags. Taking the reverse approach is also possible: developing a site around keywords that lead to a high-revenue AdSense account. That approach, which I cover later in the next section, is trickier. The middle ground between optimizing a built site and building an optimized site is adding pages to an existing site without betraying the overall topicality, primarily to enhance AdSense revenue. Keep reading to explore both these possibilities.

Shooting for More Valuable Ads

It's no secret: All AdSense ads are not equally valuable. The value of any ad displayed in your ad unit depends primarily on what the advertiser bid to put it on your page, in its position in the Ad Group. That bid is the *most* that the ad can be worth to both you and Google; Google might, in fact, charge the advertiser less, depending on mathematical considerations I describe in the AdWords chapters. And whatever the ad is worth to you and Google combined, it's worth less to you alone. You don't know the percentage of its total value that you receive per clickthrough, and you don't know the overall value in dollars and cents, either. That's a lot of not knowing. Here's the formula:

Advertiser's bid *minus* Google's discount to the advertiser *minus* Google's portion of the revenue split

With all this subtraction, it's amazing that AdSense pays out at all, but it does. Some of those advertiser's bids are sky-high (and the AdWords bid market is inflating all the time), and Google's split with AdSense publishers appears to be generous. Still, AdSense publishers who keep an eagle eye on their reports quickly learn that some clickthroughs are worth much more than others. That means that some ads are more valuable than others. Ideally, you want the most valuable ads to appear on your pages.

To some extent, the relative value of ads you receive is a factor out of your control. The best you can do is optimize each page to most clearly convey its topic and run the ads Google sends. But you can travel down two other avenues in the quest for more valuable ads:

✔ Start a new site

✔ Create new pages optimized for more valuable ads

The first option is not a possibility for Webmasters who are not devoted full-time to their Internet businesses. Even if they are working full-time online, their hands might be full with properties they already run.

I must also point out that Google discourages building a site solely as a vehicle for AdSense, but does not outright forbid such a site. Google looks for quality content, regardless of its motivation. If you slap up nearly blank pages with keywords stuffed into the `meta` tags, and start running AdSense ads on them, Google will likely shut you down. (That means closing your entire AdSense account, eliminating AdSense on any legitimate properties you might be running.)

Dire consequences notwithstanding, there isn't much difference between a new site designed for AdSense and a long-running site that just joined AdSense, *if* both sites have substantial and worthy content. A new genre of Web site has started to appear, optimized for valuable AdSense ads and created to earn AdSense revenue. If the content is good, nobody is harmed by this scenario. Visitors enjoy a positive site experience; advertisers receive high-quality clickthroughs; the AdSense publisher builds revenue; and Google maintains the integrity of its value chain. It's all about content and relevancy.

Identifying high-value keywords

So, looking back at those two methods of attracting high-value ads, the point to remember is that the processes are identical. Whether starting a new site or spinning off new pages, pulling more valuable ads from Google is accomplished by identifying high-value keywords and optimizing new content around those keywords. That's a densely packed concept, so let me unwind it:

- ✔ The value of keywords is determined by advertiser bids on those keywords.

- ✔ High bids for certain keywords represent an advertiser's wish for a top position on search results pages as well as on content pages.

- ✔ Clickthroughs on ads associated with expensive keywords cost advertisers more, and yield more to AdSense publishers, than clickthroughs on less valuable ads.

- ✔ AdSense publishers can use a variety of tools to determine the relative value of keywords.

- ✔ Given the same number of clickthroughs, optimizing content around expensive keywords versus less expensive keywords leads to higher AdSense revenue.

For existing sites, building new content optimized around high-value key-words is a three-step process:

1. **Identify current keywords.**

   These keywords are the core concepts of your page(s), which might or might not be incorporated in your `meta` tags and embedded in your page text.

2. **Research related keywords.**

   Keyword research is . . . well, *key* to the whole Google ad game, for advertisers and AdSense publishers alike. Your goal is to find keywords that advertisers are bidding up. See the tip after this list for two interactive tools that uncover this vital bidding information.

3. **Build content around high-value keywords.**

   Building content is easier said than done. Writing and assembling page content that keeps visitors coming back is a long-term process. For existing sites, the issue might be one of reorganizing existing content to optimize pages around high-value keywords.

 The two biggest providers of pay-per-click search engine advertising, Google and Overture, both provide on-screen tools for determining the relative value of keywords. Using Google's Traffic Estimator is more work than using Overture's Bid Estimator and yields less explicit results. However, the results are more pertinent because you're trying to attract high-value Google ads, not Overture ads. Successful AdSense publishers put themselves in the mind-set of an AdWords advertiser. Achieving that state of mind is best accomplished by opening an AdWords account and using the Keyword Suggestion Tool and the Keyword Estimator. There's no cost or obligation in opening an AdWords account. See Chapter 7 for complete instructions.

Making the most of AdWords tools requires a certain amount of savvy. Figure 13-1 illustrates the Traffic Estimator. You can see that certain keywords generate more clicks per day than others, meaning they are more popular search terms. You can also see that a relatively high cost-per-click (such as 38 cents for the keyword *ipod*) yields a lower ad position than a less expensive keyword (such as *imusic*). By inference, you know that *ipod* is a more valuable keyword than *imusic*, and if you create a content page optimized for *ipod* it will probably pull more valuable ads than if you optimized for *imusic*.

Overture provides a more direct view of comparative keyword value. Follow these steps to view Overture bid amounts:

1. **Go to the Overture site at** `www.overture.com`.

2. **In the search box, type a keyword.**

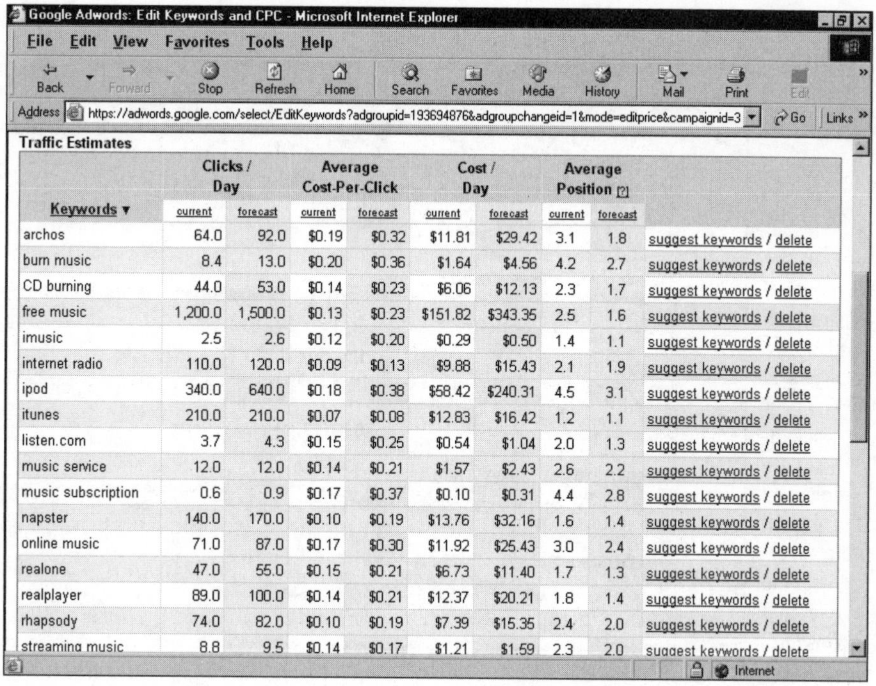

Traffic Estimates

Keywords ▾	Clicks / Day current	Clicks / Day forecast	Average Cost-Per-Click current	Average Cost-Per-Click forecast	Cost / Day current	Cost / Day forecast	Average Position current	Average Position forecast	
archos	64.0	92.0	$0.19	$0.32	$11.81	$29.42	3.1	1.8	suggest keywords / delete
burn music	8.4	13.0	$0.20	$0.36	$1.64	$4.56	4.2	2.7	suggest keywords / delete
CD burning	44.0	53.0	$0.14	$0.23	$6.06	$12.13	2.3	1.7	suggest keywords / delete
free music	1,200.0	1,500.0	$0.13	$0.23	$151.82	$343.35	2.5	1.6	suggest keywords / delete
imusic	2.5	2.6	$0.12	$0.20	$0.29	$0.50	1.4	1.1	suggest keywords / delete
internet radio	110.0	120.0	$0.09	$0.13	$9.88	$15.43	2.1	1.9	suggest keywords / delete
ipod	340.0	640.0	$0.18	$0.38	$58.42	$240.31	4.5	3.1	suggest keywords / delete
itunes	210.0	210.0	$0.07	$0.08	$12.83	$16.42	1.2	1.1	suggest keywords / delete
listen.com	3.7	4.3	$0.15	$0.25	$0.54	$1.04	2.0	1.3	suggest keywords / delete
music service	12.0	12.0	$0.14	$0.21	$1.57	$2.43	2.6	2.2	suggest keywords / delete
music subscription	0.6	0.9	$0.17	$0.37	$0.10	$0.31	4.4	2.8	suggest keywords / delete
napster	140.0	170.0	$0.10	$0.19	$13.76	$32.16	1.6	1.4	suggest keywords / delete
online music	71.0	87.0	$0.17	$0.30	$11.92	$25.43	3.0	2.4	suggest keywords / delete
realone	47.0	55.0	$0.15	$0.21	$6.73	$11.40	1.7	1.3	suggest keywords / delete
realplayer	89.0	100.0	$0.14	$0.21	$12.37	$20.21	1.8	1.4	suggest keywords / delete
rhapsody	74.0	82.0	$0.10	$0.19	$7.39	$15.35	2.4	2.0	suggest keywords / delete
streaming music	8.8	9.5	$0.14	$0.17	$1.21	$1.59	2.3	2.0	suggest keywords / delete

Figure 13-1: The Traffic Estimator in the AdWords account infers the relative value of keywords.

3. **On the search results page, click the View Advertisers' Max Bids link, near the upper-right corner.**

   The View Bids window pops open.

4. **Type the security code in the provided box.**

   This little speed bump prevents automated access of Overture's Max Bids features. Entering the code assures Overture that you are a human.

5. **Click the Search button.**

As you can see in Figure 13-2, Overture displays its advertisers' ads for the keyword you entered, listed in descending order of bid amount. This remarkably public disclosure of what companies pay for their Overture ads does not necessarily correlate with Google bid amounts, which are probably higher. But it does give you a basis for comparison, especially if you repeat the process with related keywords. (You can launch a new search directly from the results window.) A recent search revealed a top bid of 40 cents for the keyword *ipod,* and no bids at all for the keyword *imusic,* confirming the inference of Google's Traffic Estimator.

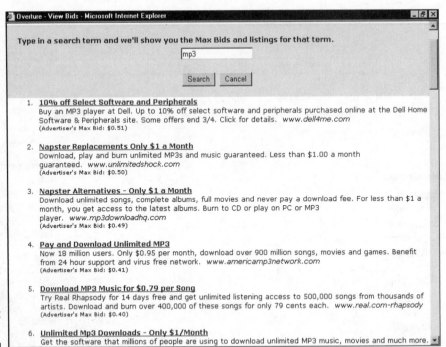

Figure 13-2:
Overture divulges its inventory of ads for search terms and the amount the advertiser bid for that keyword.

Keyword-bid research isn't of much value, however, if you can't think of related keywords. Google's Keyword Suggestion Tool (in the AdWords account) creates spectacular lists of related keywords, and is free to use after opening an AdWords account. Overture provides a similar service, at this URL:

```
inventory.overture.com
```

Figure 13-3 illustrates the results of Overture's Search Term Suggestion Tool. Notice that in addition to spitting out a list of related terms, Overture divulges the search count for each term and presents the list in order of search term popularity.

Wordtracker is another popular keyword suggestion tool, with added features that calculate how popular the keywords are as search terms in various search engines. The service is located here:

```
www.wordtracker.com
```

Wordtracker does not attempt to gauge bid value. The service is used by advertisers and site optimizers to target subject niches. I discuss Wordtracker comprehensively in Chapter 3.

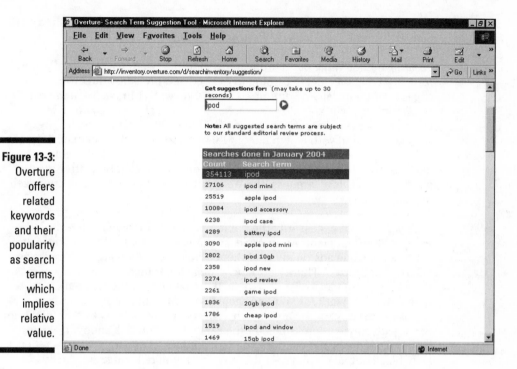

Figure 13-3:
Overture
offers
related
keywords
and their
popularity
as search
terms,
which
implies
relative
value.

Conceiving and building high-value AdSense pages

After you've identified high-value keywords, you need to find ways of extending your content to those key concepts without damaging or diluting your site's focus. If you operate a directory of bed-and-breakfast establishments, for example, you don't want to spin off pages about iPods just because of their high keyword value. You might want to start an entirely new site about iPods and digital music, but that's a big project. The goal here is not mindless opportunism. The goal is content management that leverages the best keyword value that can legitimately be applied to your site.

Although it's valuable to think like an AdWords advertiser and use the AdWords tools, remember that your priorities are the opposite of the advertiser's priorities in one respect. The advertiser seeks niche categories represented by highly targeted keywords over which there is little bidding competition. The ideal keyword is used as a search term by a specific demographic of searchers and has been overlooked by other advertisers. The AdSense publisher, conversely, seeks broad categories represented by high-demand keywords over which there is a great deal of competition. The ideal keyword is both hugely popular as a search term and in demand by other advertisers. The advertiser's pain (high bid expenses to hit the desired market) is your gain (high clickthrough revenue).

Creating higher-value pages from an existing site is often a matter of generalizing from the specific. Returning to the bed-and-breakfast directory, whose pages might naturally be optimized for the keyword phrase *bed and breakfast,* the Webmaster could realize that *hotel* is a more valuable keyword. In Overture, *bed and breakfast* draws a high bid of $0.35, while *hotel* enjoys stronger demand with a high bid of $1.04. These numbers don't speak for the bid amounts in Google AdWords, but what does it matter? The Webmaster never knows the absolute value of any ad on the page; only relative value matters. With this awareness, the Webmaster might create a page optimized in part for *hotel.*

High value is not necessarily the point. Capturing previously disregarded value is also important. As an AdSense publisher, look at all your pages. If you see the same ads on many of them, Google is perceiving your pages as similarly optimized. There's nothing wrong with topical consistency across the site, but from an AdSense perspective that consistency is inefficient. Ad replication can work for you and against you. Multiple impressions can impose awareness of the ad on your visitors, motivating clicks that might not occur with single impressions. At the same time, you risk annoying visitors with repeated ads and encouraging "ad blindness," in which visitors reflexively block out ad displays. At the very least, you're losing revenue by not exploiting ads that would be drawn to topical pages related to, but different from, your main pages. Continue adding content pages, with an eye to distinguishing their keyword optimizations.

Improving Clickthrough Rates

Whatever your site's level of traffic, clickthrough rate (CTR) is the determinant of AdSense success. All AdSense Webmasters should monitor the clickthrough rate in the account performance chart and watch its fluctuations. Divulging any site's CTR is a violation of Google's terms of service, so a discussion of specifics is out of bounds here. Shooting for a standard of excellence isn't the point in AdSense; improving CTR and maintaining that level is.

Remember, do not raise your CTR artificially. This is serious business; Google will close accounts if it detects CTR mischief. Artificial clickthroughs mean wasted advertiser money and the destruction of value in the AdWords program, over which Google is fiercely protective. Playing it safe is the only way, so avoid these three false types of clickthrough:

✔ Clicking your own ads

✔ Telling friends to visit your site and click ads

✔ Promoting ad clicks on your Web page

Fortunately, you can try a number of legitimate tactics to raise your CTR. Experimentation is key. The only way to know what works for your site is to try both sides of a strategy. The more traffic your site attracts, the more quickly you can evaluate your CTR experiments.

Placing ads above the fold

You are concerned with the *highest* fold point. The lower the screen resolution, the higher the fold point. Visitors running a monitor resolution of 640 x 480 pixels see very little of your page without scrolling. Most Webmasters no longer design for 640 x 480 viewing, but 800 x 600 is widely in use, and that resolution, too, has a high fold point. If you normally view your site with higher resolutions, the advice here is to drop down to lower rez and see where your ad units appear.

Horizontal ad layouts are far easier to squeeze above the fold than vertical layouts that stretch down the page. (See Figure 13-4.) Some AdSense veterans recommend against horizontal layouts for reasons I discuss a bit later. If you choose a skyscraper ad unit, running down the page vertically, try to place the first ad, at least, above the fold (see Figure 13-5).

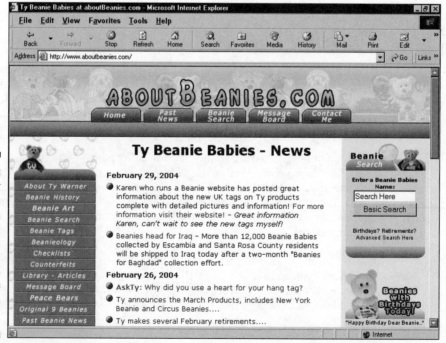

Figure 13-4: Believe it or not, this page is running AdSense ads. The ad unit is below the fold of an 800 x 600 screen.

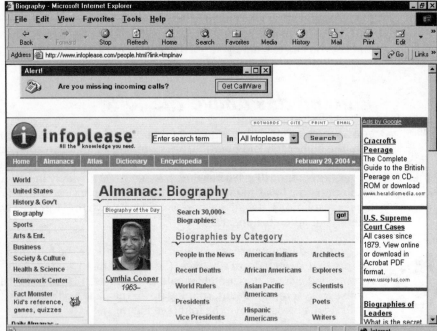

Figure 13-5:
A vertical ad layout, pushed high up on the page, where two full ads are visible above the 800 x 600 fold.

Choosing your pages

Leaving behind the fold issue, another consideration is *which* pages should host your ads. There is logic to thinking that you might as well code ads into every page of your site. Indeed, if you use templates that establish the unchanging elements of all your pages, it might be difficult to keep ads off individual pages. But two tactics for enhancing your AdSense presentation come to mind.

First, consider eliminating ads from your index page — the first page of your site. The rationale here is that an ad-free opening page welcomes your visitors and won't get their defenses up. The phenomenon of ad blindness can be instilled on the home page and persist as the visitor moves through the site. Eliminating ads from the index page makes your ad units stand out more in the inner pages.

Ad-free index pages don't work for all sites. If your index page is the highest-ranked entry page *and* exit page, the index page is your main chance to generate clickthroughs; if visitors exit the site from that page anyway, you might as well lure them into exiting through your ads. Check your traffic logs.

An experiment with exit pages

Manuel Lemos operates an information and file-download site at www.phpclasses.org focused on the PHP programming language. He is an AdSense publisher. In trying to juice up his clickthrough rate, Lemos experimented with a placement strategy using primarily exit pages. This is his account: "I formulated a thesis that stated that if, on interesting content pages the users tend to ignore the ads, the ads would be more efficient on pages that would be less interesting. To test the thesis, I figured that the less interesting pages would be the exit pages. A quick look at my site statistics showed me that typical exit pages are the download pages. The user's tendency is to come to the site, check the new components, and download them if they are interesting. So I created new pages with statistics of the files being downloaded and placed ad units on them.

"The thesis turned out to be correct. These pages have typical clickthrough rates that are three or four times greater than content pages. Users usually wait some time to download the files, and while waiting they stare at the page a bit. When the downloads end, users usually leave the site because they got what they wanted. At that time, they often click on the ads on the page."

Now look at the Infoplease.com site, shown in Figure 13-5. That figure illustrates one of the main inner pages of the infoplease domain. If you visit infoplease.com, you see that the home page doesn't run AdSense ads, though it does sprout display banners and pop-ups. While not presenting an ad-free environment by a long shot, the busy index page prepares visitors for the quieter presentation of AdSense ads displayed on the inner pages.

Another strategy of great interest and potential is to limit ad displays to boring and post-conversion pages of the site. Boring pages? Is it blasphemy to suppose anyone's pages are boring? Not at all. By "boring," I mean lacking in substantive content. Registration confirmation pages, for example, contain little information. The same is true of post-download pages. These pages represent lulls in the site experience during which the visitor might be attracted to an AdSense ad as the most interesting content on the page. Since many of these "boring" pages are presented after the visitor has been converted in some way (signing up for a newsletter, for example, or registering at the site), getting a clickthrough at that point is icing on the cake, turning otherwise useless pages into revenue earners. See the sidebar titled "An experiment with exit pages" for a real-life success story using this strategy.

Fighting ad blindness

Ad blindness affects content providers in all media. I read *The New Yorker* magazine, and occasionally I'm startled to realize that the outer borders are filled with ads that I block out of my perception. Television, of course, suffers badly from not only ad blindness but ad walkaway and ad skipthrough, both of which are a sort of self-enforced blindness. On the Internet, banners at the top and sides of pages have accustomed the online citizenry to advertising and created an immunity to it.

AdSense ads enjoy a threefold advantage over banner advertising that helps them overcome ad blindness:

✔ Text ads look different than banners.

✔ Google ads are more relevant to the page's content than most banner ads.

✔ Google ad colors can be customized to blend in with the page, appearing almost as part of the editorial content.

Despite these advantages, visitors can get used to your ads and stop noticing them. In a way, Google contributes to the problem by conditioning a huge percentage of the online population to AdWords ads in Google. No doubt many Google searchers contract AdWords blindness. On the other hand, Google has also enlightened the Internet citizenry to the possibility and potential of highly relevant advertising that doesn't flash, pop up, or balloon across the page. Searchers who have discovered good experiences clicking AdWords ads in Google are likely to extend the expectation of a good experience when they see AdWords ads on your page.

Four factors affect the ad blindness quotient of your site:

✔ Display location

✔ Color coordination

✔ Repeating ads

✔ Ad layout type

My purpose here is not to make hard-and-fast recommendations about where your ads appear, what colors you use, or which ad layout is best. Opinions in the AdSense community vary on these questions. I do think it's important to be aware of the factors under your control and to experiment. I also make the following general recommendation regarding ad blindness: Don't get into a rut. Many AdSense publishers find that their clickthrough rate degrades over time. If traffic remains steady, this distressing CTR phenomenon can easily be attributed to visitors getting so used to your ads that they simply don't see them. When this seems to be the case, the antidote is to shake up your AdSense presentation with new locations, new colors, new layout types, and (this is more difficult) new ads.

In the previous two sections I discuss display location in a few respects: placing ads above the fold, omitting ads from the index page, and concentrating ads on exit pages. Although those sections are not presented in the context of ad blindness, the location of ads certainly is part of the problem. Now I want to move on to issues of layout type and customized colors.

Fighting ad blindness with the right ad layout

In this section and the next, we move into the realm of subjectivity. No fast rules apply to ad layout. You must balance two considerations, which don't always agree:

- ✔ What looks best in your page design
- ✔ What works best in your page design

By "what works best," I mean what delivers the best clickthrough rate. Google gives you four basic ad layout choices:

- ✔ Horizontal: Leaderboard and banner (see Figure 13-6)
- ✔ Vertical: Skyscrapers, also called towers
- ✔ Button: Two styles containing one ad each
- ✔ Inline: More rectangular than horizontals and verticals (see Figure 13-7)

Note that despite terminology that includes the words "banner" and "button," both of which imply graphic ads, all Google ad layouts contain identically formatted text ads. Check out all available layout formats here:

```
www.google.com/adsense/adformats
```

One school of thought believes that leaderboard and banner layouts should be avoided, because the Web's history of banner advertising has blinded visitors to the horizontal format. Also, Google uses vertical layouts for the most part on its pages, acclimating users to seeing AdWords displayed in a tower format. Thus, deviating from established success is risky. Arguing against that viewpoint is the mandate to place ads high on the page, which is easier to do with a horizontal layout.

Google's ad layouts use inflexible dimensions and can stretch your table cells to an accommodating size. This factor is a special issue with the leaderboard horizontal layout, which is 728 pixels wide. Placing that wide unit into a narrower table cell can widen the entire table beyond its original dimensions. Such enlargement can be a problem for pages optimized for unscrolled viewing at the 800 x 600 resolution.

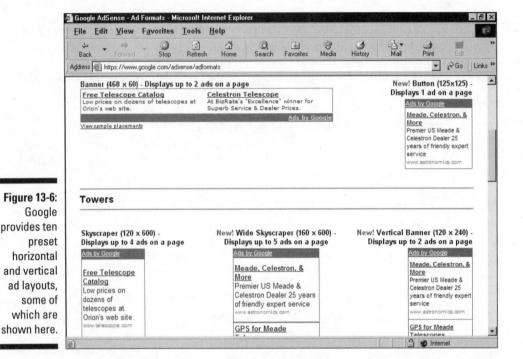

Figure 13-6:
Google
provides ten
preset
horizontal
and vertical
ad layouts,
some of
which are
shown here.

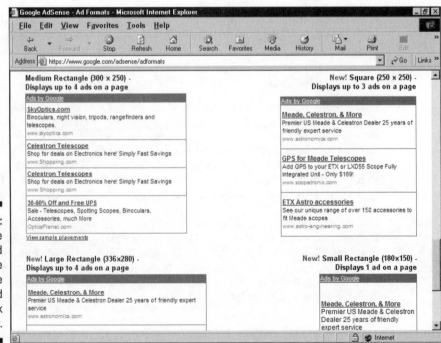

Figure 13-7:
The inline
rectangle ad
layouts are
meant to be
inserted
in a block
of text.

You must discover through trial and error whether vertical or horizontal layout works best for you. Consensus is evenly divided on the matter. Design considerations play a part in the decision; if you don't have free sidebar space for a tower above the fold, you might feel forced into a leaderboard or banner. The rectangular inline layouts work well in wide blocks of text; the text flows around the ads. (See Figure 13-8.)

The two button options provided by Google are new layout choices, and interesting ones. (By publication time, these single-ad buttons were not in wide use.) Their advantage is clear: Such a small layout footprint is easy to position all over the page. Their disadvantage is likewise obvious: With only one ad to click, you reduce clickthrough opportunities. On the other hand, people don't always respond well to multiple choices, so a single, pointed advertisement might work well in your user demographic. Are you getting the idea that AdSense success is more art than science? Actually, in the true spirit of science, AdSense responds to experimentation.

In the quest to reduce ad blindness, variety is key. Run different layouts on different pages, and change each page's layout from time to time. Track performance in your AdSense account, and shake things up when your CTR drops.

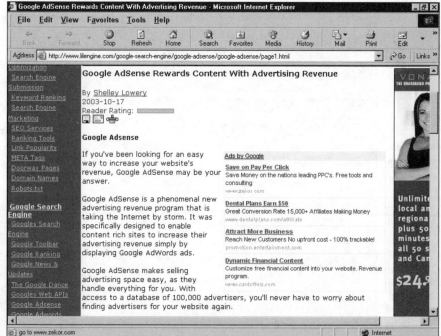

Figure 13-8:
Wide text
wraps
around
inline
rectangles.

Fighting ad blindness with the right colors

Just as ad layout issues split opinion in the AdSense publishing community, so does custom coloring of the ad unit. Many Webmasters simply don't bother with the detailed HTML tweaking necessary to fully integrate an ad unit into the look-and-feel of the host page. Others deliberately let their ad units stand out garishly on the page, to attract attention and defeat ad blindness. (Whether garish ad displays defeat or encourage ad blindness is debatable.) And a small minority of Webmasters carefully insinuate their ad units into the page design until they are nearly indistinguishable from editorial content.

You have three basic customization choices:

- ✔ **Don't do anything.** This is the choice of many Webmasters, and you see a lot of the default Mother Earth palette in the AdSense network. (See Figure 13-9.)

- ✔ **Create custom palettes in the AdSense account.** I describe how to do this in Chapter 12.

- ✔ **Fine-tune colors using HTML hex values.** This option integrates ad units into pages with complex designs or pages using background colors not found in Google's custom palette section.

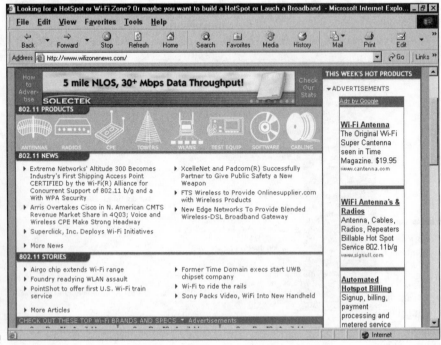

Figure 13-9: Many Webmasters use the default color palette. Here, blue ads contrast with a red-themed page.

Changing the colors of the ad unit is an acceptable alteration of the code, but no other tweaking is allowed. Do not squash the ads, enlarge them, or attempt to change the dimensions of the ad unit. Doing so violates the AdSense terms of service.

To fully customize your ad unit colors, you need a reference source of *hex codes,* which are six-digit numbers that pinpoint colors in HTML code. All browsers understand hex code. If you use a WYSIWYG (what you see is what you get) page builder, you can probably check the hex codes of the colors on your page by looking at the HTML view of that page. When customizing Google ad units, finding the page's background color is especially important. You can also use an online chart such as the one located here:

```
hotwired.lycos.com/webmonkey/reference/color_codes/
```

Each customized hex code is plugged into one of five lines of the Google AdSense code. Here is an example of those five lines:

```
google_color_border = "25314C";
google_color_bg = "25314C";
google_color_link = "FFFFCC";
google_color_url = "008000";
google_color_text = "999999";
```

You can recognize these color lines by the word color in each of them; that word doesn't appear anywhere else in the AdSense code. When you create a custom palette in your AdSense account, Google fills in those lines with hex code. Here, you're manually changing the hex code to better match your page design. Note that each line corresponds to a different element of the ad unit. You can customize five elements:

- border refers to the bottom bar and thin border extending around the ad unit

- bg refers to the background color of the ad unit

- link refers to the ad's headline, which is linked to the destination URL

- url refers to the display URL below the ad text

- text refers to the one- or two-line (depending on the display) ad text

In my experience, altering the border and bg elements makes the biggest difference when integrating ad colors with page colors. If you match both those colors to the page's background color, the ad unit seems to sink into the page. Figure 13-10 illustrates a page displaying the AdSense banner layout, displayed with the default Mother Earth colors. The border is light blue against the page's dark blue, and the ad background is white (although you can't see this in the grayscale screen shot). The ad unit stands out boldly against the page.

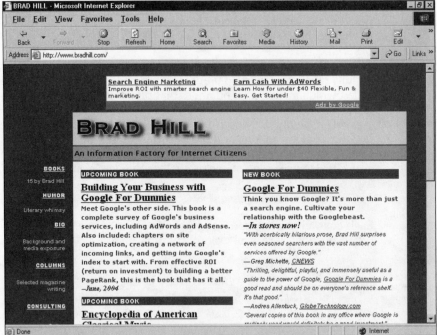

Figure 13-10:
Uncustom-
ized ad units
stand out
boldly from
the page.

Figure 13-11 shows the same page with customized ad colors; the border and background elements now match the page's background color. The ad colors in Figure 13-11 match the code in the example; the background color's hex code is 25314C. I altered the other elements too, but they don't matter as much. Making the border and background disappear into the page creates the important effect.

Be creative! If you combine customized colors with a specially prepared table cell, you can construct an ad display that blends in (and even enhances) your page's look-and-feel, while subtly calling attention to the ads. Figure 13-12 shows such a page; the ad unit sits in a specially built table cell with complementary colors. The ad's headline color matches the background color of the column below, and the background color exactly matches the overall black background of the page.

The question remains: Do slickly customized ad units *work* as well as uncustomized units? That question can be answered only by experimentation on a site-by-site basis. If your site pulls extremely relevant ads, and your visitors respond to ads best when they seem to blend into editorial content, customize away. If you prefer grabbing your visitors' attention forcefully, perhaps the ugliest possible ad display works best for you.

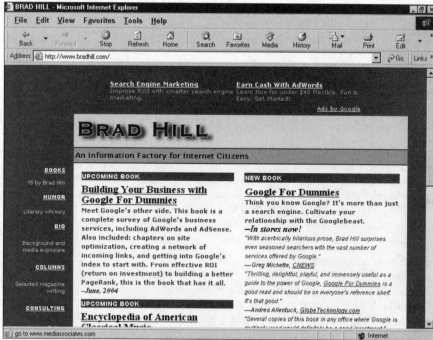

Figure 13-11:
A customized ad unit, with border and background colors matching the page's background, seems to sink into the page.

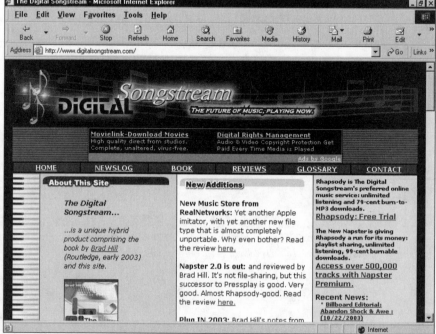

Figure 13-12:
The ad unit blends into the page yet looks distinctive, thanks to color management and a special table cell.

TIP

Don't be afraid to mix customized ad units with uncustomized units on the same site. (Only one ad unit per page, of course, per the AdSense terms of service.) Remember, part of defeating ad blindness is surprising your visitors' expectations.

When CTR doesn't matter

Some AdSense publishers don't give a hoot about CTR. To them, it's all about total revenue. This approach works well when the Webmaster adds new pages regularly. If the CTR slips downward, the deficit is made up by higher click volume. Rob Arnold, Webmaster of www.linear1.org, shares his experience:

"AdSense complements my content well. My readers clearly find it useful; the clickthrough rates reflect that. I had a significant body of text to begin with, and coherent navigation and layout. If you're starting up a site you'll need a few hundred thousand words of content, organized coherently, to achieve good results. I also spent a short time in the early stages investigating the impact of ad placement and color changes. But what has proven to be the most effective use of my time is producing quality content. If you can add a page a day of quality content to your site, that can matter more than tweaking your ad layout or positioning."

Rob Arnold's total AdSense presentation includes highly color-coordinated palettes and above-the-fold leaderboards, as shown in the figure. Custom colors can make ad units blend into the page as if they were part of the editorial content.

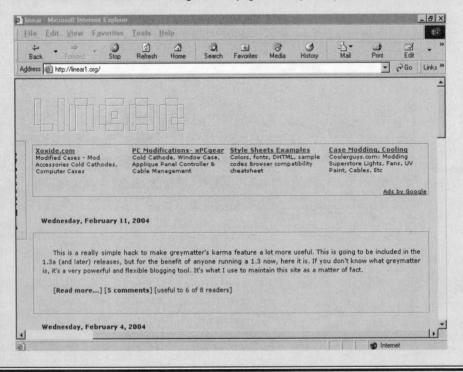

Filtering Ads

Understandably, you might not want to display AdWords ads from your competitors. If you and your competitors operate information sites, the competition doesn't matter as much — if a visitor clicks away from you to a competing site, you gain a bit of income without losing a sale. But if you sell products through your site, losing a sale for a clickthrough might not be good business. In that case, consider blocking your competitors' URLs. This type of filtering targets the destination URL of an AdWords ad, not the display URL. You have two basic methods at your disposal:

 ✔ Make a list of your known competitors, and filter out their home-page URLs.

 ✔ Systematically check the destination URLs of ads that appear on your pages, and keep adding competing URLs to your filter list.

Your best bet might be to combine the two methods: Start with a known list of competing URLs, and then keep your eye out for others.

When it comes to the easiest way of determining the destination URLs of any ad unit, disregard the complicated procedure provided in the AdSense Help section. Instead, just click the Ads by Google link at the edge of any ad unit. (You can do this on any AdSense page, not just your own.) A new browser window pops up with an explanation of AdWords that includes the URLs of the specific ad unit you clicked, as shown in Figure 13-13.

However you come up with your list — through your own knowledge of competitors or by vigilantly watching your ads and clicking Ads by Google — use the URL filter page in your AdSense account to maintain your list of blocked URLs. Follow these steps:

 1. **In your AdSense account, click the Settings tab.**

 2. **Click the URL filter link.**

 3. **Click the Add/Edit sites button.**

 4. **Type URLs into the box, one per line.**

    As shown in Figure 13-14, you add the URLs of sites whose ads you want to block from your site.

 5. **Click the Save changes button.**

    New filters should take effect within a few hours of adding them to your list.

Figure 13-13:
You can see the destination URLs of specific ad units.

Figure 13-14:
Add URLs of sites whose AdWords ads you do not want appearing on your pages.

When adding site URLs to your list, you can block the entire site by eliminating the *www.* prefix. Using the *www.* prefix tells Google to block that distinct page location, which is usually the index page of the filtered site. In that case, AdWords ads that point to an inner page as the destination URL can still be displayed on your sites.

Using Alternate Ads

In rare cases, Google can't deliver ads to an AdSense page. You might want to signify a stand-by ad source, or even a noncommercial image, to slip into the spot normally occupied by Google's ad unit. You may indicate that alternate source at any time in the AdSense account. Here's how:

1. **In the AdSense account, click the Setting tab.**

2. **Click the <u>Ad layout code</u> link.**

3. **Scroll down to the Alternate Ads box, and enter the *http://* destination of your alternate ad or image source.**

4. **Click the Update code button.**

5. **Copy and paste Google's updated script into your HTML document.**

Even though the Alternate Ads box is located on the Ad Layout Code page, along with choices of ad layout and palette, this setting has nothing to do with the ad layout or palette. But you must make the settings of the Ad Layout Code page conform to the ad settings used on your site page, so that the appearance of your ad units doesn't change when you paste the new code into your page.

Part IV
Google Business for the Larger Company

The 5th Wave   By Rich Tennant

©RICHTENNANT

"Just how accurately should my Web site reflect my place of business?"

In this part . . .

As a technology company, Google has built its business on the grassroots level with its AdWords and AdSense programs. And if offers premium programs for large accounts and enterprise-level search customers.

This part explains how companies can submit product information to Froogle, Google's shopping engine, and Google Catalogs, a service for mail-order houses. Chapter 14 offers detailed help with maximizing your products' exposure in Froogle.

The AdWords and AdSense programs both offer enhanced services for large companies. Chapter 15 is a summary those services. Custom search solutions are described in Chapter 15 as well.

Chapter 14

Getting into Froogle and Google Catalogs

*B*ecause of the huge amount of publicity doled out to AdWords and AdSense, you might think that Google's business services are only advertising services. Not true. Google is really in the exposure business, increasing visibility for both advertisers and sites listed in the Google indexes — including its two shopping indexes, the subjects of this chapter. To put Google's business services in an even broader light, you might say that Google is in the keyword business. As a keyword services company, Google brings together those who seek with those who provide, matching them through the powerful relevancy of keywords.

When it comes to seeking and providing, shopping is at the center of the mating dance, on equal footing with information and services. Froogle and Google Catalogs, Google's two keyword-based shopping portals, employ dedicated engines that match Google searchers to products on the Web (Froogle) and to products in mail-order catalogs (Google Catalogs).

The following section describes the kind of shopping portal Google aspires to be, and is.

Google as the Ultimate Shop Window

Through Froogle and Google Catalogs, consumers experience a digital twist on the time-honored pastime of window shopping. Rather than strolling from window to window, consumers gaze through the single Google window as its contents change on demand.

Froogle and Google Catalogs are hybrid directories/engines that respond to keyword searches. The main difference between Google's shopping services and those in other major portals is that Google doesn't get its hands on the money. Customers don't buy anything through Google. Both Froogle and Google Catalogs function purely as directories to products, sending consumers elsewhere to make their purchases.

Following are two important points for merchants:

- ✔ Google has no revenue-sharing arrangement with any merchant represented in either Froogle or Google Catalogs.
- ✔ Preferred placement in the search results for Froogle or Google Catalogs is not available.

Although you can't buy your way to the top of a Froogle or Google Catalogs search results page, Google does place AdWords ads on Froogle pages. Froogle ads might be the most powerful possible deployment of a product-oriented AdWords campaign because those ads share the page not with information links (as is likely on a Google search page), but with product links. Essentially, *every* link on a Froogle page is an ad, so AdWords ads don't stand out *as ads* to the same extent as on any other page.

If you're a merchant who wants to extend your AdWords campaign to Froogle, you need only set your ads to appear in Google's network of search sites, in the Campaign settings of your AdWords account (see Chapter 7). However, you can't limit your ads to Froogle pages — you must accept AdWords distribution throughout Google search pages. (See Chapters 6 through 10 for an extensive discussion of AdWords.)

Google doesn't assist you in setting up an e-commerce shop or transacting business. Compare this approach to Yahoo! Shopping, which is a virtual mall where any merchant can rent space. Yahoo! helps design and implement the online store and offers extensive transaction services, including a universal shopping cart and easy payment-data collection through Yahoo! Wallet. Banners of featured stores clutter the main pages. The underlying search engine has some smarts. All this is useful, and Yahoo! houses many of the most important online retailers in the business. AOL and MSN have similar programs.

You may operate your online store at Yahoo! Store (or in AOL or MSN) and still be represented in Froogle and in Google Catalogs. In fact, many Yahoo! Stores are included in Froogle thanks to a Yahoo! setting that makes the store's products compatible with Froogle's crawler. (The setting turns Yahoo! Store product information into something similar to a Froogle data feed, which I describe in the next section.) Besides the Yahoo! Store quirk, Google is store-agnostic; it doesn't care where you're located or who handles your transactions.

Systems like Yahoo!'s and AOL's, modeled on shopping malls, are purchase oriented. Google is search oriented. Google is not currently interested in selling products directly, taking payment information, or hosting stores. There's no Google Wallet.

The Google shopping portal is a search engine that separates products from stores to deliver targeted search lists. Furthermore, it uses evaluations similar to those in a Web search to determine which products matching your keywords are most important and should be listed first. Froogle and Google Catalogs recognize merchant branding but downplay it. The product is far more important than the store, because Google recognizes that priority in the minds of most shoppers. The pages of Froogle and Google Catalogs are as banner-free as all other Google pages, as you can see in Figures 14-1 and 14-2.

When it comes to buying through Google, *through* is the right word, as opposed to *from*. Froogle search results are like Web search results, insofar as they link you to target sites, in this case e-commerce sites with their own shopping carts and payment systems. Google Catalogs provides mail-order phone numbers and — where possible — links to Web sites.

Figure 14-1:
Froogle search results and AdWords ads.

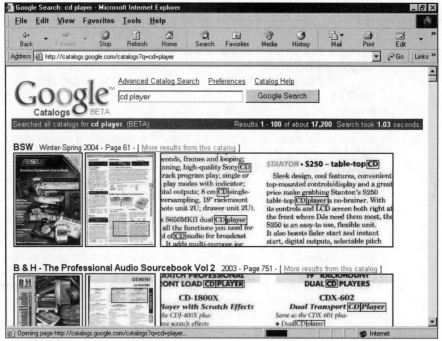

Figure 14-2:
Google
Catalogs
search
results.

Understanding Froogle's Index and Search Results

Getting into Froogle resembles getting into Google's Web index. Two methods are at your disposal:

- ✔ Let Froogle find your products
- ✔ Submit your products to Froogle

Submitting to Froogle is a more complicated affair than submitting a site URL to Google's Web index and requires a familiarity with database files. More on that a bit later.

Being crawled by Froogle

Froogle's strength, like that of Google's flagship service, lies in its crawling and ranking engine. This dedicated engine crawls deeply through the Web, as Google's Web spider does, and uses contextual analysis to find product pages. From those pages Froogle extracts categories of information — product type, name, description, price, and a photograph if there is one. Then Froogle ranks the page, places the product into a category of the Froogle directory, associates the page with keywords, and incorporates all this in its index. When a consumer searches Froogle by keyword, the crawled product appears in the results list according to its rank and relevancy.

Most of this index-building works remarkably well. Froogle is good at recognizing products and e-commerce pages in the colossal mass of Web content that it sifts through. If your product pages contain standard indicators of e-commerce, such as prices, references to a shopping cart, and product descriptions, Froogle can identify those pages as relevant to its mission and extract the information more or less accurately.

Will Froogle find the pages in the first place? Your visibility to Froogle is based on the same principles as your visibility to Google's Web index: Primarily, you must be linked to be found. Froogle finds products the same way Google's engines find anything — by crawling links. At least one link to your product page must exist, somewhere, for Google to make the connection. That link can come from your own site, as long as that site is represented in Google's Web index. If Google knows about you in the Web index, Froogle knows you exist also, and can put your products in the Froogle index.

Search results in Froogle

Froogle's search results are delivered in two categories:

- ✔ Confirmed results
- ✔ Total results

For the most part, confirmed results are submitted products. The rest of the total results (which I call unconfirmed results, but Froogle doesn't call anything) consist of product information extracted from the Web and assembled by Froogle's spider. Confirmed results are distinguished by three important features that merchants should be aware of:

- ✔ Confirmed results always appear first, above the unconfirmed results (refer to Figure 14-1).
- ✔ Confirmed results always include the store name.
- ✔ Confirmed results are always accurate, to the degree that they are submitted accurately. Unconfirmed results might be accurate too, but the merchant has only indirect control over their accuracy.

The separation of confirmed results from total results is a relatively new Froogle feature, and it puts pressure on merchants to submit their products lest they be dropped lower on the results list. The next section discusses the Froogle data feed by which products are submitted.

Froogle's eligibility rules

Froogle listings are free, and merchants are welcome to aggressively submit products to Froogle's index. A few requirements hold sway:

✔ You must be an e-merchant, and your site must transact sales online. Specifically, you must accept online payments. Merely promoting products on a Web site is not good enough if you require offline transactions such as phone orders or mail orders.

✔ You must transact payments in U.S. dollars.

✔ You must fulfill your orders yourself. The important point of this rule is: no affiliates.

For example, a member of the Amazon.com affiliate program may not put books from Amazon's catalog into Froogle, linking to the affiliate's site, from which users would click through to Amazon and generate a commission for the affiliate.

✔ You must specify product pricing on the product page of your site.

✔ You must sell a product, not a service. Your wares needn't be tangible — software is acceptable — but a travel agency, for example, is not suitable for Froogle.

Froogle search results default to the order in which Froogle ranks the product pages, displayed as a vertical list of links with pictures. Users can reorder Froogle results in various ways:

✔ **Grid view.** Arranging results in a grid displays more products "above the fold" — that is, before you have to scroll down the page (see Figure 14-3).

✔ **Sort by price.** Users may arrange results from low price to high, or high price to low.

✔ **Sort by price range.** Getting more specific about price sorting, users may define low and high prices in dollars. Froogle then displays products within that range.

✔ **Group by store.** This setting arranges Froogle results by merchant. Stores with higher PageRanks appear higher on the list, unless the user is sorting the page by price.

Froogle results are independent of Google Web results. You need not choose between the two indexes; neither blocks the other. Being listed in one index does not improve your rank in the other index.

Sometimes, however, Froogle items appear on Google Web search results pages. Google began promoting Froogle more assertively in December 2003, and placed Froogle results near the top of Web results for keywords related to products. Froogle listings placed atop Web search results are called *Product search results* (see Figure 14-4). This crossover is unpredictable: Some product-oriented keywords produce the Product search results while others do not. Even keywords that do generate Product search results do not necessarily display them every time.

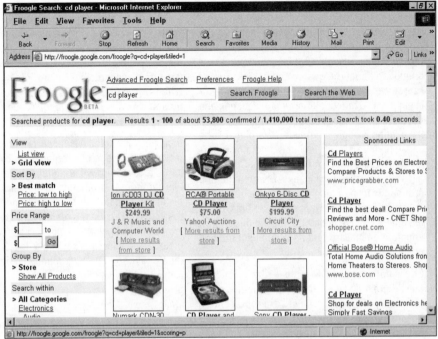

Figure 14-3:
Froogle
search
results in
grid view.

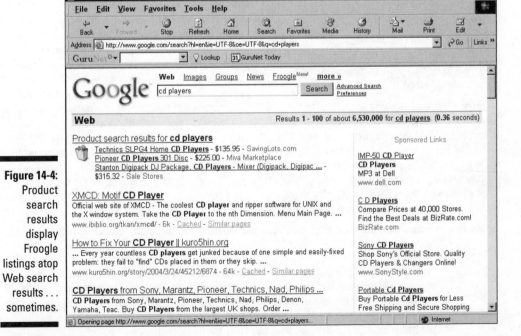

Figure 14-4:
Product
search
results
display
Froogle
listings atop
Web search
results . . .
sometimes.

The quality of Froogle searches

Portions of the Froogle merchant community are grumbling about the quality and consistency of search results. Froogle is a beta product, meaning that, while functional, it is still in a testing and development phase. As a consumer myself, I have found Froogle searches rewarding. In one instance, my sister-in-law could not find a certain lace tablecloth for her mother's Christmas gift after searching for weeks. My wife found it in seconds using Froogle. So Froogle can cut to the chase impressively. At the same time, many observers believe the technology of this search engine is immature and its results sometimes chaotic.

Size is not an issue in Froogle — the index contains a gigantic repository of product information, and many major retailers are represented. The main issue for merchants is the relevancy of results. Indeed, it's easy to bring up results pages whose products are less relevant and appealing than the accompanying AdWords ads in the right column. A recent search for *mp3 jukebox*, for example, returned several instances of one particular model atop the list — no other products appeared above the fold of an 800 x 600 screen. The accompanying AdWords ads linked to review-and-comparison sites where one might narrow the search more intelligently.

From this experience you might think that Froogle responds better to longer keyword phrases and keywords that include the exact model being searched (if you've already narrowed the search to an exact model). Indeed, searching for *archos jukebox recorder* (a model of mp3 jukebox) delivered more productive results, roughly on par with the accompanying ads. However, a recent search for *ipod* resulted in several top listings for an arm band accessory that fits on the iPod mp3 device, when one might have expected to find iPods themselves populating the top results.

Perplexing problems pop up when you spend time with Froogle. A search for *formal wear* yielded a full page of evening gowns and other items for women, while the accompanying ads were uniformly promoting tuxedo shops. Being a man, I found the ads far more compelling than the listings. The top ten results for the keywords *antique books* included a model of an antique car, a globe, a bookend, a set of old dolls, and a vintage post card. The accompanying ads offered Alibris.com, eBay, BookFinder.com, and other productive results.

The observation that Froogle's ad column often presents better results than the editorial listings leads to an oft-expressed wish in the merchant community for a cost-per-click model in Froogle. If that were the case, merchants would bid for position in the listings and pay for each clickthrough — very much like the AdWords program. Generally, sound business favors paying for a good service over tolerating a questionable service that's free. This is not to say that Froogle is useless by a long stretch. If it were, major companies would not bother making gigantic, regular submissions of their online product information. Companies of all sizes that track the sources of their incoming customers often find that Froogle generates respectable traffic and important sales. All the same, almost everyone believes that there's room for improvement in the Froogle engine.

Froogle ranking depends on an algorithm no more publicized than the Web index's PageRank. In fact, more mystery enshrouds Froogle's ranking. Nobody outside Google knows whether PageRank (from the Web index) has any sway in Froogle. I spoke to one merchant who created a new product page with no incoming links, and submitted that page's product to Froogle. Thanks to relevancy, a good category fit, price, and other factors, this merchant's product shot up to a top spot for certain keywords. Since the new page didn't exist in Google's Web index (the merchant did not submit it there, and without incoming links the spider could not have found it), the merchant concluded that Web PageRank doesn't exist as a factor in Froogle ranking. The possibility remains, though, that this merchant's product rode the coattails of its *site's* PageRank in the Web index, even if its specific product page had no PageRank.

The mystery remains. But two factors improve a merchant's product positioning in Froogle:

✔ Manual submission of product information

✔ Optimization of product pages

The following two sections cover these points.

Submitting Product Information to Froogle

The only advantage to submitting a site to Google's Web index is getting into the index — there are no additional advantages such as a higher or more accurate listing. If the spider can find your Web page without a manual submission, there's no advantage at all to submitting manually. Froogle is different. Submitting product information requires some work, rewarded by these advantages:

✔ Guaranteed inclusion in the Froogle index even if your products aren't already included.

✔ Fast, automated service — submitted information is included within a few hours at most, and sometimes within minutes.

✔ Assured accuracy, if the information you submit is accurate.

✔ Better placement on the Froogle results page. Before the separation of confirmed results from unconfirmed results (see the preceding section), better placement did not necessarily follow submission. Now, when the searcher is running default Froogle settings, submitted (confirmed) products always appear before unconfirmed products.

✔ Quick changes of your product lineup as represented in Froogle.

Submission to Froogle is accomplished in a data feed. Throughout this chapter, when I refer to submitting "your product," I mean product information — don't send actual products to Google. A Froogle *data feed* is a text document submitted to Froogle through FTP (file transfer protocol). This process sounds technical — and it is, somewhat.

Submitting to Froogle requires an acquaintance with database creation and FTP. It's beyond the scope of this book to instruct you in the creation of a database, especially because many different database programs are available. Likewise with FTP uploads. Furthermore, the details of creating the data feed, and the categories of product information it may contain, might change. For all these reasons, the best way to proceed is through Froogle's forms and instructions. I'll get to them in a moment. First, a few bits of information about what's in the data feed.

As I mentioned, the Froogle data feed is a simple text file. This text file is derived from a database file. You create the database file by inserting product information according to certain Froogle-approved categories (fields). Then you save the file as a *tab-delimited* text file. Just about all database programs offer this option in the Save window. After you have that tab-delimited text file containing your product information, you upload it directly to Froogle's FTP address (which is supplied to you when you request the data feed forms), using a unique username and password (also supplied to you).

Submitting a data feed is not a one-time event. Merchants may submit revised data feeds daily, weekly, or monthly. Some e-tailers even experiment with submitting multiple revised feeds during the course of a single day. These rapid-fire feeds are sometimes rejected, but there's no punishment for a rejected feed. In some cases, multiple daily feeds are accepted and take effect in the Froogle index quickly. Although submitting multiple feeds during the day leads to unpredictable results, merchants may certainly update their product information as frequently as every 24 hours. Anecdotal reports of latency (the amount of time required for updates to take effect) vary from near-instant to a few hours.

After submitting your first Froogle data feed, you're committed to a monthly update schedule. You may update more frequently, at your discretion. But you *must* update within a month, or the products represented in your latest feed disappear from the Froogle index. To retain your Froogle listings unchanged, simply upload the same data feed every month.

A Froogle data feed has seven standard product information fields:

- ✔ **Product URL.** The page at which your product resides. Froogle guidelines insist that a visitor be able to purchase the product from that very page. The page can't be merely promotional; it must be transactional.

- ✔ **Name.** The name of the product, which usually includes the brand and model number or name. You may allot up to 80 characters to the product name.

- ✔ **Description.** The product description may be as long as 1000 characters, but many fewer characters will be selected by Froogle for display on any search results page. The description text is selected automatically by the Froogle engine, based on its understanding of the description context and its match to the keywords used to bring up the results page.

✔ **Price.** The product's price.

✔ **Image URL.** Products sell better with pictures than without them. In this field, you insert the URL of the product's photograph on your server.

✔ **Category.** You may insert the category in which the product resides at your site, but merchants report greater visibility in search results when they identify the correct category in the Froogle directory for each product.

✔ **Offer ID.** This field contains a product-unique alphanumeric tag. This value must remain constant across all data feeds containing the product.

In addition to the standard product information fields, Froogle data feeds may contain any combination of several available extended fields. The *extended fields* offer slots to input additional product information such as shipping cost, product availability (yes or no), UPC code, color and size, quantity discounts, and the expiration date of an offer. Perhaps most important among the extended fields is the Product ID, which you can use with the Offer ID (see the preceding list). The Product ID represents groups of products, such as music CDs, and the Offer ID represents a single item. Read Froogle's current information on data feeds to find which extended fields it accepts.

When you upload a Froogle data feed, it ***fully updates*** the previous data feed. The new data feed ***does not supplement*** the previous data feed. Therefore, do not create a new data feed containing only new products if you still want the previous products to remain in Froogle. If you upload such a feed, Froogle replaces the old products with the new products. To supplement your product inventory on Froogle, create a new data feed containing the old products ***and*** the new products. (You may change the information fields of a continuing product, but use the same Offer ID as in the previous data feed.) To eliminate a product from your Froogle inventory, submit a new data feed containing all previous products except the one you want to remove.

You now have an overview of the Froogle data feed, but you need to get up-to-the-minute information and explicit instructions from Google. Remember, if you sell products online, you're probably already represented in Froogle. You don't *need* to submit a data feed. But your performance in the Froogle index — in other words, your Froogle visibility — will probably benefit from embarking on the monthly (at least) commitment to creating and uploading data feeds. Get started by filling out the on-screen form located here:

```
services.google.com/froogle/merchant_email
```

Optimizing for Froogle

Did you think I would end my discussion of Froogle without a section on optimization? I hammer home this subject throughout the book because it's an essential nail in the marketing edifice.

Google doesn't provide guidance about Froogle optimization, as it does (to a limited extent) for Web index optimization. But common-sense rules combined with anecdotal reports from Froogle merchants yield principles for creating product Web pages that Froogle ranks high on the results page.

It's (still) all about keywords

Keywords are at the heart of everything related to Google. Chapter 4 emphasizes the importance of identifying keywords as the first step in effective page optimization. That principle holds true for Froogle optimization. Read Chapter 4 to understand the principles of assigning core keywords to a page and embedding them in the page's content.

Principles of keyword optimization break down somewhat on the pages of e-commerce sites, mainly because those pages are often dynamically generated — their content is pulled from an underlying database, and the exact content depends on what the customer has clicked or entered. Static Web pages are unchanging and can be optimized individually. Most e-commerce sites display thousands of differing dynamic pages with certain common elements. Those elements, which are usually part of a site-wide template, can be optimized. Consider these points:

- ✔ Surround your product displays with commercial words such as *buy, cart, basket, product,* and *purchase,* dollar signs, and so forth.

- ✔ Insofar as keywords apply to your entire site, target keyword strings of two words and longer. Optimizing for specific searches results in higher placement on Froogle pages seen by your best prospects.

- ✔ Use brand names.

- ✔ Optimize your site's `meta` tags and link text according to the principles described in Chapter 4. In particular, use the `keywords` tag to include brand names you sell and product-specific keywords that you can't place on the text of individual pages.

Optimization is particularly important for merchants who do not submit Froogle data feeds and instead rely on the Froogle spider to find, understand, and rank product pages.

Create sales

One of the best ways to increase visibility on Froogle is to create product sales and submit the lowered prices in a Froogle data feed. Underselling competing merchants is a tactic with major visibility advantages:

✔ When a Froogle user isolates your product category and reorders the page by price (lowest to highest), you rise to the top of the page.

✔ When Google lists Froogle results on a Google Web search page for keywords relevant to your product, the three lowest-priced Froogle instances of that product tend to be the ones listed on the Google results page. Anecdotal reports strongly suggest that clickthrough rates for Froogle listings increase dramatically when the listings appear on Web search pages.

One way to lower prices is to extract products from packaged groups and list them separately on-site. Then create separate entries for each product in your Froogle data feed. You may, if you want, keep track of products broken out in this fashion by assigning each one the same Product ID but a unique Offer ID. If you don't submit data feeds, breaking out products on individual Web pages increases your visibility to Froogle's spider.

Optimizing your product description

Froogle snips descriptive material from the target page (or from the submitted data feed) for its list description just as Google does for its Web search listings. It is therefore important to optimize the descriptive text surrounding your product on the target page. Under no condition does Froogle excerpt more than 1000 characters of descriptive material. As you easily notice when browsing through Froogle, most descriptions are much shorter than 1000 characters. Remember, as with the Web results, Froogle selects excerpts that seem to match the keywords of the results page. To best optimize your descriptive content, remember these two rules:

✔ Keep the total description less than 1000 characters.

✔ Embed keywords in your description to target Froogle users searching for those keywords.

If you follow these two golden rules, none of your description will be lost to Froogle (first rule), and the relevant portion of your description will appear in Froogle's descriptive snippet of your product.

If you want to avoid having your product descriptions excerpted — in other words, if you want entire descriptions to appear — keep them short! Short means fewer than 200 characters. Follow this route only if keeping the description intact is more important than striving to match snippets to a range of keywords.

Two final optimization tips

Remember that the product category is a standard field in the Froogle data feed, and therefore open to experimentation. Informal merchant reports indicate that finding the right category has a vital influence on a product's position in search results.

Finally, if you're displeased with your Froogle positioning, search for your product and note which stores and items are listed first. Visit those pages and note how they are optimized. Emulate whatever principles seem evident — not to the extent, of course, of copying artwork.

Getting into Google Catalogs

Google Catalogs is a listing and search service for companies that sell mail-order products and publish mail-order catalogs. This section of the chapter is short, because getting into Google Catalogs and staying in its index is far simpler than in Froogle. In fact, a two-step process does the trick.

First, put Google on your catalog mailing list. Subscribe this address:

```
Google Catalogs
171 Main St. #280A
Los Altos, CA 94022
```

Then, write Google an e-mail notification of the incoming catalog. Write to

```
catalog-vendors@google.com
```

When Google receives your first catalog, it scans the entire thing and incorporates the content in Google Catalogs. Once in the index, your catalog (and subsequent editions received by Google) becomes fully searchable by keyword.

Google Catalogs does not link to specific product pages. The service does link to the merchant's main Web address, but that link is difficult to find. The primary mission of this service is to present scanned, searchable catalogs. For the most part, customers are converted, or not, in Google Catalogs — not on your Web site. If they want to purchase something, they call your order number like any other customer.

Chapter 15

Premium Services

. . . .

. . . .

*G*oogle provides premium versions of its three major programs for high-traffic and high-budget sites. Those three programs are AdWords (see Part II), AdSense (see Part III), and on-site Google searching (see Chapter 5). This chapter describes the high-end versions of these programs, premium AdWords, premium AdSense, Custom WebSearch, and Silver and Gold Search.

Premium AdWords

Google AdWords is not just for small businesses and entrepreneurs anymore. Small accounts put the program on the marketing map, but now corporations of all types are represented in the advertising column on Google search results pages. When Google eliminated its Sponsored Link program, which sold placement on a pay-by-impression basis, the corporate segment of its advertising clientele was rolled into AdWords — probably with little complaint. The efficiency and control afforded by AdWords applies just as happily to large companies as to small ones.

Large advertisers are eligible for a special program called premium-level AdWords. (No one, even the largest, most budgetarily advantaged advertisers, is forced to use the program.) Similar to regular AdWords, the premium program offers a more involved customer service experience throughout the campaign. Many a small-business owner wishes he or she could enjoy the service perks built into premium-level AdWords.

To qualify for premium-level service, AdWords advertisers must commit to spending a minimum of $30,000 over a three-month period and at least $10,000 per month. (There is no charge beyond the spending minimum.) Because AdWords is a pay-per-click system, a natural question arises: What if the company's ads don't generate $10,000 worth of clickthroughs in a month? After all, it can be difficult for little businesses to keep their clickthrough rates high enough to spend money seriously. This is where Google steps in.

Each premium AdWords account is assigned a customer service team that assists the client at every step, from soup to nuts. This level of assistance includes industry-specific marketing advice, creative help writing ads, hands-on account maintenance if desired, campaign structuring, keyword generation, account planning and optimization, performance analysis — basically, everything an excellent third-party agency would do when implementing an AdWords campaign for a client.

Conceiving of Google as a specialized ad agency brings up an interesting issue: Should a high-spending company operate in non-premium AdWords with the help of a hired ad agency? Or is it better to enter premium AdWords and let Google be your de facto agency? Going with Google saves money — that's one consideration right off the bat. However, if AdWords is part of a large, multifaceted marketing campaign, the ideal situation might be to manage the entire effort under one roof, which would not be Google's roof. Then again, just as Google doesn't manage non-AdWords aspects of the campaign, most traditional ad agencies do not specialize in AdWords. So getting it all under one roof — either Google's or a hired agency — is difficult.

A few miscellaneous notes about premium AdWords:

- ✔ Despite the special service provided to premium AdWords clients, Google doesn't bend basic AdWords rules. The ads are the same — small boxes of text. The competitive environment for placement on the page is identical to the competition faced by regular AdWords customers, and premium-level advertisers bid on keywords in the same fashion as non-premium-level users.

✔ The pay-for-placement Sponsored Links, which were once placed atop search results pages, no longer exist as pay-for-impression ads. AdWords ads receiving the top two spots on pages populated by ten ads go in those top-of-page slots, but they're paid for by the click just like any AdWords ad. Premium-level AdWords doesn't offer pay-for-placement service.

✔ Just as with regular AdWords, participation in premium AdWords doesn't affect a site's listing or PageRank in Google's Web index.

✔ Although account management is offered to premium-level accounts, those clients are free to use the standard AdWords reporting and administrative tools available to everyone.

If your company is interested in the premium level of AdWords and meets the spending commitment requirement, you notify Google of your interest by filling in an on-screen form. The form, shown in Figure 15-1, requests basic contact, industry, and URL information and serves as an introductory letter to Google. Find that form here:

```
services.google.com/ads_inquiry/en
```

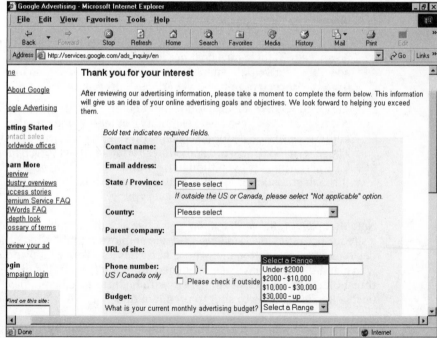

Figure 15-1:
This form serves as an introductory letter to Google for prospective premium-level AdWords customers.

Premium AdSense for Content Sites

As it does with AdWords, Google offers a premium-level version of AdSense. Because AdSense publishers at any level do not pay Google, the requirement for breathing the thin air of premium membership is not a financial commitment, but a traffic threshold. Sites serving at least 20 million page views per month (not unique visitors, but total page views) are eligible to apply.

Whereas premium-level AdWords provides essentially the same AdWords features but with enhanced customer service, premium-level AdSense for content sites differs a bit from standard AdSense. These variations include the following:

✔ Custom ad layouts and formats diverge from the presets in regular AdSense. However, many premium publishers use the standard ad layouts. (See Figures 15-2 and 15-3.)

✔ Dedicated account management is available, offering site optimization and technical support as needed.

✔ Standard AdSense allows publishers to block ads from competitive domains (see Chapter 13). In premium AdSense, competitive filtering of unwanted ads is a more serious and robust tool.

✔ The AdSense for content program pays selected publishers to sell their ad space to Google on a cost-per-impression basis for running AdWords ads. Prospective publishers must qualify for this program independently from the normal premium-level AdSense program.

✔ Although regular AdSense publishers enter, start, pause, and exit the program at will (given basic eligibility), at least some premium clients contract with Google for a certain term (for example, six months). These term contracts are sometimes terminated by Google for poor CTR performance. Even though the publisher is not aware of the click-through statistics associated with ads appearing on the publisher's site, Google definitely keeps track of everything.

Note that page traffic of 20 million views per month doesn't necessarily qualify a site for premium-level AdSense. Google employs unpublicized criteria when deciding who is admitted and who is not. I have spoken with owners of sites who claim that they have been declined although their traffic exceeds the threshold. Other AdSense publishers with high traffic claim to have received unsolicited invitations to shift to premium AdSense.

Interested companies may start the application process by filling in an introductory on-screen form here:

```
services.google.com/ads_inquiry/ct?hl=en
```

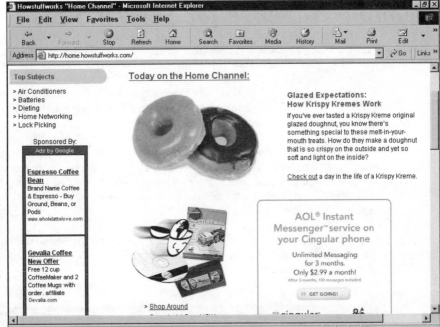

Figure 15-2:
Premium
AdSense
publishers
may use
slightly
modified ad
layouts not
available in
standard
AdSense.

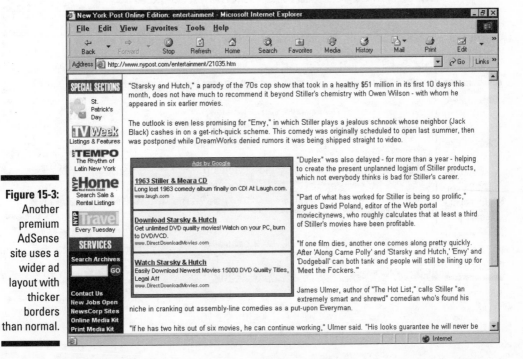

Figure 15-3:
Another
premium
AdSense
site uses a
wider ad
layout with
thicker
borders
than normal.

Premium AdSense for Search Sites

Premium-level AdSense is available to search portals in formats that don't resemble normal AdSense publishing. Just as Google sometimes displays AdWords ads at the top of its own pages (and that format is not available to AdSense publishers), so too does Google provide layout alternatives to other search engines who want to share Google's advertising engine and revenue. AOL Web Search is a good example; this major portal licenses both editorial search results and related advertising from Google. AOL's entire search results page is driven by Google engines, yet it's displayed in AOL's proprietary formats and page templates. (See Figure 15-4.) Amazon.com is an example of a destination portal that functions as a search site thanks to its massive traffic, and uses Google engines to deliver both objective and pay-per-click search results. (See Figure 15-5.)

Google supplies this specialized version of premium AdSense to Netscape, Excite, AskJeeves.com, Go.com, About.com, Teoma, iWon.com, Disney, and many others.

Figure 15-4:
AOL Web
Search is a
high-profile
client of
premium
AdSense,
displaying
pay-per-
click ads on
its result
pages.

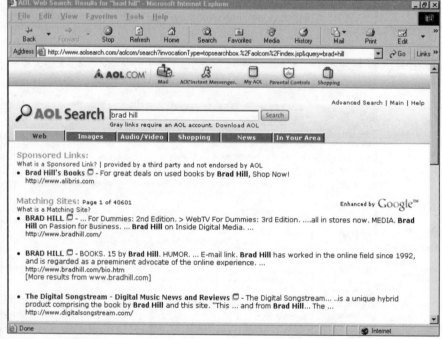

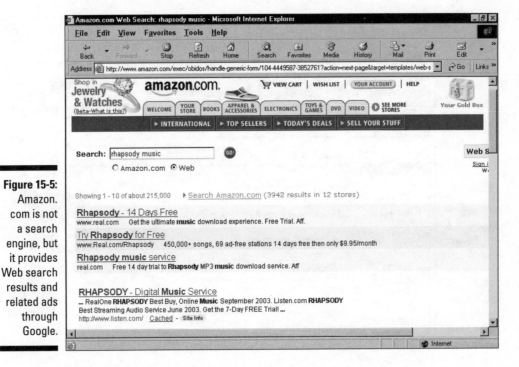

Figure 15-5:
Amazon.
com is not
a search
engine, but
it provides
Web search
results and
related ads
through
Google.

Custom WebSearch

In the preceding section I discuss the premium AdSense program for search sites, which delivers Google AdWords on search results pages presented at large sites with search engines. Google's Custom WebSearch is similar, except it provides editorial search results, not ads. Custom WebSearch enables a site with sufficient traffic to become a search destination, with results provided by Google. This program is a premium version of Google's free search, which is described in Chapter 5.

Custom WebSearch is acquired through a licensing arrangement with Google. A company gets started by sending Google an online form located here:

```
services.google.com/licensing/request
```

Custom WebSearch works similarly to Google's free search service: The client site puts a search box on its pages. When users enter a search, the keywords are sent to Google, which returns results to the host site. The host site then presents the results on its site, formatted to look like that site. The results don't necessarily look much like Google (see Figure 15-6), but it is Google.

Figure 15-6: Custom WebSearch results are formatted with the host site's look-and-feel.

Most of the familiar features of Google, including Advanced Search, Similar Pages, and site descriptions, are available to Custom WebSearch clients.

Note: Custom WebSearch sites may sell advertising on search results pages. An easy way to monetize those pages is through Google's AdSense for content program. But if a site is already in the advertising business, delivering search results pages is a swift method of dramatically increasing the site's advertising inventory to its existing advertisers and agencies.

Silver and Gold Search

Two on-site Google search programs are available to sites with solid search traffic but less traffic than Custom WebSearch clients: Silver Search and Gold Search. These two services are similar to Google's Free Search described in Chapter 5. As with Free Search, Silver and Gold customers place a Google search box on their pages, and their users are taken to Google for semicustomized search results. Three major differences distinguish Silver and Gold Search from Free Search:

✔ The Silver and Gold results are more customizable than in Free Search. Free Search users may place a logo atop the search results and modify colors. Silver and Gold customers may create an elaborate header and footer for their pages, extending those elements into full-blown HTML tables that include sidebars.

✔ Silver and Gold customers may serve advertisements on the search results pages.

✔ The Silver and Gold services are not free.

The monthly fee distinguishes Silver from Gold. At the time of this writing, Silver Search costs $599 per month, plus $10 per thousand search queries over one million per year. Gold Search, which is designed for sites that normally experience more than four million queries per year, costs $1999 each month plus $8 per thousand queries over four million per year.

Google doesn't allow Silver and Gold Search pages to display AdWords ads or any other advertising on results pages. Sites that have implemented Custom WebSearch, however, may sell their own keywords advertising against search results.

Part V
The Part of Tens

The 5th Wave   By Rich Tennant

"This is a 'dot-com' company, Stacey. Risk-taking is a given. If you're not comfortable running with scissors, cleaning your ear with a knitting needle, or swimming right after a big meal, this might not be the place for you."

In this part . . .

Carrying on the *For Dummies* tradition, this part gathers lists of destinations and tips that don't fit elsewhere in the book.

The first chapter spotlights ten site optimization resources. The second chapter is gold: SEM (search engine marketing) tips from the pros. These are the folks who run optimization companies and consulting services. You might not end up hiring them for your optimization and search-marketing needs, but they give away some of their hard-won wisdom in these pages.

Chapter 16

Ten Site Optimization Resources

*O*ptimizing your Web site is not a Google-exclusive tactic. A site optimized according to globally recognized standards attains better stature than a non-optimized site in every search engine. The SEO (search engine optimization) field predates Google's index and PageRank algorithm. Living as we do in the Google era, however, SEO is mainly concerned with Google-specific page optimizing. In this regard, most professional optimizers are one of two types: general optimizers who work across the board or Google optimizers.

The truth is, optimizing exclusively for Google is needlessly fanatical. First, Google doesn't publicize its algorithm tweaks and the subsequent recalculations of PageRanks and reordering of search results. Following a silent but influential Google upgrade, wails of anguish from Webmasters around the world can be heard as their sites drop from previously hard-won positions. As a community, Google optimizers try to figure out what changed and how to reoptimize their domains. This manic-depressive process is ongoing and necessary, but it probably shouldn't be the only page-tweaking task on your plate.

Second, and the main reason that general optimization is the way to go, all important search engines respond well to the same basic optimization improvements. If your site needs an optimization overhaul, chances are the most basic spider-friendly improvements will dramatically raise your visibility in Google — and in any other index that lists your site.

Hitch your wagon carefully

This chapter spotlights optimization sites, tools, gadgets, and more. When following these suggestions and exploring on your own, you're bound to encounter some strong come-ons from optimization companies and specialists. SEO is a competitive field, especially with the Google feeding frenzy. Some optimization pitches resemble get-rich-quick spam. Outlandish promises are followed by unrealistic (and probably untrustworthy) guarantees. However, I'm not one to throw out the baby with the bathwater. (Who coined that barbaric expression?) Plenty of great optimization specialists are just a link away. You just need to know the telltale signs to avoid.

Guarantees of any sort should set off alarms in your head. Google's indexing can lead to unpredictable results — and no optimizer can seriously promise a specific search ranking or ad position. The more dramatic the guarantee, the less you should trust it. Guaranteed number-one placement on a search results page is frankly absurd. You might indeed claim the top spot for certain keywords, but don't believe anyone who promises you such a thing. Another enticement is the promise of placement on the first page of listings — this is both unrealistic and a bit sleazy. The first results page in Google can be as short as 10 listings or as long as 100, depending on the user's Preferences setting.

Automated optimization is troublesome. Certain handy tools automate the creation of meta tags; I cover these tools in this chapter and they're fine. Automated measurements — of keyword density and crawler readiness, for example — might or might not be accurate or helpful, but they're not dangerous. But automated rank-checking engines violate Google's terms of service and can get your site into hot water. Optimization is mostly a hands-on affair. Some SEO companies sell software packages that assist the process with a combined set of online and offline tools. Various invasive elements can be planted in your computer whenever you install a new program, and I've never found it necessary or desirable to employ desktop applications when optimizing.

Speaking of automation, some companies offer bulk submissions to hundreds of search engines. According to traffic measurement statistics, more than 95 percent of all search engine traffic derives from a handful of top engines. Hiring somebody to bulk-submit your site globally might not be the best investment.

Link farming (see Chapter 3) is not optimizing. Be wary of any SEO company that proposes mutual links between its site and yours.

Finally, understand the difference between optimized results and paid results. Some search engines (not Google) accept fees for placement *in* their search results (not off to the side). Nothing is inherently unethical in this business model, even though it did give the entire search industry a bad reputation in the 1990s. But a lack of ethics is at play when an optimization consultant spends your money gaining paid placement in some search engines instead of spending it working up the Google results page. Sometimes this strategy is used to fulfill a promise of top-page search listing — a promise that should never be made to begin with.

Google optimization, as a specific tactic, comes into play when a Webmaster limits the entire marketing plan to Google. There's nothing wrong with that at Google's current levels of traffic. (See Chapter 1 for a discussion of Google's competition and the prospects for the future.) Another example of Google-specific optimization is a highly optimized site that tweaks its page features specifically to eke out better returns from Google. In both cases, optimizations made for Google tend to help in other search engines, just as general optimization helps in Google.

The resources suggested in this chapter fall into three categories:

- ✔ **Do-it-yourself optimization.** These sites offer tutorials, interactive tools, directories, and other resources, some of which might cost money. Don't expect consulting, site management, or individualized optimization reports.

- ✔ **Don't-do-it-yourself optimization.** These companies and individuals cater to Webmasters and businesses that don't want to master optimization fundamentals or plunge their hands into code and keywords. This category also includes many of the questionable SEO practices that leverage their clients' naiveté and need to outsource, promising unrealistic results and employing unwholesome strategies. At the same time, this space is where you find the many honest, smart, and skilled optimization specialists who can deliver personalized site evaluations for a reasonable cost, tighten your code, deepen your keyword identity, and multiply your Google-derived leads in a single crawl cycle. Don't be afraid of SEO specialists; just be cautious.

- ✔ **Hands-on tools.** Online gadgets! Keyword analyzers, `meta` tag generators, page evaluators, and other interactive assistants populate this category. These tools are for the do-it-yourself crowd.

Some sites cover all three bases. SEO specialists usually (but not always) include some do-it-yourself content on their sites.

Search Innovation

www.searchinnovation.com

Search Innovation is a search engine marketing company with a strong optimization streak. Two sections of this site generously provide information: the Articles and Resources sections.

The site's articles, mostly written by founders Daria and Dale Goetsch, are detailed, serious, and informative. These pieces cover such topics as effective keywords, "organic" SEO (the practice of optimizing toward high placement in search listings, as opposed to purchasing placement on search pages), optimizing dynamic pages (a tricky subject many optimizers don't go near), link building, SEO myths, crawler methods, building site maps, writing effective link text, and content writing.

The articles at this site are enough to get this site mentioned in this chapter, but the Resources page shines just as brightly. Here you find a directory of forums, newsletters, blogs, interactive tools, seminars, and Web sites that are resourceful in other ways.

HighRankings.com

www.highrankings.com

Operated by Jill Whelan, an optimization consultant, the HighRankings site is distinguished by a friendly atmosphere, a generous allotment of free articles, a free, almost-weekly newsletter, and a discussion forum dedicated to optimization.

The High Rankings Advisor newsletter, contains articles by Whalen and guest writers. Many of these pieces are archived in the Advisor Articles section; new and mid-level optimizers would do well to read through the whole lot of them. The articles tend to be detail-oriented, with, for example, entire tutorials devoted to a single `meta` tag. You can also find great information about getting framed sites indexed in Google, submitting to directories, and other basic tasks sometimes ignored by high-pressure optimization shops. HighRankings.com maintains a vigorous do-it-yourself sensibility, even as it offers site evaluations, writing services, and content editing.

The discussion forum is possibly the most thorough and SEO-dedicated set of message boards anywhere. This forum hosts well over 1000 topics and about 15,000 messages covering every possible aspect of site optimization. (See Figure 16-1.)

Jill Whalen is an active participant and friendly moderator of the voluminous Webmaster chatter. Conversations, like the articles, tend toward technical details. Participants use the space to work out fine points of site coding, CSS style sheets, supplementary programs that bundle code in spider-friendly ways, strategies for organizing page elements at the code level, and so forth. I recommend the HighRankings forum most highly to serious optimizers and Webmasters at all levels who have questions.

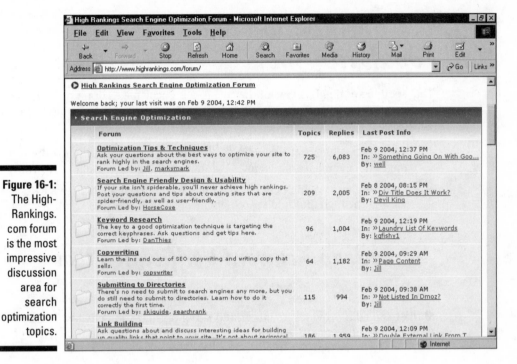

Figure 16-1:
The High-
Rankings.
com forum
is the most
impressive
discussion
area for
search
optimization
topics.

Mediumblue.com

Newsletters and newsletter archives are a terrific resource for optimization tips. Beyond the sheer informational value, receiving newsletters sparks continued work on your site, reminding you that optimization is an ongoing (frankly, never-ending) occupation. True, you can't avoid repetition when scanning dozens of articles, but sometimes we need to be nudged repeatedly to do our online chores.

Medium Blue is an optimization and marketing consultancy with a free monthly newsletter. Less chatty and varied than Jill Whalen's High Rankings Advisor (see the preceding section), the Medium Blue sheet is informative in its formal way. Each newsletter is a single article utterly lacking in chatter, ads, links, and other distractions.

Past editions are archived back to November 2001, forming a useful knowledge bank covering subjects as diverse as keywords (of course), evaluating site performance, monitoring search engine positions, long-term techniques to attain high rankings, and site traffic analysis. Broad rather than detailed, the articles don't divulge finicky matters of HTML tagging or keyword density. One newsletter from 2003 contains an interview with the founder of Wordtracker (see Chapter 4).

Keyword Verification and Link Popularity Tools

This section spotlights a few interactive tools. These pages don't provide optimization tools per se, such as `meta` tag generators. Rather, these gadgets check on the results of your optimization efforts in two areas:

- ✔ Keyword verification, which checks a URL's presence on the results pages of several search engines, when searching for certain keywords
- ✔ Link popularity, which checks the number of incoming links to a URL, as viewed through multiple search engines

Marketleap Keyword Verification tool

www.marketleap.com/verify

Marketleap.com provides an integrated set of optimization checks. The two tools described here are beautifully designed and create elegant displays of results. These gadgets are free to use.

Figure 16-2 shows the Keyword Verification tool. It tells you whether your site (or specific page) is returned in the search results of 11 major search engines and, if so, on what search results page it appears. (The definition of a results page is not provided; my experiments indicate that a page probably equals 10 results.)

Follow these steps:

1. **Enter a URL.**

   If you're checking an inner page of your site, you don't need to enter the full address of that page, although it doesn't hurt to do so. Marketleap finds inner-page matches to your keywords to whatever extent the tested search engines can find them.

2. **Enter a keyword or phrase.**

   Type whatever you've optimized for, as if a Google user were searching for that phrase. You're likely to get more encouraging results if you enter a phrase, not a single word. Placing quotes around the phrase, for an exact match to word order, creates more hits, but doesn't necessarily create a realistic report of your site's visibility to the average Google user.

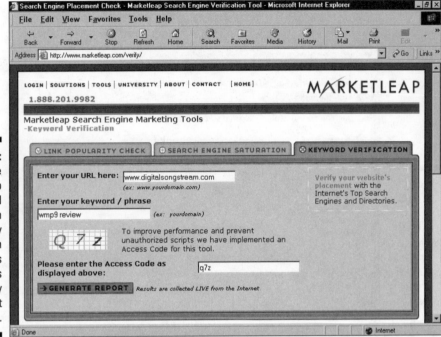

Figure 16-2:
The
Marketleap
Keyword
Verification
tool, ready
to search
the engines
for a site's
visibility
against
keywords.

3. **Enter the displayed access code.**

   Simply type the code that appears in colored letters. Forcing users to replicate the code prevents this tool from being overused by automated scripts.

4. **Click the Generate Report button.**

   A moment after the results first appear, they're redrawn in a table, as shown in Figure 16-3.

Note in Figure 16-3 that some engines match your keywords with a targeted inner page (in this example, the page that's best optimized for the keyword phrase), and other engines can't see that deeply. Google has crawled the site carefully, but AltaVista has not.

Marketleap doesn't check any engines beyond the third page. If your page doesn't appear in the results table, the omission is not necessarily an indicator that your page has not been crawled by that engine. However, it does indicate that the page is not optimized powerfully for that engine. In the context of this book, Google is the top priority, so all is well with the results shown in Figure 16-3.

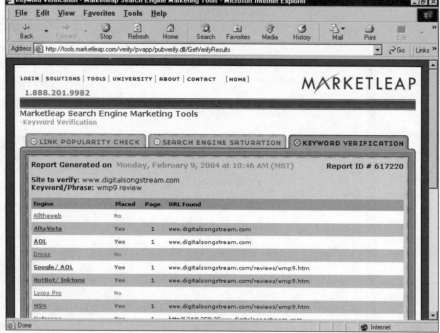

Figure 16-3:
Results
of the
Keyword
Verification
test. Some
engines see
the inner
page; some
do not.

Marketleap Link Popularity Check

www.marketleap.com/publinkpop

Marketleap's second optimization tool measures your incoming link network (see Chapter 3). In an attractive twist, this little engine also lets you compare your main link with three comparison URLs, as shown in Figure 16-4.

Finally — and this goes above the call of duty — the results page fills in gaps by supplying total incoming links for many other URLs, providing a broad context in which to evaluate your site. The result can be discouraging, but here goes:

1. **Enter your site's URL, and then enter three comparison URLs.**

   In both cases, enter the exact page you want to compare, with the understanding that in most cases it should be the home, or index, page. Most incoming links aim straight for the front door. However, if you have been optimizing and networking an inner page, this is the place to check out the results.

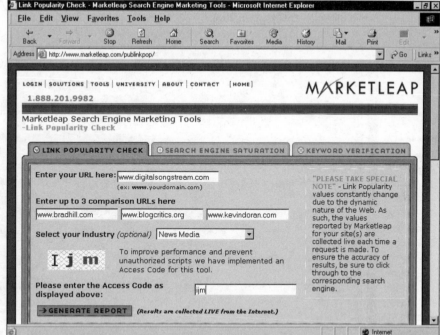

Figure 16-4:
The Link
Popularity
Check,
ready to
compare
the backlink
totals of four
sites in five
search
engines.

2. **Select an industry from the drop-down list.**

   This selection determines the nature of the fill-in sites that Marketleap provides on the results page. The more accurately you choose the industry, the more meaningful the context of your results.

3. **Enter the access code.**

   Again, this step blocks automated scripts.

4. **Click the Generate Report button.**

   Wait a few seconds for the results to appear on your screen. This tool is usually slower than the Keyword Verification device.

Figure 16-5 illustrates a results table. You see only part of the table; the comparison results continue down the page, ending with media juggernaut CNN.com and its impressive 6.6 million backlinks.

Note that Google often shows fewer incoming links than the other four search engines in the table. It can be a shock to think that your site's hard-won backlinks are incompletely represented in Google. Actually, Google doesn't necessarily divulge all incoming links in its index for a given page.

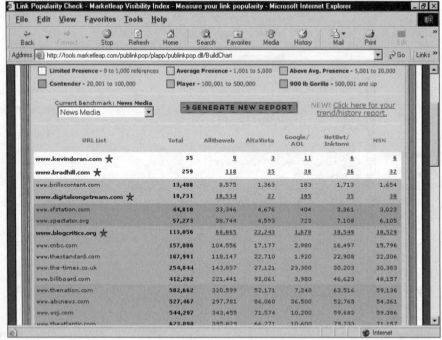

Figure 16-5:
The Link
Popularity
Check
results
table. You
can search
again
against a
different
comparison
industry.

Google excludes similar results, which, in many cases, means inner pages of sites. Those inner pages might be in your own site, if you generate a lot of your own incoming links (most sites do). Furthermore, Google (at its discretion) excludes the display of incoming links with low PageRanks. The result of these omissions can make it seem that other engines do a better job of assessing a site's backlink network. That might or might not be true in any given crawl cycle. The more common truth is that Google withholds some results of some searches using the `link:` operator. Google explicitly warns Webmasters not to trust the `link:` operator (used here for Google's column in the results table) for a full backlink picture. The value of this table lies in the comparisons it affords.

From the search results table, use the drop-down menu to run the search again against a different industry.

Mike's Link Popularity Checker

`www.mikes-marketing-tools.com/link-popularity/`

An alternative to the Marketleap tool described in the preceding section, Mike's backlink checker does not include results from HotBot but adds Teoma to the mix. Google, of course, is included. The results are packaged in an attractive table, and several preset sites from diverse industries are checked along with yours, for comparison, as shown in Figure 16-6. Google is one of those comparative sites — notice that Google's assessment of its own backlink network is much lower than the networks of MSN, AllTheWeb, and AltaVista.

Mike's backlink checker conveniently remembers the five URLs you last searched. Each search after your first includes the results for your previous five searches.

When you get to the page listed in the URL, scroll down a bit to find the Link Popularity Check button and URL entry box.

TopSiteListings.com

```
http://www.topsitelistings.com/optimization.php
```

TopSiteListings is an optimization consultancy with an abundance of do-it-yourself information on the site. The preceding link leads you directly to a section of the News & Article archive devoted to optimization.

Your Link Popularity Report - Microsoft Internet Explorer

Your report is being processed. Please wait...
If you're still waiting after 60 seconds, please close this window and try again.

Your Link Popularity Report

Created by www.Mikes-Marketing-Tools.com ▢ Searched URL ▢ Last 5 Searched URLs

Notes: Divide Google results by 2 to get the actual number of incoming links. The stats don't really mean much. What is important is that your site's link popularity is higher than your competitors'.

Site URL	Google	MSN	AllTheWeb	AltaVista	Teoma	Total
http://www.digitalsongstream.com	105	16	18,768	27	205	19,121

Compared to other sites...

Site URL (Check Time)	Google	MSN	AllTheWeb	AltaVista	Teoma	Total
http://www.google.com (02/09/2004 - 02:15 PST)	307,000	2,312,571	18,661,506	5,064,016	184,200	26,529,293
http://www.yahoo.com (02/09/2004 - 02:46 PST)	537,000	2,508,866	7,098,795	2,184,159	82,700	12,411,520
http://www.alltheweb.com (01/04/2004 - 08:26 PST)	27,800	237,613	5,802,356	303,707	22,200	6,393,676
http://www.harvard.edu (01/02/2004 - 07:41 PST)	32,200	31,815	164,587	54,889	6,560	290,051
http://www.ezskins.com (02/01/2004 - 05:59 PST)	706	1,090	57,288	6,482	569	66,135
http://www.psychology.org/ (09/05/2003 - 05:21 PST)	611	1,552	14,767	3,431	894	21,255
http://www.digitalsongstream.com (02/09/2004 - 19:01 PST)	105	16	18,768	27	205	19,121
http://www.mikes-marketing-tools.com (02/09/2004 - 07:15 PST)	348	230	10,357	2,618	148	13,701

Figure 16-6: Results of Mike's Link Popularity Checker.

These articles are for serious, technically minded Webmasters. The articles don't shy away from thorny subjects such as dynamic page optimization and using your server logs as optimization indicators. Mathematical formulas are sometimes used to convey a point. This archive might be the spot where you find answers to nagging questions, such as how to optimize a graphical site without devolving to all text, thus destroying its look and feel. TopSiteListings, as a company, responds quickly to Google emergencies such as the late-2003 algorithm change that sent many top listings plummeting down the search results page. Bookmark this page and check it often. New articles are posted weekly, more or less.

SEO Consultants Directory

www.seoconsultants.com/

SEO Consultants is what it says it is, and more. Although the site focuses on SEO issues, the company also consults on the larger field of search engine marketing. The directory published at this site is excellent. Click the SEO Resources button in the left navigation panel to get started.

This site provides a definite rarity: a Froogle optimization tutorial. Click the Froogle SEO button in the left navigation bar. If that button doesn't exist when you read this, try the following link:

www.seoconsultants.com/articles/1383/froogle-optimization.htm

Search Engine World Tools

www.searchengineworld.com/misc/tools.htm

Search Engine World is a terrific search marketing resource that every Webmaster should know about. Here, I want to point you to three tools related to optimization.

Webpage Size Checker

You don't need a special tool to see the file size of your Web page; a quick glance on your hard drive can tell you that. But this gadget gives you more than just the raw file size, as shown in Figure 16-7.

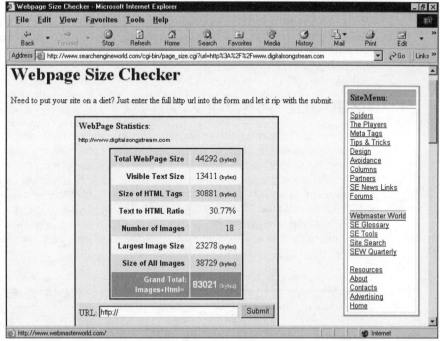

Figure 16-7:
The
Webpage
Size
Checker
results.

Below the Total WebPage Size in the results table are three related statistics: Visible Text Size, Size of HTML Tags, and Text to HTML Ratio. In Figure 16-7, you can see that the text in the HTML tags (all of which are listed below the table) outsizes the text on the page body by more than two to one. Troubling? Well, it depends on the page's intent. Low text-to-HTML ratios often indicate pages hosting many links, because links take up a lot of HTML space. So a directory page, for example, *should* have a low text-to-HTML ratio.

The next three statistics in Figure 16-7 are also related to each other: Number of Images, Largest Image Size, and Size of All Images. From the standpoint of usability and optimization, you want these numbers to be low: few images (because the Google crawler doesn't understand what the images are saying), small images, and low total size of images (for the user's benefit when loading the page).

Sim Spider

Sim Spider presents a view of any Web page as a search engine spider sees it. Spiders also crunch the page down into a compressed index form, which you don't see.

Figure 16-8 shows what Sim Spider looks like after it has finished surveying a page. The illustration shows only a small part of a moderate-sized page. Beneath the text summary is an inventory of every link on the page. You can launch a Sim Spider crawl through that link with a single click.

Keyword Density Analyzer

The Keyword Density Analyzer, shown in Figure 16-9, is frequently used by Webmasters who optimize. This famous, indispensable gadget crawls whatever page you put into it and computes the frequency with which your chosen keywords appear on the page. Keyword density is usually regarded as a crucial optimization consideration. Generally, the more dense, the better. This means that the more instances of your keywords on the page, the more readily Google can understand what the page is about and rank it accurately. However, too many mentions of a keyword can be interpreted as spam by Google, serving to lower the page's rank rather than raise it.

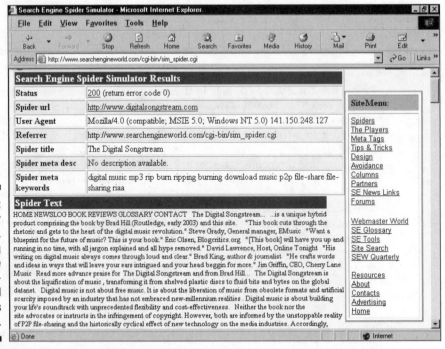

Figure 16-8:
Sim Spider results, summarizing a Web page with all formatting and graphics removed.

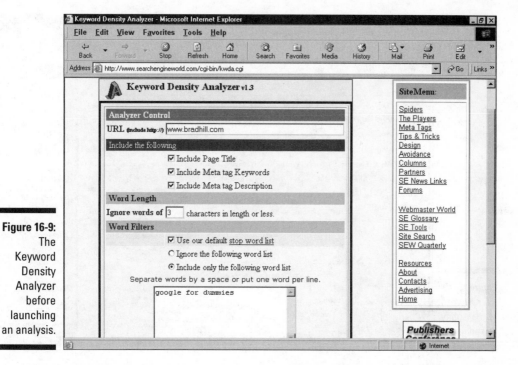

Figure 16-9:
The
Keyword
Density
Analyzer
before
launching
an analysis.

Figure 16-9 shows this tool just before launching a search. Note the following:

- ✔ It is important to include the page title, `meta` keywords, and `meta` description in the analysis. Remember that the density should be much higher in those fields.

- ✔ The default word length is set to four letters and above; this is reasonable. I've never changed it.

- ✔ Using the stop word list prevents small words from mucking up your results. Click the <u>stop word list</u> link to see a complete list of excluded words.

- ✔ For a general analysis of every word that appears on your page, select the radio button next to Ignore the following word list. To analyze specific keywords, select the radio button next Include only the following word list, and then enter your keywords in the box.

Figure 16-10 shows the keyword density results. Note that the engine analyzes all possible variations of your keywords, even if they make no sense. Those tables can be ignored.

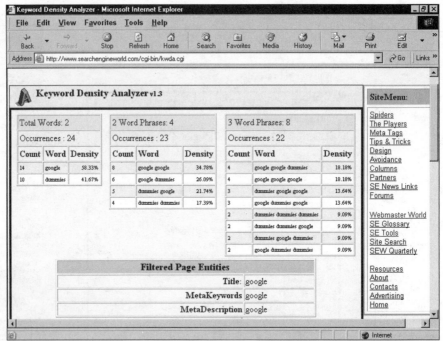

Figure 16-10:
A Keyword Density analysis.

JimWorld

www.jimworld.com

Another articles-and-forums site, JimWorld is stronger in the latter department. A slim but useful selection of articles leads to a fine optimization forum
featuring four major discussion areas and about 60,000 messages divided into
some 8000 topics. Registration is free.

Finding SEO forums

Optimization results are hard-won, involving
fastidious work and patience while waiting for
its rewards. Community forums are wonderful
places for would-be and experienced optimizers to visit. Finding a home in one or more of
these forums gives you someplace to go when
you need a question answered. Beyond that
convenience, the message boards make good
and informative reading.

The best communities maintain a topical focus
broader than just site optimization, ranging over
the spectrum of search engine marketing. Here
are two that cover optimization issues within
their diverse marketing topics:

✔ www.webmasterworld.com

✔ www.ihelpyouservices.com/forums

Eric Ward

`www.ericward.com/articles`

Eric Ward is a link-building specialist, and this site is a must-bookmark for any Webmaster who focuses on the networking aspect of Google optimization. Because Google plainly states that backlink networking is the single most important factor in PageRank, every Webmaster should be concerned with incoming links. An astonishing persistence of focus on backlinks creates the most concentrated resource site on this crucial topic I've ever seen. Tons of articles explore every angle of creating backlinks. Legal issues of deep-linking are covered. Guest writers contribute generously.

SEO Directory

`www.seolist.com`

This optimization directory seeks to be a topical link farm, but that aspect isn't as important as its articles. The site is young, and the selection of articles is a bit sparse. Let's hope it grows with an emphasis on the editorial side.

Pros and cons of hiring an SEO company

The time might come when you decide that you're not an optimization do-it-yourselfer. Don't be embarrassed; endlessly tweaking your tags and headers might not be the best delegation of your time and energy.

The main advantages of hiring an SEO firm for ongoing work are threefold: you buy expertise, you buy resources, and you save time. Those resources can be in the form of in-house staff at the SEO firm and proprietary technology such as evaluation software.

The main disadvantages of hiring an SEO firm are also threefold: loss of control, loss of awareness about what's going on in your site, and cost. Be sure to find a communicative company that's willing to keep you in the loop, so you understand the game plan for your site every step of the way.

When is it time to hire an SEO company? Not finding your site on a search results page might not be a clear-cut indicator that you need professional help. Perhaps you're searching with keywords that don't represent your site or don't represent your customers. However, if you see competitors in Google while you remain invisible, you know that your site is failing to expose your company.

Chapter 17

Ten SEM and SEO Tips from the Pros

*1*n this chapter I turn the floor over to professionals in the closely related fields of search engine marketing (SEM) and search engine optimization (SEO). Optimization is one small but vitally important aspect of online marketing in general and search engine marketing in particular. (Chapter 4 tackles the subject of optimization with gusto.)

You'll see some affirmations of principles I talk about throughout the book, especially in Parts I and II. More than parroting, though, this chapter offers diversions, alternative thinking, and some contrary views. Marketing is as much art as science, and this chapter gives space to several top-flight marketing artists.

These professionals were not paid for their contributions, nor did they pay to be represented in the book. I selected these individuals for the excellence of their Web-published articles and contacted them with invitations to provide some words of wisdom. I was frankly astonished at the generosity and enthusiasm that met my unassuming invitation. As you can see in this chapter, many of the quoted responses are extensive, but I was reluctantly forced to cut out much more material than I included. These folks are passionate about SEO and SEM! They gave and gave, and offered to give more. My sincere thanks to each person who made this chapter possible.

This chapter is structured as a sort of printed roundtable, over which I moderate. However, the chapter is not a transcription, and I didn't converse with these folks in real-time. The words of our experts were gathered one by one, through e-mail, as answers to a broad series of questions. I have culled highlights and organized them according to topics that were most prominent in the entire body of responses.

Many of the quotes are Google-specific, but I also encouraged the experts to speak broadly about search-marketing and optimization issues. Indeed, many principles of sound Google marketing match broader marketing rules. If there's one unanimous theme among these experts, it's that the connection between site usability and effective customer conversion transcends the mandates of a specific search engine. In other words: Implement the basics, and you'll do well in Google.

SEM Is (Somewhat) Revolutionary

Search engine marketing represents a radical break from traditional media promotion. How important is this marketing channel? Should every company be addressing SEM issues and making an effort to extend their brand onto search results pages? Opinion differs on the revolutionary effect of SEM, but every expert in this roundup agrees that targeting searchers is a marketing approach with unique advantages. David Wallace, the C.E.O. and founder of SearchRank emphasizes the readiness-to-consume among Google users who are searching for something, as opposed to the relative inertia of consumers watching traditional advertising.

> Search engine marketing is revolutionary in that it targets people who are actively looking for the services you offer. Conventional advertising such as television, radio, print, and the like, will try to get a person's attention. That person could be watching a football game or listening to their favorite radio station. Then an advertisement appears and tries to get them to change whatever they are doing or thinking about in order to focus on the product or service that is being offered. With search engine marketing, that person is already thinking about a particular product or service and they are actively searching for a business that offers it. Therefore the business simply needs to make sure they can be found. With conventional marketing, you find customers. With SEM, they find you!
>
> David Wallace, www.searchrank.com

Andy Beal, Vice President of Search Marketing at KeywordRanking notes the sheer volume of consumer traffic through search engines, and compares SEM to advertising in the Yellow Pages.

> Search engine marketing is one of the most cost-effective methods of marketing available. Over 500-million searches are conducted worldwide each day, and every one of them is a request for a product, a service, or information. For an investment that often equates to the price of an annual Yellow Pages listing, a business can reach an audience that far exceeds even that of a Super Bowl commercial. Bottom line, if you have a Web site for a commercial reason, whether to sell a product or promote a brand, you will benefit from search engine marketing.
>
> Andy Beal, www.keywordranking.com

Kalena Jordan, C.E.O. of Web Rank Ltd., demurs on the revolutionary aspect of search marketing. She describes a future that realizes a more mature venue in which advertisers will connect with qualified leads.

> SEM is not so much revolutionary now, as evolutionary. Most people don't know how to search the Web properly, meaning they are often frustrated with the results presented. Search engines are recognizing this and have begun to promote their "Advanced Search" features more transparently and educate users on how to get the most out of advanced search techniques rather than use "hit-and-miss" techniques. As the search engines learn more about their users, better technology is being developed to meet the needs of those users.
>
> The better the search engines become at providing high quality, relevant search results, the more people will come to rely on them to find goods and services. This provides an enormous opportunity for companies to use search engines as vehicles to be seen by a local, national, or global audience. Savvy companies have already implemented SEM. Search engine marketing is very inexpensive compared to offline advertising and much more effective in terms of ROI because of the targeting potential, so it simply cannot be overlooked by any company serious about their online business. SEM and SEO should be seen as a vital and compulsory component of any Web site budget. After all, what's the point of launching a web site if you are going to sabotage its ability to be found?
>
> Kalena Jordan, www.webrank.biz

Search engine marketing is indeed revolutionary, and is a great fit for most businesses. Some companies still continue to believe that their buyers are not online, but an analysis of the popularity of keywords and key phrases related to their business will usually demonstrate otherwise. Typically, if people are looking for something offline, they are also looking for it online (and a recent study conducted by the Georgia Institute of Technology found that 85% of prospective Web customers use search engines to find product solutions and vendors).

Another revolutionary aspect of search engine marketing is that results are directly quantifiable, much more so than any other form of advertising. When you spend time and effort to increase your search engine positions or spend money on pay-per-click advertising, the results of your efforts are directly available in real-time. Sophisticated and affordable analytic tools tell you how many additional visitors you are getting, what phrases are bringing you the most traffic, and even which phrases are bringing you the most valuable traffic (whether "value" is defined as buying your products, visiting your contact page, filling out a request form, or downloading a product demo). Try getting those types of metrics the next time you run some newspaper ads!

Scott Buresh, www.mediumblue.com

Barry Schwartz, President of RustyBrick, Inc., notes that SEM is 10 years old and most Web designers and developers are not aware of optimization basics. On that basis, "revolutionary" is not an appropriate descriptor for SEM; Barry believes that SEM should be mainstream.

I would not say SEM is revolutionary, as it has been around for 10 years — ever since the search engine was developed. Many small businesses are not really aware of SEM, and I have seen several big businesses that do not utilize Google AdWords, let alone the SEO basics. The beauty of SEM or SEO is that if you are paying for or optimizing for the correct keyword phrases, then leads from search engines are already qualified prospects for your business. It is probably the best type of lead a company can obtain, except for a client referral. Putting ads in newspapers or specialized Web sites are not as good by nature.

Today, I think the most crucial aspect of SEO for all businesses is that the Web designer or Web developer is often lacking the knowledge of what "Search Engine Friendly Design" is all about. Many, many Web developers just do not understand the basics of SEO and deploy Web sites that do not comply with simple standards.

Barry Schwartz, www.rustybrick.com

To Michael Marshall, C.E.O. and founder of Internet Marketing Analysts, LLC, perhaps the most revolutionary aspect of search marketing is the democracy of it; small businesses can compete effectively with larger corporations on the same search page.

> Search engine marketing is revolutionary in the sense that it is an advertising medium that levels the playing field to a significant degree. A small or new business can compete with older and larger businesses because what makes the difference in successful advertising in search engines is more a matter of what you know, not who you know or how much money you can throw at it. Furthermore, if you have optimized your site correctly, ALL of your search engine traffic is pre-qualified targeted traffic! What you have is the least expensive (often free), just-in-time (exactly when they want your product) advertising. This is why every company should be directing resources along this avenue. Chances are your competition already has.
>
> Michael Marshall, www.internet-marketing-analysts.com

Finally, Prabuddha Raychaudhuri, C.E.O. of Search Engine Optimization Guru Pvt. Ltd., quotes marketing figures to make his point that most companies should be more involved in search marketing.

> A company should invest in all avenues of internet marketing, including SEO/SEM to maximize its ROI of marketing spending. According to one SEO report by CyberAtlas, it was found that "nearly 46 percent of the marketers surveyed said they allocate less than 0.5 percent of their annual marketing budgets on search engine optimization (SEO) services, while only 10 percent spend more than 25 percent of their marketing budgets on increasing their visibility on the Web.
>
> Prabuddha S. Raychaudhuri, www.searchengine-optimization-guru.com

On Keyword Targeting

Of all aspects of search engine marketing, identifying core keywords at the center of every campaign and Web site is the most crucial.

> The most important aspect of any SEO/SEM campaign is to determine what keywords your target audience is searching for and ensure that your web site content is the most relevant to that search. Google is looking to display the most relevant search

results, and in doing so, looks for web pages that appear to focus on the keyword searched. Optimizing your web site does not mean tricking the search engines, but involves enhancing the theme within each page to demonstrate to Google that your site is the best match to the entered search.

Andy Beal, www.keywordranking.com

Kalena Jordan emphasizes the easily forgotten, yet obvious, point of including keywords in page text. She also recommends strict divisions in a site's page structure based on highly niched product categories and their associated keywords.

The secret is to focus. Search engines aren't going to rank your web site about socks highly if your body copy talks about foot sizes. You need to get specific. It sounds really obvious, but if you sell socks, make sure your site copy has plenty of references to the word socks! If you sell green wool socks, target the phrase "green wool socks" and not "foot apparel in lovely shades of emerald"! Who's going to search for socks using that phrase? At the risk of sounding like Dr Seuss, if you want to be the destination site for big socks, small socks, cotton socks, and wool socks, then mention them all. Better still, sort your copy into categories based on your various products and services. If you sell wool socks AND cotton socks, then have a page dedicated to each kind. This allows you to target niche keywords within your copy and meet the search engine's relevancy guidelines for related search queries.

Kalena Jordan, www.high-search-engine-ranking.com

Kalena also offers practical advice for deterring the most effective keywords.

When choosing keywords and phrases to target, ask yourself "What would I type in to a search engine to find my product or service?" If you don't feel confident choosing your own keywords, use a keyword research tool such as Wordtracker.com to determine what people are typing into search engines. Ask your friends, family, and colleagues what words they would use to locate sites like yours.

Kalena Jordan, www.high-search-engine-ranking.com

Using multiple keywords is important — nearly everyone agrees on that. Single keywords tend to be more competitive, more expensive to target, and less effective from an ROI perspective. Consumers searching on Google are realizing a similar insight: searching on multiple-word strings gets them to the best sites faster than entering broad, one-word queries.

Recent studies indicate that as the Web evolves, searchers are becoming much more skilled at finding what they need, and are using multiple terms in their search queries. As this trend continues, the multiple-word keyphrase you target today will be even more valuable tomorrow.

Scott Buresh, www.mediumblue.com

Instead of trying to achieve top-ten positioning on Google for a handful of one-word, highly competitive (and highly ambiguous) search terms, consider targeting hundreds of two- or three-word search terms instead. You'll not only achieve faster results, but also attract better qualified traffic.

Andy Beal, www.keywordranking.com

Alan Webb, C.E.O. of ABAKUS Internet Marketing, warns of two mutual dangers: targeting too narrowly and too broadly.

Establishing the best keywords for your domain is crucial for success. There is no point being on top for a search term that is either irrelevant to your content or hardly ever gets searched for. You can also, however, go the other way and optimize for terms that are too broad. They may receive hundreds if not thousands of searches per day, but are in many cases extremely difficult to rank well and are simply not targeted enough in most cases to what your web presence actually offers. An example would be a games console repair company targeting the keyword "playstation." How many searchers Googling that keyword are actually looking for a games console repair company?

Alan Webb, www.abakus-internet-marketing.de

On Finding the Balance between Free and Paid Marketing

Chapters 2, 3, and 4 of this book are devoted to free methods of heightening a site's visibility in Google. Chapters 6 through 10 discuss the complex, fast-lane method of bidding in the AdWords program for instant, first-page positioning on Google's results pages. In Google and in the larger world of search marketing, a balance must be struck between free and paid methods of attracting customers. In the discussion of free marketing vs. paid marketing, the free, so-called *organic* methods consist primarily of site optimization and its spinoff, link building. (See Chapter 3 for ways to build a network of incoming links.) The paid method under consideration is cost-per-click (CPC) advertising, also known as pay-per-click (PPC) marketing.

Most of our experts recommend a blend of optimization and paid placement. Andy Beal gets specific about this balance:

> In an ideal world, a business would simply need organic search engine optimization in order to drive traffic and increase online revenues. Unfortunately, in the real world, that is often not possible. Many businesses discover that they need to include some CPC advertising in order to fully benefit from search engine traffic. CPC is especially useful for any type of marketing that needs to be launched in a timely manner. If you implement a well-considered and targeted organic search engine optimization campaign, CPC advertising should not account for more than 15-20% of your overall search engine marketing efforts.
>
> Andy Beal, www.keywordranking.com

In Kalena Jordan's universe, the optimal balance varies depending on situation and should be determined by return on investment.

> The optimum balance is one that provides you with a solid ROI on your SEM investment. For example, you might have successfully optimized your site to rank highly for targeted keywords and phrases via the organic search listings, but have trouble cracking the top-ten rankings for more generic competitive terms. That's when you implement a pay-per-click campaign to purchase the more generic terms and out-bid your competitors for those. That way your site is always in front of eyeballs in the search engines — whether in the organic listings or on the advertising side.
>
> Kalena Jordan, www.high-search-engine-ranking.com

Barry Schwartz makes a compelling case for intensifying one's attempt to land on a search page as *both* an organic listing and a paid advertiser. Scott Buresh makes the same point, by comparing search advertising to magazine advertising, in which a company's ads might appear in the same issue as editorial content that mentions the company. Forced to choose, though, Scott would probably take the organic approach — not for the cost savings, but because of the greater perceived integrity of a high organic listing on a search results page.

> Some companies just allocate budgets to SEO or PPC but not both. This is a huge mistake. You have a 94% chance of achieving a click if your listing appears both in the organic results and the paid results on the same page. That is huge. In addition, if Google

makes a major change to their ranking algorithm you can drop off the organic (free) results and your business can tank with no warning. If you do not allocate your SEM budget properly to both SEO and PPC then you have a lot to worry about.

Barry Schwartz, www.rustybrick.com

Ideally, a company would want to be represented in both the organic results and the paid results of a search engine. To draw a comparison, consider a trade publication related to your business. The publication is full of articles, editorials, and stories about your industry, akin to the "organic results" of a search engine. In addition, there are numerous ads, akin to the "paid results" of a search engine. Many people will skip over the ads entirely and delve straight into the articles. Some will also take note of the ads. Being represented in both will give you the best chance to reach your prospects.

If you had to choose one strategy for long term results, however, you would probably opt to be included in the organic results. Much like the articles in a trade publication, these results are purported to be non-biased, and people tend to be less skeptical of them than of paid advertisements. However, properly optimizing a website can take a great deal of time, much like developing sustained PR exposure. With paid advertisements, your ad appears more or less immediately, but once you stop paying, your exposure disappears.

Scott Buresh, www.mediumblue.com

Michael Marshall returns the focus to the bottom line — the company's ROI, while also sketching the ideal situation of low CPC expenses in marketing high-margin products. Mike points out what is, to his view, the most potent advantage of CPC over organic listings: the instant results of buying placement on the first results page. Organic marketing, which requires gradual improvement of a site's marketing efficiency and relies on Google's crawl schedule, is the slower path to visibility. On the other hand, the results of optimization endure beyond the expense of creating a highly optimized site, whereas the advantages of CPC placement end the moment you stop spending for them.

The optimum balance for organic marketing and ad marketing (CPC) should be gauged by (1) the ROI for you of these different approaches, and (2) the needs and goals of a particular marketing campaign. For example, if you need exposure quickly and because of a time-sensitive promotional, CPC may be the way to go. Similarly, if you are fortunate enough to a have a low CPC cost in combination with a high ticket-price item you're selling, your conversion ratio may make this approach well worth the money spent (lost) on the visitors that don't buy.

Now, in many cases it is possible to achieve all of the benefits of CPC by using organic marketing (search engine optimization). The main difference and primary advantage of CPC over organic marketing is a faster "speed to market" for your ad. However, it is possible to structure and optimize your site in such a way that when adding a new page to the site, it might take only a couple of days for that page to show up in the search engines and if it is optimized well it will achieve a high ranking for its keyphrase(s) as well. Achieving this via organic marketing requires more skill on the front-end of optimizing your main site prior to whatever special promotional needs or goals you have that are time-sensitive. So if you haven't already done that and you're in a hurry, CPC will still be your best bet for your goal.

Michael Marshall, www.internet-marketing-analysts.com

Dave Davies of StepForth Placement Services doesn't deny the time advantage of paid marketing but still emphasizes organic placement as the preferred form of visibility.

Generally speaking, top organic placements are the most effective (organic placements get more attention) and lucrative form of promotion in the online marketplace. Organic marketing should be the first target for any Internet promotion plan. Even second-page organic placements, however, can take time to achieve, so, depending on the budget available, it is recommended that a small CPC campaign be implemented to generate interim traffic while organic placements are assessed. This two-pronged approach will ultimately provide the marketer with a clearer picture of which marketing tool is more efficient for their targeted terms, thus determining the proper balance for ROI. The exception is where the competition is so well entrenched that obtaining a top place-ment is expected to take a great deal of time to attain. In this case, a larger CPC campaign should be created to generate traffic to the web site while organic placements slowly improve.

Dave Davies, www.stepforth.com

Karyn Greenstreet, a freelance SEO specialist and founder of Passion for Business, purports the most radical viewpoint in this section, recommending that a marketing plan should forget about organic methods entirely when competing in high-profile, broadly targeted search areas.

If your site is based on very competitive keywords, dump search engine optimization efforts altogether and spend the money on pay-per-click advertising such as AdWords. For instance, if you type in "online advertising strategy" in Google and see 3 million responses, you know it is time to turn to pay-per-click. How will you know which to choose (SEO vs. AdWords)? Do the math.

Calculate your cost to hire someone to do SEO work for you (or calculate the hours you'll spend in both initial SEO work and monthly SEO updates), and compare that cost to a fixed monthly budget for AdWords. Since you get to set the daily budget amount in AdWords, you may find that AdWords is the better deal in the long run.

Karyn Greenstreet, www.passionforbusiness.com

Optimization versus Incoming Links

In the area of site optimization, another balance must be decided: the one between page optimization (including tag authoring, keyword embedding, content design, and other considerations covered in Chapter 4) and link building (constructing a network of incoming links from other sites in your topical field). These two tasks are the twin drivers of organic list position in Google, determined by Google's PageRank, Google states clearly that incoming links (the number and quality of those links) represent the greatest single factor in a site's PageRank, but some of our experts surprisingly put their weight into the optimization side of the equation.

Every search engine marketing campaign should start with a focus on the actual content and structure of the website. Not until you have conducted your keyword research, improved the keyword density of your text and ensured a search engine friendly structure, should you consider building the number of inbound links. However, you should not consider building links as a separate practice. Obtaining quality links from external sources should be an integral part of any search engine marketing campaign.

Andy Beal, www.keywordranking.com

Building links and optimizing your site are both important. Personally, I would give primary importance, between the two, to optimization of the site itself. Backlinks, links pointing to your site from other sites, can improve the ranking of your site quite considerably. It must be understood, however, that it's not simply a matter of the number of backlinks but the quality of backlinks that counts. You must have the right kinds of sites linking to you in the right kinds of ways. Having the right kind of site linking to you in the wrong way may cause you to lose the benefit from that link you could have had. Having the wrong kind of site linking to you (link farms, for example) might even cause a decrease in your ranking.

Michael Marshall, www.internet-marketing-analysts.com

The more competitive the keyword the more you need to build
links. Always, always need to optimize your site — that is always
step one no matter what.

Barry Schwartz, www.rustybrick.com

David Wallace makes an interesting comparison between incoming links and
political endorsement. It's a good point, and the endorsement angle is exactly
why Google rewards highly linked sites.

Optimizing a Web site for keyword phrases that are relevant to
one's business and obtaining quality external links are equally
important. Think of it as a political race. A candidate can have a
good character, support relevant issues, and have a great message.
However, if no one endorses or votes for them, they are not going
to hold office for the position they are running for. A Web site is
the same in that it may have great content and be aesthetically
pleasing, but if no one links to it, it is not going to hold a very
high position in a search engine.

David Wallace, www.searchrank.com

Dave Davies takes the middle road: Optimization and incoming links are
equally important. Why not cover all bases?

Link building and site optimization are equally important.

A well optimized website allows clear paths for not only Google,
but all search engine spiders. As it stands today Google relies
heavily on relevant inbound links for ranking websites. With an
aggressive link building campaign it is quite possible to rank in the
top ten without having done any optimization work. But keep in
mind; if Google makes an adjustment to its algorithm to give links
less weight, your rankings could plummet. If you pursue a well-
rounded campaign combining optimization with link building, not
only do you have a stronger chance to achieve top rankings in the
first place, but your placements are more likely to remain in place
after an algorithm change.

Google loves links, and lots of them. At the time this answer was
written, the most important factor to a strong ranking at Google
is highly relevant links coming in from sites with higher page ranks
than yours. We see lots of sites that, in our opinion, should not be
ranking at Google. However, these sites always have a ton of links
coming in from highly relevant and high PR sites.

Dave Davies, www.stepforth.com

On Content and Site Design

This section is all about optimization.

> If your web site doesn't contain any body text on the home page, give yourself a good smack and go to your room without supper. When you're ready to behave and design your site with the search engines in mind, come back out and start over.
>
> Kalena Jordan, www.high-search-ranking.com

> You need rich, relevant content to support your keyphrases, and I advise having at least 200 words on any page that is optimized for search engine ranking.
>
> Michael Marshall, www.internet-marketing-analysts.com

Does each page of your site stand on its own as a content page? Scott Buresh recommends building pages around keywords, not finding space on preexisting pages for new keywords.

> Treat each page of your site as a separate potential entry page. Many "optimized" sites are really only optimized for the home page — a tremendous waste of potential. Use software like Wordtracker to find out what your potential customers are typing in search engines, and make sure that you directly address these areas of interest on your site. Don't be afraid to add content to your site to cover additional topics — especially if you know that your visitors are interested in them. As a rule of thumb, don't ask "Where am I going to fit these keyphrases on my site?" Ask instead "Why do I not have a page of my site devoted to this popular topic?"

> Make your website an authority on your area of business. After optimizing their website, people are often dismayed to discover that it is very difficult to collect relevant incoming links. They don't realize that webmasters of quality sites will often link to sites that provide valuable information without even being asked. Make sure you devote a large portion of your site to informational content that people in your industry would find useful. There is a direct relationship between valuable content, incoming links, and search engine rankings — but very often people try to achieve the last two without devoting any energy toward the first.
>
> Scott Buresh, www.mediumblue.com

Genius is in the details! Lee Traupel, founder and C.E.O. of Intelective Communications, likes to place important keywords toward the top of each optimized page:

> Google's "spider" (automated bot that visits and archives information) also "likes" sites that have keywords that are closer to the top of a page — the spider does not like to wade through a great deal of HTML code to find keywords. So, utilize your keywords at the top of the page in titles, headers, first two to three sentences, etc.
>
> Lee Traupel, www.intelective.com

> The single most important aspect to consider when optimizing your website is to approach it from a user's perspective. The folks at Google conduct extensive studies on what types of results and websites their users like to see, and naturally tailor their algorithms accordingly. While there are many tricks du jour that will work in the short term, the real secret to long term success on Google is to piggyback on the knowledge that they have acquired about web searchers. By deducing through the Google algorithm what the preferences of Google searchers are and applying these qualities to your site, you are making your site more attractive not only to Google, but also to the user.
>
> Scott Buresh, www.mediumblue.com

> Very important is the structure of the site. Are all pages fewer than three clicks away from the homepage, for example? Are the links normal href links and not javascript, flash, or image map links?
>
> Alan Webb, www.abakus-internet-marketing.de

> The simple truth is this: search engines read text and not much else. You absolutely, positively need to use text on the pages of your site that you want indexed and ranked highly. Not graphical text that you created in your fancy design software, but actual, visible body text. Whether it's Google or AskJeeves or AllTheWeb or AltaVista or whoever, you need to include visible text on your site pages if you want them indexed and found by potential visitors.
>
> Kalena Jordan, www.high-search-engine-ranking.com

Finally, a technical note from Scott Buresh:

> Sites built completely in Flash are a nightmare from a search engine perspective, since very few search engines can properly index the technology. In the past few years, many big-name companies have spent big dollars on Flash sites, only to discover that Flash rendered their site essentially invisible to search engines. Another thing to avoid is framesets, since they hinder the spider's

ability to distinguish between individual pages on the site. Also, the text on your site should be in standard HTML. While using graphic text might give you more aesthetic options, a search engine spider can't read it, and therefore the engine won't be able to tell what your page is about. Finally, if you are going to use certain navigation schemes, such as javascript pulldown menus, make sure that you also create an alternate text navigation scheme to ensure that the spider has a path to follow. Many sites unintentionally limit the spider's access to only the homepage.

Scott Buresh, www.mediumblue.com

On the All-Important Title Tag

You might think that asking several SEO experts what they think is the most important optimization detail would yield a fierce and diverse argument. Amazingly, one simple answer emerges with remarkable agreement. The good news is that the single most important optimization trick is also one of the easiest to accomplish.

The title might be the single most important on-page SEO element, because (1) it tells search engines what to find on that page, and (2) search engines use that title in the search engine results page. So if you have your company name in the title of your page and it does not accurately describe what that page is about (example: your product) then the search engine will not rank that page well for your product. In addition, if you do rank for that page, the search engine user (searcher) will see just your company name and say, "What does this have to do with my search?" and skip over to a more relevant listing.

Barry Schwartz, www.rustybrick.com

How many times have you looked at a web site where the page Title in your browser reads "Welcome to [company name]'s web site" or simply "[Company Name]"? Nothing wrong with that, I hear you say? Well if you want to achieve high search engine rankings, there's PLENTY wrong with it. You see, while it may not be common knowledge amongst webmasters or (shock, horror!) even some web designers, most search engines index the content of the Title Attribute and consider it to be one of THE most important factors in their relevancy algorithm. What you place in your Title can make or break your ranking for particular search terms on the various engines. If you don't include your most important search phrases within your Title tag (and target the content of each Title to the content on each page), you are overlooking a vital opportunity in your quest for higher search rankings.

Having said this, you should try and keep your Title to a maximum of 200 characters, as that is the average limit most search engines will truncate to. If you really insist on including your company name in your title and you're willing to sacrifice good keyword real estate to do so, put it at the very end of the tag, because search engines give more relevancy "weight" to content at the start of your tag.

Kalena Jordan, www.high-search-engine-ranking.com

As for what is known as 'on-page' optimization, which involves the source code on your website, probably the most important thing to get right is the Title tag. This has to be the most weighted tag on a webpage, and if your keywords do not show up in it, then you can expect poor rankings.

Alan Webb, www.abakus-internet-marketing.de

The two most important aspects when optimizing a site for Google or any other crawler-based search engine are the title tag and content of each page. One should make sure that the keywords that are relevant to each page are represented in the title tag of the page as opposed to saying something like "Welcome to our site!". One must also make sure they have well-written HTML text that also represents the keywords they wish to target. With Google, more often than not, content is king.

David Wallace, www.searchrank.com

Aiming for the Top Ten

It is perhaps not surprising that a crew of SEM consultants would wax optimistic about the chances of cracking the top ten search results in Google. They're not likely to conclude that the quest is hopeless. But every one of the pros recognizes the daunting challenge of competing for top listings for single, generic keywords. The recipe for success pulls together marketing precepts scattered throughout the book.

It is quite realistic to aim for top ten (or, what is often just as effective, top twenty) search results. In fact, you should aim for nothing less. It is a well-known fact of searching behavior that most people do not look at more than the first 2 pages (top 20) in the search results before either revising their search term or switching to another search engine if they don't find what they want on those first 2 pages. You can crack the competition by following long-standing, tried-and-true SEM principles (no tricks or spamming).

Principle #1: Find what terms and phrases (related to your business) people are using in their searches. Principle #2: Give the search engines what they want, and they will give you the traffic that you want. Principle #3: Always follow a search engine's own guidelines for URL submission. Principle #4: Always follow a search engine's own page guidelines for avoiding penalties. Principle #5: Once you've ascertained the specifics related to principle #2, analyze what your competition is doing that you can improve upon, or what they are not doing that will give you the edge. Principle #6: Develop a strategy that is long-term, not a quick fix. If you want results that last and grow, run this race as a marathon, not a sprint. Principle #7: Don't put all your efforts into just one strategy or search engine. Principle #8: Track results in a nice closed-loop fashion to better assess ROI and which strategies do and don't produce desired results. Principle #9: With regard to the quality of link partners you choose, guilt by association is just as important as good reputation by association, in the eyes of the search engines. Principle #10: Be Patient!

Michael Marshall, www.internet-marketing-analysts.com

It is entirely realistic for a small business to crack the top ten under almost any two-keyword phrase but it is pretty difficult to crack the top ten under a one-keyword phrase. When considering keyword targets, we generally advise clients to select a variety of highly relevant two- or three-keyword phrases. This is almost always more beneficial for smaller websites simply because the more words are associated with the keyword-target, the better chance we have of getting the top-ten listing.

It is also advisable to map out your search engine placement campaign in stages, taking the easier-to-reach keyword targets first and getting the more competitive phrases later. This method establishes your site as a top-ten player, likely garners you more initial visitors in a short time (which is noted and tracked by Google), and gives you a strong platform from which to chase more competitive phrases.

Dave Davies, www.stepforth.com

Achieving top-ten Google and other search engine rankings through a natural (organic) process is realistic and possible, even for the most generic and highly competitive terms like "internet marketing," "weight loss," etc. However, successful organic SEO campaigns need continuous SEO efforts and patience (may take 5-6 months) before a web site attains top-ten rankings.

Vudatala Meena, www.searchengine-optimization-guru.com

It's not very realistic for many small businesses to achieve top-ten search results on Google unless they are utilizing keywords that are not too competitive but that will still drive traffic. The "less competitive" traffic may not be as great as what a top-tier keyword might provide; but in the end, a conservative strategy will frequently pay off with quality traffic that generates a desired action like a lead or revenue generation.

Lee Traupel, www.intelective.com

On Large and Small Companies

One of the most potent attractions of search engine marketing, as well as a reason for its surging influence in online promotion, is its accessibility. Any site can increase its business with Google. In fact, small businesses often have advantages over corporations in this realm, because they tend to be more nimble and, in certain ways, more resourceful. Search marketing isn't a puzzle that can usually be solved by throwing money at it. So the deep-pocket path to dominance in media promotion doesn't work when it comes to optimization and CPC battles. Small businesses are racing to gain traction in the most democratic of all marketing venues.

Small businesses can indeed compete with larger companies on search engines, and in fact have certain advantages. They are typically able to make necessary search engine adjustments to the company Web site without running it through multiple departments and then making a board presentation (all the while defending against complaints from IT and Marketing about perceived infringements on their turf). Also, large corporations are much more likely to assign the task to an internal person, who typically has no background in search engine marketing and has many other job functions to fulfill. This is a primary reason that some of the most egregious search engine errors you will ever see consistently come from household name companies.

Scott Buresh, www.mediumblue.com

For small-business owners and entrepreneurs, the advantages of search engine placement are enormous. SEO is still one of the most affordable forms of advertising available. In no other way can a business promote their products/services to a worldwide market for the costs associated with SEO.

Compare, for example, the cost of SEO to Yellow Pages ads. A full SEO campaign can often be undertaken for a fraction of the cost of a single Yellow Pages ad yet make your site visible to a worldwide market rather than just the local market served by the Yellow Pages.

Additionally, once the SEO is complete, the cost to maintain it is relatively low. In traditional forms of media, the high cost of continued marketing is generally maintained with little reduction over time.

Dave Davies, www.stepforth.com

SEO/SEM is an area that can be harnessed by the small-business owners to the fullest extent. In other words, SEO/SEM is a tool that can aid the small-business owners to fight with their bigger brothers on the same platform and even surpass them. Though small businesses are often impaired by limited advertising/ marketing budgets, proper utilization of that budget through SEO/SEM can provide high returns for them. In a nutshell, the most crucial aspect of SEO/SEM for a small-business owner or entrepreneur is the unlimited business opportunity that it achieves through top-ten Google ranking of their Web site even when pitted against some of the major corporations.

Prabuddha S. Raychaudhuri, www.searchengine-optimization-guru.com

A small business should concentrate on not just creating a few brochure pages, but making their Web site a resource that is worthy of bookmarking. Check the top results for your main search term and see how many pages those sites at the top have listed. To do that, type into the Google search box "site:www.domaintobe checked.com" (without the quotation marks). Then build your site with at least as many pages as they have, if not more. Also be sure to actively seek links to your site. A small business doesn't have to have a small (and insignificant) Web site!

Alan Webb, www.abakus-internet-marketing.de

Sumantra Roy, founder of 1st Search Ranking, has a few priority guidelines for larger companies.

For the larger enterprise (I am talking of very large companies with well-known brands like IBM, Nokia, etc.) link popularity presents less of a challenge. Their reputation ensures that lots of other Web sites will link to them without being asked to do so. For larger enterprises, the most important thing would be to ensure that the thousands of pages they have in their sites are properly optimized in terms of proper placement of keywords in the Title tag and in the main content. Secondly, large organizations need to have a proper internal linking strategy so that all the pages in the site can be spidered by the search engines. Lastly, large organizations need to have proper documentation and quality assurance policies in place so that any changes that are made to a page in order to boost its rankings in the search engines are properly documented. This ensures that after a page has been optimized, the changes are not reversed by someone else in the organization who does not know that these changes are supposed to be there.

Sumantra Roy, www.1stsearchranking.com

Building Incoming Links

While the important backlink network isn't part of on-site optimization, it is definitely part of marketing the site to Google. So, optimization specialists cannot, and do not, ignore this crucial area.

The best way to get incoming links from other webmasters is of course to have quality content. Consider a FAQ, tutorial, forum, glossary, unique online tool, detailed product pages, and technical pages.

Alan Webb, www.abakus-internet-marketing.de

The most important thing that a small business should do is to improve the link popularity of its website. Link Popularity is by far the most important factor as far as getting top rankings in Google (and many of the other major search engines) is concerned. You can't build your link popularity simply by setting up multiple websites and having them link to your website. You also can't build your link popularity by submitting your website to hundreds of free-for-all pages. You should first submit your site to directories like the Open Directory and to other industry-specific directories. Then, you should have an ongoing reciprocal linking program for your website, i.e. you should approach other sites that are related to your site and ask them whether they would be interested in linking to your site in exchange for your site linking to them.

Sumantra Roy, www.1stsearchranking.com

On-the-page techniques alone can often get great results for less competitive keyphrases without requiring a great deal of link building. However, on-page factors can only take you so far. As your less competitive keyphrases become more competitive (and if they are valuable they almost certainly will), your site will inevitably show a steady decline in rankings over time as competing sites concentrate on both aspects of optimization. And if you target more competitive phrases at the outset, you will almost certainly need to do some quality link building if you intend to crack the top twenty.

On the other hand, if you concentrate on link building alone, you run the risk of being judged solely by the company you keep. If you don't pay attention to any on-page factors (especially technical issues), Google might decide what your site is about only by the type of sites that are linking to you, not by the type of information you provide. This makes it very difficult to target the wide range of phrases that are necessary for a successful search engine optimization initiative.

Scott Buresh, www.mediumblue.com

Getting links from other sites will help to boost your rankings in Google. But not just any site will do. Choose sites that have a high Google Page Ranking (use the Google Toolbar to see a site's page ranking). Also, choose sites which are rich in content, as they will attract the most visitors, who will also see your site. Finally, sites with high Page Ranking and rich content tend to score better on Google's search results rankings, so having a link from their site to your site will drive business to you as a secondary click off a high ranking search result (from Google's results, to the high ranking page where your site is listed, to your page).

Karyn Greenstreet, www.passionforbusiness.com

It is also advisable to cultivate several highly relevant links from sites with page ranks higher than yours. Use the anchor text in these links wisely by having a variety of keyword phrases used across different sites.

Dave Davies, www.stepforth.com

The Most Important Tips

This section is for final arguments — the crucial, boil-it-down, golden-rule words of wisdom.

Karyn Greenstreet and David Wallace agree that the emotional strategies of patience and tenacity are as important as anything you do on the screen.

The most important part of search engine optimization is patience, patience, patience. Many search engines update their database every four to six weeks. If you just missed an update, you might have to wait a month before your listing is added or modified. Patience is also key if your rankings drop. Don't feel pressured to make SEO changes to your site if you know you did a good job optimizing it originally. Hold on for a few weeks to see if your ranking in reinstated before updating your site.

Karyn Greenstreet, www.passionforbusiness.com

The most crucial aspect of SEO or SEM for both small business and large business is to be tenacious. SEO/SEM is not a "one time shot-in-the-arm cure" as many people believe it to be. It is much like body-building, which requires a lot of hard work and a continuous effort. Someone who is going to build muscle mass must commit to it for the rest of their life or else it will eventually turn to fat. SEO/SEM is the same. It will take a lot of hard work in the beginning and even some trial and error to earn high positions. Once a person has those positions, it requires a continuous effort to keep them. It is the classic "king of the hill" battle: It is tough to get to the top and even tougher to fight the elements to stay there.

David Wallace, www.searchrank.com

It's no surprise that keyword targeting comes up again in the "most important" section.

The most crucial aspect of SEO or SEM for any size business, entrepreneur or enterprise, is choosing the right keyphrase(s) as the focal point(s) of your search engine marketing strategy. Choose the wrong keyphrase(s), and everything else you do will be a waste of time, effort, and money.

Michael Marshall, www.internet-marketing-analysts.com

Whether you are a large company or a one-person home biz, whether you are optimizing your web site for performance in the traditional free or "organic" search engine listings or are purchasing pay-per-click ads, sponsored listings, or paid listings, the MOST crucial element to successful search engine marketing is keyword targeting. The Internet is no place for verbosity. People are in a hurry — they want to find what they seek quickly and easily with the least hassle possible. You can help them in this quest by ensuring that your site copy uses simple language, easy to grasp concepts, and logical keywords that they are likely to look for.

Kalena Jordan, www.high-search-engine-ranking.com

Are you in Google? Barry Schwartz reminds you that you're not "in" unless *all* of you is in — every page of your site.

Your Web site, each and every page, must be in the Google index. To check this you can type into the Google search box "allinurl: www.domain.com site:www.domain.com" and it will bring back all the pages of your Web site that are included in the index. If all your pages are not in the index, then that is the most crucial part to work on.

If you are in the Google index, then you need to make sure that each one of your pages is targeting a unique and meaningful keyword.

Barry Schwartz, www.rustybrick.com

The following comment from Scott Buresh shows a deep understanding of how SEM should fit into a company's overall marketing effort.

The most crucial aspect of SEO or SEM is almost certainly recognition of the value of the channel and a commitment to using it to further your business objectives. It isn't a good idea to pursue an SEO or SEM campaign simply because you can't find your site on a search engine. Leave your ego at the door — it's more important to consider how showing up on searches for certain terms might benefit your business than how it will impress your friends, neighbors, and colleagues. Search Engine Optimization or Marketing should be no different than any traditional advertising or marketing program. Goals should be established at the outset, along with the means to measure the progress and return of the channel.

Scott Buresh, www.mediumblue.com

In my opinion, there are two essential components to a good Google placement campaign. First of all, the text used in all site elements is extremely important. Clear, concise, and relevant text used in titles, description tags, and body text is the most important element for Google or any other search engine. With Google specifically in mind, incoming links from relevant sites is the second most important.

The key that binds text and incoming links is theme-relevancy. The site linking to your site must address a similar topic or theme.

Dave Davies, www.stepforth.com

There are two vital components to optimizing a web site. The first is to ensure that every page that you wish to market contains a unique Title Tag that includes two or three of your targeted search terms in its text. Relevant, focused Title Tags appear to be important across all search engines when trying to improve your search engine positioning. The second most important component is to ensure that the page you are optimizing actually contains the search terms that you are targeting. It's not enough to have relevant graphics or use text that implies the content; you need to be explicit in your wording and actually use the phrases that searches enter at Google each day.

Andy Beal, www.keywordranking.com

Karyn Greenstreet wraps up this chapter with a reminder of the ultimate goal: conversion and sales.

> No matter how much effort you put into your search engine marketing efforts, you will not get paying customers unless your website leads the customer through the sales process.
>
> Karyn Greenstreet, www.passionforbusiness.com

Glossary

SEO Terms

Above the fold (ATF): Originally a newspaper term, above the fold means on the top half of the page. Placing a story above the fold makes it more visible. In Web publishing, in which no fold exists, premium placement generally means toward the top of the page, in a position where visitors don't have to scroll down. Screen resolutions differ, of course, so if you design your page using a resolution of 1280 x 1024, for example, your own fold is way down the page. The higher the resolution, the more material you can put into each "fold" portion of the page, because high resolutions make text and graphics smaller. (In effect, high resolution makes the screen bigger.)

For years, I optimized my page design with the assumption that my visitors were viewing the site on a 640 x 480 screen. I now regard that resolution as sufficiently obsolete to upgrade my optimization to 800 x 600 screens, which are still prevalent on laptops. (My apologies to 640 x 480 users, who must scroll vertically and horizontally at my sites.) Keeping all this in mind, and perhaps viewing your pages through different resolutions, try to place your most magnetic content so that it's visible without scrolling.

Backlink: A link at another site, leading to your site. Also called an *incoming link.* The number and quality of backlinks represent the most important factor in determining a site's PageRank. The value of any backlink is determined partly by the PageRank of the linking site, which is determined partly by the quality of *its* backlinks, and so on.

Bridge page: *See* doorway page.

Cloaking: A type of search-engine subterfuge in which an indexed Web page is not shown to visitors who click its link in Google (or another search engine). The cloaking works two ways: Visitor content is cloaked from Google, and Google's indexed content is cloaked from visitors. This serves to give a high PageRank to content that ordinarily would rate a low PageRank. Cloaking is not always illicit. A certain type of cloaking are used to deliver pages tailored to a visitor's ISP (America Online, for example) or specific Web browser.

Crawler: *See* spider.

Cross linking: Intentionally or unintentionally, cross linking creates large backlink networks among sites that exist in the same domain or are owned by the same entity. Unintentional cross linking happens when a site generates a large number of pages with identical navigation links or when at least two sites mutually link related content. When cross linking is done intentionally, the Webmaster is seeking to raise the PageRank of the involved sites. Excessive cross linking can backfire. If Google decides that the resulting enhanced PageRank is artificial, any or all of the sites might be expelled from the Web index. Innocent cross linking between two related sites is usually not a problem.

Deepbot: The unofficial name for Google's monthly spider. Freshbot is the unofficial name of Google's frequently crawling spider. The official name for both crawlers is Googlebot.

Domain: The first- and second-level address of a Web site. Top-level destinations are defined by the domain extension: `.com`, `.net`, `.org`, `.biz`, and others. The second level adds a domain name: *yoursite*`.com`.

Domain name: The second-level domain address that identifies and brands a site, such as `google.com` and `amazon.com`.

Domain name registration: The process of taking ownership of a domain name. Registrations are processed by dozens of registrars approved by ICANN (Internet Corporation for Assigned Names and Numbers). The cost of domain ownership is no more than $35 per year. (Hosting the domain's Web site is an additional expense.) Registration takes place online, and the activation of a new domain (or moving a domain from one host to another) generally requires no more than 48 hours.

Doorway page: An entry page to a Web site, sometimes known as a splash page. Doorway pages endure a negative connotation due to illicit techniques that send visitors to an entirely different site than the destination they clicked in Google.

Dynamic content: Web pages generated by an in-site process that depends on input from the visitor. Most dynamic content comes from a database operating behind the scenes, feeding information to a Web page created in response to a visitor's query. Search engines are among the largest producers of dynamic content; every Google results page, for example, is pulled from the background index in response to a keyword query. Google's spider generally avoids portions of sites that rely on dynamic page-generation, making it difficult to index the content of those sites.

Entry page: *See* doorway page.

Fresh crawl: Google's frequent scan of Web content that occurs between the deep monthly crawls. Google does not publicize the schedule of its intermediate crawls or its target sites. The term "fresh crawl" is an unofficial one used by Webmasters, site optimizers, and other Google obsessives.

Freshbot: The unofficial name for Google's near-daily spider. Deepbot is the unofficial name of Google's monthly-crawling spider. The official name for both crawlers is Googlebot.

Googlebot: Google's Web spider.

Incoming link: *See* backlink.

Index: In the context of Google, the index is the database of Web content gathered by the Google spider. When Google receives a search query, it matches the query keywords against the index.

Keyword: As an optimization term, a keyword represents a core concept of a site or a page. The site's content, HTML tagging, and layout strategies are based on effective deployment of keywords, which could also be key phrases. Google matches search results to keywords entered by its users and assigns a PageRank in part on how consistently a site presents its keywords.

Keyword density: A proportional measurement of keywords embedded in a page's content. High keyword density focuses the page's subject in a way that Google's spider understands. The spider can interpret too high a density as spam, which results in a lower PageRank or elimination from the index. Most optimization specialists recommend a density between 5 and 15 percent.

Keyword stuffing: The attempt to gain a higher PageRank (or higher ranking in any search engine) by loading a page's HTML code or text with keywords. In most cases a visitor can't see the keywords because they're buried in HTML tags, camouflaged against the background color of the page, or reduced to a tiny typeface. Keyword stuffing violates Google's guidelines for Webmasters and can result in expulsion from the index.

Link farm: A site whose only function is to display outgoing links to participating Web sites. Link farms are disreputable versions of legitimate, topical link exchange sites through which visitors gain some content value. Link farms often have no topicality and present no guidelines or standards of submission. Google does not explicitly threaten expulsion for joining link farms, but it discourages their use.

Meta tag: Positioned near the top of an HTML document, the `meta` tag defines basic identifying characteristics of a Web page. Often, several `meta` tags are used on each page. In those tags you set the page's title, description, and keywords.

Mirror site: Mirror sites duplicate content and are used for both legitimate and engine-spamming purposes. Legitimate mirror sites assist in downloading when a great deal of traffic is trying to reach a page or acquire a file. Illicit mirror sites attempt to fill a search results page with multiple destinations owned by a single entity. When Google discovers a mirror site whose only purpose is to dominate a search page, that site risks expulsion.

Optimization: A set of techniques to improve a Web site's presentation to visitors and its stature in a search engine's index. As a specific field, search engine optimization has suffered in reputation due to unscrupulous individuals and companies using tactics that degrade the integrity of search results and violate guidelines set by those engines. Generally, any optimization scheme that tricks a search engine also tricks visitors to that site, making online life worse for everyone involved. Pure optimization, though, helps everyone: the Webmaster, the search engine, and the visitor. The true values of optimization are clear content, coherent navigation, wide reputation for quality, and high visibility in search engines.

Outgoing link: A link from your page to another page. Outgoing links don't build PageRank by volume, as incoming links (backlinks) do. However, Google pays attention to the text elements of outgoing links, and a page's optimization can be strengthened by consistent placement of key concepts in that text.

Page redirect: A background link that sends site visitors to another site. Page redirects can be used legitimately, as when a site moves from one domain to another. In that scenario, the Webmaster sensibly keeps the old domain active for a while, seamlessly sending visitors to the new location when they click the old one. As an illicit optimization technique, page redirects deflect visitors from the site indexed by Google to another site that would not be able to gain as high a PageRank. This type of redirect, when uncovered by Google, risks the expulsion of both sites from the index.

PageRank: A proprietary measurement of Google's proprietary ordering of pages in its Web index. PageRank is the most intense point of focus, speculation, observation, and desire in the Webmaster and optimization communities. More than any other single marketing factor, PageRank has the power to determine a site's visibility. A high PageRank moves a page toward the top of any search results page in Google when that page matches the user's keywords. Obtaining a PageRank high enough to break a page into the top ten is the primary goal of Google optimization. An approximate version of any page's PageRank can be checked by displaying the page in Internet Explorer while running the Google Toolbar. Hover your mouse over the PageRank cursor to see the current page's rank on a 0-to-10 scale.

Robots.txt file: A simple text file that stops Google (and other search engines that recognize the file and its commands) from crawling the site, selected pages in the site, or selected file types in the site.

SE (search engine): A site, such as Google.com, that matches keywords to Web page content.

SEO (search engine optimization): SEO seeks to increase a site's visibility in search engines and enhance its value to visitors through topical page design, consistent HTML tagging, and focusing content on core keywords.

SERP: Search engine results page. A page of links leading to Web pages that match a searcher's keywords.

Spam: Generally refers to repeated and irrelevant content. As an optimization term, spam refers to loading a page with keywords or loading a search engine's index with mirror sites. Google reacts strongly to spamming, and takes harsh measures against Web sites that use spamming techniques to improve PageRank.

Spider: An automated software program that travels from link to link on the Web, collecting content from Web pages. Spiders assemble this vast collection of content into an index, used by search engines to provide relevant sites to searchers. Spiders are also called crawlers, bots (short for robots), or Web bots. Google's spider appears in Webmaster logs as Googlebot.

Splash page: *See* doorway page.

AdWords and Search Advertising Terms

Account: A Google AdWords account provides the Web space in which you design and operate a campaign. Opening an account costs nothing; activating your account costs five dollars. Account holders have access to Google's keyword research and traffic estimation tools, even before activation. Therefore, you can conceive and budget a complete ad campaign before spending a dime.

Activation: To activate a Google AdWords account, you select a payment method and currency and provide billing details. After you activate an account, you're ready to launch a campaign.

Activation fee: A five-dollar fee is charged when AdWords advertisers first activate their accounts. An additional five-dollar fee is imposed every third time you reactivate a campaign after Google has stopped it due to underperformance.

Actual cost-per-click: As compared to cost-per-click, the actual cost-per-click is the billable amount charged by Google when a searcher clicks your ad. This amount might be the same as or lower than your maximum bid for your ad placement, but it's never higher.

Ad Group: The main subdivision of an ad Campaign, an Ad Group consists of one or more ads associated with one or more keywords. Keywords define the Ad Group. New Ad Groups in a Campaign are associated with different keywords, though they might have the same ads.

AdRank: Advertisements are placed in sequence based on AdRank, with the top-ranked ad at the top of the column. AdRank is measured as a combination of bid value (maximum CPC set by the advertiser) and clickthrough rate (CTR). Successful ads with high CTRs are sometimes ranked and placed higher than less successful ads with higher CPC bids. The measurement, ranking, and placement of ads are automated.

AdWords column: The right-hand stack of AdWords advertisements on a Google search results page. Ads are placed in that column according to AdRank, which is a calculation of maximum CPC and clickthrough rate.

Affiliate (aff): Affiliate marketers direct their clickthroughs to third-party destinations that sell products or services. The affiliate receives a commission when the clickthrough results in a sale. Google's guidelines require advertisers to indicate in their ad copy if they're engaging in affiliate marketing. To save space, the *aff* abbreviation is often used.

Broad match: The default keyword-matching setting in Google AdWords. Broad match displays your ad on search results pages that match your keywords and a large peripheral universe of keywords that Google determines is relevant — so your ads appear on the results pages of keywords you might not have directly chosen. Broad match is an easy way to spread your ad out to keywords that haven't occurred to you. In choosing this option, however, you're relying on Google's relevancy algorithm to choose keywords related to your selections. (See also *keyword-matching options*, *expanded match*, *exact match*, and *negative match*.)

Call to action: Google recommends using short phrases that command the viewer to do something. These calls to action encourage clickthroughs with phrases such as "Learn more," or "Download now for free." Some marketers dispute the effectiveness of calls to action. A good way to test the value of calls to action is to use multiple ads in an ad group, some with calls to action and others without.

Campaign: The largest subdivision of a Google AdWords account, a Campaign holds one or more Ad Groups. Campaigns can be paused, resumed, budgeted, networked, and scheduled — these settings affect all Ad Groups simultaneously and equally. Ad Groups have their own settings for finer control.

Clickthrough: Clickthroughs occur when a viewer clicks your AdWords ad. Clicking through generates a charge to your account.

Clickthrough rate (CTR): The CTR is a calculation of an ad's clickthroughs divided by its impressions (the number of times it's displayed). CTR measures the effectiveness of an ad.

Content network: Non-search-engine sites that publish Google AdWords make up the Google content network. These sites participate in the AdSense or premium AdSense programs. AdWords advertisers decide whether or not they want to release their ads to this expanded network.

Content-targeted ads: AdWords ads targeted to the information pages of the content network and distributed through Google's AdSense program.

Control Center: The Control Center is the entire suite of ad-creation and campaign-reporting tools located in Google AdWords.

Conversion: Conversion occurs when a site visitor performs an action planned and desired by the Webmaster. In a business context, conversion usually involves a capture of information (such as registering at the site or joining a mailing list) or a transaction (such as buying a product). In the context of AdWords, conversion is the final step of a successful clickthrough.

Conversion rate: A calculation determined by dividing a site's conversions by AdWords clickthroughs. Conversion rate measures the success of an AdWords ad and, ultimately, the return on investment (ROI) of the campaign.

Conversion tracking: A tool in the AdWords Control Center that measures conversions resulting from ad clickthroughs.

Cost-per-click (CPC): The maximum or billable cost of a viewer clicking an AdWords ad. In Google's system, unlike competing systems (at the time of this writing), actual CPC is often lower than the maximum CPC established by the advertiser. Cost-per-click is assigned to an entire Ad Group, or to individual keywords of that Ad Group, or both. You can think of your maximum CPC as a bid for placement in the AdWords column.

Cost-per-thousand (CPM): A measurement of the cost for each thousand impressions (displays) of an ad. CPM is not used in Google AdWords, which employs a cost-per-click (CPC) system. However, some other search engines sell advertising on a CPM basis.

Creative: The text copy of an AdWords ad. Google is reducing its use of this word to describe ad text, but it remains in widespread use in forums and articles about the AdWords program.

Daily budget: Set at the Campaign level, the daily budget establishes a ceiling on Campaign expenses. Google recommends a daily Campaign budget based on projected impression frequency and clickthrough rate. The actual ceiling is set by the advertiser.

Destination URL: Not necessarily visible in the ad, the destination URL points to the ad's landing page.

Display URL: Visible in the ad, the display URL doesn't necessarily match the destination URL. The main purpose of a different display URL is to reduce the destination URL to a size that fits in the small ad box. The shortened URL makes it easy for viewers to see the ad's target site before clicking.

Distribution preference: This setting allows the advertiser to release or not release a Campaign's ads to Google's content networks.

Exact match: One of Google's keyword-matching options, exact match forces Google to display your ads only on search results pages that exactly match your selected keyword or key phrase. Exact match may be selected for individual keywords in an Ad Group. (See also *keyword-matching options, broad match, expanded match*, and *negative match*.)

Expanded match: Expanded matches are variations of your selected keywords (such as plurals, synonyms, and misspellings) that Google deems relevant and helpful to your ad's success. Expanded matching is included in the broad match option. (See also *keyword-matching options, broad match, exact match*, and *negative match*.)

Geo-targeting: Google enables advertisers to target ads by geographic region, according to a preset list of countries, American states, and certain American metropolitan areas. Geo-targeting works by identifying the searcher's IP (Internet Protocol) address, thereby locating the searcher geographically. Geo-targeted ads are displayed only to searchers viewing Google in the targeted area.

Google advertising network: The total reach of Google AdWords, consisting of Google.com, Google Groups, the Google Directory, and Froogle, plus its search partners (AOL Search, Netscape, AskJeeves, and others), and the Google content network of AdSense sites.

Impression: A single ad displayed on a user's screen.

Keyword: The specific word combinations and phrases users search on and advertisers bid on.

Keyword Suggestion Tool: This interactive tool is Google's in-house keyword generator for AdWords users. The Keyword Suggestion Tool spits out long lists of words and phrases related to a selected keyword.

Keyword-matching options: Google offers four keyword-matching options for expanding or restricting how your ads match keyword searches. These options are broad, expanded, exact, and negative. Refining the keyword-matching options can turn around a faltering campaign.

Landing page: A Web page represented by the destination URL. The landing page usually seeks to convert visitors to customers.

Negative match: This option prohibits an ad being displayed once a negative term has been applied. (See also *keyword-matching options, broad match, exact match*, and *expanded match*.)

Optimization: In the context of Google AdWords, optimization has nothing to do with Web site design (see Chapter 4). AdWords optimization is about the distribution of multiple ads in an Ad Group. Google tracks the relative success of ads and manages their rotation accordingly. This optimization can be turned off by advertisers who prefer a random rotation of ads in an Ad Group.

Overdelivery: Overdelivery refers to Google's optimization allowance. In the Terms of Service agreement, Google is permitted to exceed your daily budget by 20 percent but must reconcile this overdelivery of ad impressions (and resulting clickthroughs) every month. Your monthly budget, which is determined by multiplying the daily budget 30 or 31 times, can't be overcharged. Furthermore, if Google overshoots the daily budget by more than 20 percent, it issues an overdelivery credit for the additional clickthroughs.

Paid placement: Search result listings paid by sponsors, these listings might be indistinguishable from index results. Some search engines accept paid placement as a form of advertising, but Google does not.

Pay-per-click (PPC): Pay-per-click is another term for cost-per-click (CPC).

Phrase match: One of Google's four keyword-matching options, phrase match forces Google to restrict the placement of your ad to search results pages that exactly match your key phrase, including matching the word order. Other words might be included in the user's keyword string, but the exact phrase specified in your phrase match must be present.

Return on investment (ROI): A general business and advertising term, return on investment measures the profitability of a campaign. Simplified, ROI calculates a formula by which expenses are subtracted from sales to measure revenue gain. As an AdWords measurement, ROI is about conversions exceeding clickthrough expenses.

Rotation: Rotation is the formula by which multiple ads in an Ad Group are selected for display. In Google, rotation may be random or optimized.

Start and end dates: Google enables AdWords advertisers to determine in advance the start and end dates of a Campaign.

Traffic Estimator: The Traffic Estimator is an indispensable tool in the AdWords Control Center that enables advertisers to gauge the clickthrough rates of individual keywords.

AdSense Terms

Ad layout: An ad configuration for AdSense publishers. Google offers ten ad layouts; you can choose horizontal or vertical layouts containing one, two, four, or five ads. AdSense publishers cannot alter the configuration of ads within the bars and banners that constitute ad layouts, but they may change the colors in which text and borders are displayed.

Ad unit: One set of AdSense ads displayed in an ad layout.

AdSense code: The snippet of HTML and javascript that Webmasters paste into their pages to begin serving AdWords ads.

Alternate ads: AdSense publishers may specify non-Google ad sources for the space occupied by an ad unit, in preparation for those occasional times when Google can't deliver ads. Once specified, the alternate ad source is bundled into the AdSense code, and the replacement of Google ads by alternate ads occurs automatically if Google has no relevant ads to serve.

Banner: One type of ad layout. Three banners are available; one vertical and the other two horizontal. Each banner contains multiple ads.

Button: A type of ad layout that holds a single ad.

Clickthrough rate (CTR): Calculated by dividing the number of clicks by the number of displays (impressions). AdWords advertisers are charged for clicks through their ads. AdSense publishers are paid for clicks through the ads they host, sharing the revenue with Google.

Color palette: Individually adjusted colors for each of five elements in AdWords ads: headline text, ad text, URL text, border, and background. Google supplies several preset color palettes.

Content-targeted advertising: The generic name for Google's distribution of AdWords ads to AdSense sites. The AdSense network is also known as the *content network*. The word *content* is important in this context because Google uses its analysis of an AdSense page's content to determine which ads should be served on it.

Cost-per-click (CPC): A monetary amount charged by Google, and paid by the advertiser, when a user clicks through an ad. Advertisers bid for placement by offering a maximum CPC per keyword; Google charges the minimum amount beneath that amount (called the *actual CPC*) required to hold the best possible page position for the advertiser. AdSense publishers are paid an undisclosed percentage of the actual CPC.

Cybersquatting: The practice of unfairly capitalizing on ownership of a domain name that infringes a trademark or copyright. Google doesn't allow AdSense publication on a cybersquatting Web page.

Destination URL: An underlying URL in an AdWords ad that specifies the destination of clickthroughs. The destination URL is not necessarily the same as the URL displayed on the ad (called the *display URL*). When you set up a URL filter, the destination URL is blocked.

Distribution preference: Set by AdWords advertisers to include, or exclude, the content network of AdSense sites. AdSense publishers run AdWords ads only when those advertisers opt to have their ads appear on content pages.

Double serving: The practice of placing AdSense code in more than one location on a single page. Doing so violates Google's terms of service and is grounds for a warning and possibly expulsion from AdSense.

Impressions: Ad displays. AdSense measures and reports the impressions of all your ad units.

Inline rectangle: A type of ad layout meant to be placed within bodies of text, not in sidebars. Google offers four configurations of inline rectangle.

Leaderboard: A type of ad layout featuring four AdWords ads arranged horizontally. Leaderboards are designed to be placed at the top of Web pages but can be placed anywhere on the page.

Public service ad (PSA): Used to fill an AdWords ad before an AdSense site is crawled for the first time or if topical relevancy can't be established for some reason.

Publisher: An AdSense account holder and operator of a content site.

Skyscraper: A vertical arrangement of ads. Two skyscrapers are available, one holds four ads and one holds five.

Towers: All the vertical ad layouts: two skyscrapers and one vertical banner. Towers are usually placed on AdSense pages in the sidebars.

Typosquatting: The practice of purchasing and capitalizing on a misspelling of a prominent domain name, such as `googal.com`.

URL filter: A means of blocking specific AdWords ads from displaying on an AdSense site. This feature is normally used to prevent competitors from advertising on your site, taking away your visitors. Webmasters need to know the destination URL of any ad to block it.

Index

Notes

Notes

Notes

Notes

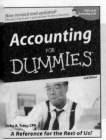

FOR DUMMIES®

A world of resources to help you grow

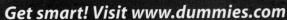
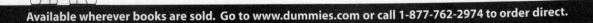

FOR DUMMIES

Helping you expand your horizons and realize your potential

INTERNET

0-7645-0894-6

0-7645-1659-0

0-7645-1642-6

DIGITAL MEDIA

0-7645-1664-7

0-7645-1675-2

0-7645-0806-7

GRAPHICS

0-7645-0817-2

0-7645-1651-5

0-7645-0895-4

FOR DUMMIES®

The advice and explanations you need to succeed

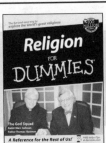

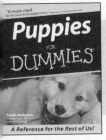

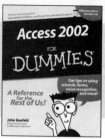